NO-BRAINER'S GUIDE TO THE BIBLE

NO-BRAINER'S
GUIDE TO THE
BIBLE

WRITTEN BY **JAMES S. BELL,** JR. AND **JAMES DYET**

 TYNDALE HOUSE PUBLISHERS, INC., WHEATON, ILLINOIS

Visit Tyndale's exciting Web site at www.tyndale.com

Library of Congress Cataloging-in-Publication Data

Bell, James S.
  No-brainer's guide to the Bible / by James S. Bell Jr. and James Dyet
    p. cm.
  ISBN 0-8423-5426-3 (sc)
  1. Bible—Introductions. I. Dyet, James T. II. Title.
BS475.3 .B45 2001
220.6'1—dc21   00-047967

Printed in United States of America

08 07 06 05 04 03 02 01
9   8   7   6   5   4   3   2   1

CONTENTS

Appendixes

PART ONE

A Few Basics

CHAPTER ONE

What's So Special about the Bible?

Abraham Lincoln is credited with the statement: "I believe the Bible is the best gift God has given to man. All the good from the Savior of the world is communicated to us through this book." Was Honest Abe right? Judge for yourself as you take an up-close and personal look at the Bible using this guide. For a starter, you may be wondering, *What's so special about the Bible?* This guide can't answer your question in great detail, but it can highlight some features of the Bible that will answer it in a general way.

1. As we read and apply it, we learn that the Bible has some important benefits for our life that no other book contains.

2. The Bible is unique in a number of ways because God is its author.

3. There is a rich history of Bible translation leading up to our foundational English Bible, the King James Version.

The Greatest Love Story Ever Told

If it is true that all the world loves a lover, then all the world ought to love God, because love is an integral part of God's nature, and He loves everyone. The Bible's central and recurring message affirms these facts.

Perhaps you have noticed a John 3:16 sign lifted prominently behind the goalposts of a football game or behind home plate at a

SETTING FUTURE DATES

Although the Bible informs us about certain future events—the second coming of Christ, for example—it does not reveal dates or encourage our speculation. The future belongs to God and is therefore not ours to schedule.

baseball game. While not everyone would agree with this in-your-face style of telling people about Jesus, no one can fault the message of John 3:16. It announces that God loved the world so much that He gave His Son Jesus to be our Savior. Through a simple act of faith, whoever believes in Jesus receives everlasting life. Now that's incomparable love—and it's the message of the Bible.

The Bible was not written to teach us calculus or world history or linguistics or any other academic discipline. Although the Bible lays a good foundation for all learning, it was written primarily as a history of redemption, showing how God reaches out in love to humanity, offering every person a loving and harmonious relationship with Him. From Genesis through Revelation we read of God's quest for wayward humanity and the invitation He extends to come back to Him. Only God's deep love explains such a persistent and gracious pursuit. And the only acceptable and reasonable way to respond to God's love is to love Him in return. As one of the writers of the Bible pointed out, believers love God because He first loved us (1 John 4:19)!

Promises That Deliver: God's Big Instruction Book

The Bible doesn't promise its readers a huge bank account, an enormous house with a three-car garage, children with straight teeth, or worldwide fame, but it does promise God's direction for a fulfilling and significant life. You may want to check this out for yourself by reading Joshua 1:8; Psalms 1:1-3; 19:7-11; 119:24, 97-105, 129-130; Proverbs 3:1-6; and 2 Timothy 3:15-17.

Countless thousands of people have turned to the Bible for comfort, hope, and encouragement in difficult times. The Bible offers hundreds of promises that assuage hurts, wipe away tears, and lift a fallen spirit. It helps us see beyond our problems and find help within its pages. The book of Psalms, especially, offers a rich supply of promises intended to soothe the soul and cheer the heart. For just a sample of such help, read Psalms 42; 46:1-3; and 121.

Past, Present, and Future: It's All Here

History tells us where we have been and where we are now, but it can only arm us with lessons for facing the future. If we refuse history's lessons, we will most likely repeat the errors of the past. But the Bible provides more than history lessons; it explains the past and the present and reveals enough of the future to round out the big picture of human history. We interpret the news headlines to grasp what lies ahead for our planet—and us. By reading the Bible you can say with confidence that you have read the last chapter of the Book and know that God has everything under control.

What an Inspiring Author

If you have ever sat down to write a book, you know the words don't jump out of the computer of their own accord. You have to dig down inside yourself for creative juices, the right words, and the best way to organize those words. Then you add sweat, toil, and tears to each paragraph until paragraphs become chapters and chapters become a book. Having done all that, your next challenge involves finding a publisher. Finally, if you get your book published, you must face the fact that it may not stay on the best-seller list (or the back-seller list) for long.

Kind of makes you appreciate the Bible, doesn't it? It has been around for centuries, and no book has outsold it. It has survived the attacks of its enemies and the arguments of its critics. And it has impacted countless lives for the better, even transforming hardened criminals into wholehearted Christians. If the Bible were simply a book conceptualized and crafted by human authors, it would have faded from memory a long time ago. But it is God's book. He inspired it, and it's here to stay.

Second Timothy 3:16 is a key verse underscoring the fact that God inspired the Bible. It says simply that all Scripture is inspired by God, but the word *inspired* means "God-breathed." God breathed out the words of the Bible, which have been translated over the years into many languages and translations.

The process by which His breathed-out words were written in the Bible is fascinating. God guided the writers of the Bible to write exactly what He wanted written—nothing more and nothing less (2 Peter 1:20-21). Further, He allowed each of them to write within his own vocabulary range and with a writing style that reflected his unique personality. The result? The Bible shows both the human element and the divine authorship, giving it reliability, infallibility, and authority.

The Bible Has Its Act Totally Together

If you could select 40 writers from various occupations and backgrounds, would you expect to find a perfect unity in their finished product? Hardly! Now, complicate this situation by picking those same writers over a 1,500-year time period so they would not have a chance to collaborate. What are the chances of finding a perfect unity in the written product? Zilch?

Yet, this is exactly what God did. He chose from among kings, prophets, priests, farmers, fishermen, and tax collectors to bring us a Book written by about 40 people over a period of 1,500 years. But this remarkable book carries His authorship and is structured around a perfectly constructed theme—His love expressed in redemption. As you read the Bible, you won't go running down rabbit trails; you will follow a trail that leads to God's heart of forgiveness.

The Bible is special for other reasons too, but you can have the fun of discovering them for yourself as you read this incomparable book.

Terms Related to Inspiration

Here are a few definitions of words theologians use when they refer to the Bible's inspiration:

- **Verbal inspiration:** The very words of Scripture are God's words.
- **Plenary inspiration:** Every part of the Bible is equally as inspired as all the other parts. This means, for example, that 2 Kings 7 is as inspired as Psalm 23 or the Gospel of John.

- **Reliable:** The Bible is totally true and trustworthy.
- **Authoritative:** Because the Bible is God's Word, it commands the right to frame our beliefs and values and set the standards and guidelines for our behavior.
- **Inerrant:** The Bible contains no errors in the original written documents.

INFO BYTE
OUCH! WHAT'S AN UNCIAL?

Uncial comes from the Latin word for *inch*. The uncial manuscript writers used only large capital letters nearly an inch high.

From God to Us with Love

Here's a brief overview of how the Bible, which communicates God's love, came to us.

The Old Testament was handwritten in Hebrew in manuscript form between 1400 B.C. and 400 B.C. The New Testament was also written in manuscript form in the first century, after the resurrection of Jesus Christ. Although we have no original manuscripts, we have hundreds of copies that were prepared and checked with eagle-eye attention to detail. The earliest complete copies of New Testament manuscripts date to around A.D. 350 and are known as the *Sinaitic* and *Vatican* manuscripts. The *Sinaitic* Manuscript was found in 1844 in a monastery at Mount Sinai. The British Museum is now the custodian of this manuscript. The Vatican has held the *Vatican* Manuscript in its library since 1448.

The British Museum also holds the *Alexandrian* Manuscript, copied around A.D. 400. The patriarch of Constantinople presented it to King Charles I in 1628. Earlier, it had resided in Alexandria, Egypt.

More than 100 other manuscripts copied between the fifth and tenth centuries exist as *uncial* manuscripts. Hundreds of other manuscripts were written in cursive style between the ninth century and the introduction of printing.

What's Your Version of the Story?

As Christianity began to spread throughout the world in the first few centuries A.D., many books began to circulate that falsely claimed divine inspiration. Discerning believers noted the false teaching in these books, and, after a series of church councils,

church leaders decided which books should be considered Scripture. The list of books that were considered Scripture is called the *canon* of Scripture. The Old Testament books cherished for centuries by Jews as having God's authorship were in. Also, books written by the apostles and recognized clearly as divinely inspired were in.

Next came versions of the Bible. When it comes to Scripture, the term *versions* does not mean different retellings of the Bible, much like we have different "versions" of the story of King Arthur. Instead, Bible versions are simply different translations of the Bible into other languages. The Old Testament was translated into Greek around 150 B.C. This translation is called the Septuagint. The Bible was translated into Syriac in the second century. A Latin version called the Vulgate, meaning "common" or "popular," was completed around A.D. 400. Other versions were completed around this same time in Coptic, Gothic, Ethiopic, and Armenian.

The Bible—namely the Gospel of John—was first translated into English (Anglo-Saxon, actually) around A.D. 735 by a monk who is often referred to as the Venerable Bede. King Alfred translated portions of the Bible in 900. In 1380 John Wycliffe translated the Latin Vulgate into Middle English. His efforts, however, were seriously opposed by the established church. William Tyndale provided the New Testament in English, and later completed translations of Old Testament books. His contribution was distinct, because he translated directly from the original Greek (New Testament) and Hebrew (Old Testament) texts of Scripture. Because the printing press had now been invented, the Scriptures became readily available.

Not everyone appreciated the availability of the Bible in English, but its wide acceptance persuaded Henry VIII to approve the Coverdale Bible, a translation completed by Miles Coverdale in 1535.

The strong-handed efforts of Queen Mary Tudor to restore England to the Roman Catholic Church drove many British scholars to Europe. In Geneva, William Whittington and others published the Geneva Bible in 1560. It was based on earlier English translations and dedicated to Elizabeth, England's new queen. Because some of the marginal notes offended many bishops in the Church of England, the church produced its own version in 1568, the Bishops' Bible.

In 1611 the King James Version was published by the authority of King James I. The 54 scholars who worked on this version relied heavily on the Bishops' Bible, but they also used earlier English translations, Luther's German translation, Greek and Hebrew texts, the Syriac, the Septuagint, and Latin versions.

Today, many easy-to-read translations exist, and the Bible is readily accessible to those who want to read the Bible—from God to us with love.

CHAPTER TWO

Introduction

SOME THINGS YOU'LL DISCOVER IN THIS CHAPTER

1. The Old Testament is divided into different types of books—the law, history, poetry, and prophecy.

2. The New Testament is similarly divided, with books of history (or the Gospels and Acts), letters (or the Epistles), and prophecy (Revelation).

The Bible Is Sort of like the Universe

If you look at the universe, you see everything existing in an orderly fashion and following established natural laws. You won't find the sun rising one day in the east and another day in the west. The moon passes through established cycles, and gravity always exerts a pulling force. You will never perform a vertical leap without coming down again. You see, God the Creator does everything in an orderly way. He is infinitely well organized. So we shouldn't be surprised to learn that His written Word, the Bible, is well organized.

The Bible contains two parts: the Old Testament and the New Testament, so named because they involve two great covenants (testaments). These are the Mosaic Covenant given at Mount Sinai (Exodus 24:8) and the New Covenant introduced by Jesus at the Last Supper (Matthew 26:28).

The Old Testament contains 39 books, and the New Testament has 27 books. So there are 66 books in the Bible. If you remember that the Old Testament has 39 books, you can easily determine the number of New Testament books by multiplying 3 by 9 (3 times 9 equals 27).

11

Laws and the Prophets Who Preached Them

It seems at first the Old Testament was perceived as having two parts: the Law (Genesis through Deuteronomy) and the Prophets (Joshua through Malachi). Jesus referred to the Law and the Prophets in Matthew 5:18. A threefold division also became recognized (Luke 24:44). This division included the Law (Genesis through Deuteronomy), the Prophets (Joshua, Judges, Samuel, Kings, Isaiah, Jeremiah, Ezekiel, and the Twelve Minor Prophets), and the Writings (all the other Old Testament books). In English translations of the Bible, the Old Testament is structured as the Law (Genesis through Deuteronomy), History (Joshua through Esther), Poetry (Job through Song of Songs), and the Prophets (Isaiah through Malachi).

In the threefold Jewish arrangement of the Old Testament noted above, the Prophets are also divided into the Former Prophets and the Latter Prophets. Joshua, Judges, 1 and 2 Samuel, and 1 and 2 Kings comprise the Former Prophets and take us from Israel's occupation of Canaan to the fall of the Kingdom of Judah. The Latter Prophets (Isaiah, Jeremiah, Ezekiel, Daniel, Hosea, Joel, Amos, Obadiah, Jonah, Micah, Nahum, Habakkuk, Zephaniah, Haggai, Zechariah, and Malachi) cover a period of history from just prior to the time Israel and Judah collapsed through the time of their exiles and return to their homeland. The Former Prophets are largely historical; the Latter Prophets contain mainly the messages delivered by the prophets. In this guide we will follow the order of the books as they appear in the English Bible.

The Greatest Story Ever Told (in Different Ways)

How many books does the New Testament contain? Let's see, the Old Testament has 39 books, and 3 times 9 is 27, so the New Testament has 27 books. Here's the order: History (the Gospels and Acts), Letters (Romans through Jude), and Prophecy (Revelation).

Here's a trick for remembering the order of four of Paul's New Testament letters. It's easy to get them out of order, but knowing your vowels is the key to keeping those letters straight. The vowels are A E I O U. You can forget the U, but notice how prominent each vowel is in the following letters from Paul (in the correct order):

A—Galatians
E—Ephesians
I—Philippians
O—Colossians

As we noted in the first chapter of this guide, the Bible is constructed around a single theme—redemption—so the writing stays on track from Genesis through Revelation. It has been said that the New Testament is concealed in the Old, and the Old Testament is revealed in the New. The fact is the Old Testament prophesied the salvation (redemption) Jesus would bring, and the New Testament shows how Jesus fulfilled those Old Testament prophecies.

Complementary Books That Compliment God

Certain Old Testament and New Testament books complement each other, and studying them together can uncover a lot of meaning for the reader. Listed below are a few complementary books:

- Genesis/Matthew
- Leviticus/Hebrews
- Isaiah/Romans
- Daniel/Revelation

Chronological Order

The books of the Bible do not appear in chronological order. Here is an overview of their chronological sequence.

Old Testament

Genesis and Job
Exodus and Leviticus
Numbers and Deuteronomy
Joshua
Judges and Ruth

IN CASE YOU'RE WONDERING
WHAT'S IN THE MIDDLE?

The middle verse of the Bible is Psalm 118:8. It advises us that trusting in the Lord is better than putting our confidence in people. We may not be able to believe everything we read in the newspapers, but we can believe everything God tells us in the Bible.

1 Samuel

2 Samuel and Psalms

1 Kings and 1 Chronicles, Song of Songs, Proverbs, Ecclesiastes

2 Kings and 2 Chronicles, Obadiah, Joel, Jonah, Amos, Hosea, Micah, Isaiah, Nahum, Zephaniah, Habakkuk, Jeremiah, Lamentations

Daniel and Ezekiel

Ezra, Esther, Haggai, Zechariah

Nehemiah and Malachi

New Testament

James (A.D. 45–50)

Galatians (49)

1 and 2 Thessalonians (51)

Mark (50s or 60s)

1 Corinthians (56)

2 Corinthians (57)

Romans (58)

Luke (60)

Ephesians, Colossians, Philippians, Philemon, Acts (61)

Matthew (60s)

1 Timothy and 1 Peter (63)

Titus (65)

2 Timothy and 2 Peter (66)

Hebrews (64–68)

Jude (70–80)

John (85–90)

1, 2, and 3 John (90)

Revelation (90s)

The apostle Paul is credited with writing 13 New Testament letters, although some insist that he also wrote Hebrews in addition to those 13. In each of his epistles a pattern shines through. He wrote doctrinal instruction first, then told how this doctrine applies to daily life. You will observe this pattern as you read Paul's letters.

How to Get the Most Out of This Guide

Lack of space in this book doesn't permit a detailed study of the Bible. Our goal is to give a clear picture of what the Bible is all about. By all means, proceed through this book at a comfortable pace. If something you read triggers a desire to study a passage of the Bible in depth, why not read that passage, jot down a few notes, and enter your findings in a journal? Here are a few things you can do to further your understanding of the Bible:

Select a Bible that fits your needs

You won't have to look far to find the Bible that's right for you. There are plenty of translations, and they come in many sizes. Select one you can read easily without having to squint.

Read the Bible alongside this guide

First, read what this guide says about a book or books of the Bible. Then read that book or those books of the Bible—slowly and thoughtfully. You don't have to rush. (There's no reward for winning a Bible-reading sprint!)

Read the sidebars

The sidebars are identified by the titles "Info Byte," "In Case You're Wondering," "What's Up with the Good Book?" and "It's a Promise." These little devices offer helpful insights into biblical people, places, times, and promises, as well as famous quotations about the Bible.

Take the quizzes

Monitor your progress by taking each fun quiz, "Let's Get Testy," at each chapter's end. You will be pleasantly surprised to see how well your Bible education is progressing as you journey through this guide. And if you miss a few answers, don't sweat it; you can learn from the mistakes and go on.

Keep a journal

Why not prepare a journal of your experiences with this guide? For example, you might want to record the date, the book or books of the Bible covered in each reading, any particularly helpful information, and surprising information.

A page in your journal might look like this:

Date: May 14

Book(s): Genesis 12–50

Helpful Information: God works everything out for good in the
lives of His people, even when they experience many troubles,
as Joseph did.

Surprising information: Joseph requested that his body be carried
from Egypt and buried in the Promised Land.

One more tip

God responds well to prayer. Ask Him to make your reading of this
guide and any Bible reading you do profitable. You will be in good
company if you pray for understanding. One of the writers of the
Psalms prayed that God would open his eyes so he would see the
wonderful things written in God's Word (Psalm 119:18).

PART TWO

The Old Testament

CHAPTER THREE

Getting into Your First "Law" Book (Genesis 1–11)

SOME THINGS YOU'LL DISCOVER IN THIS CHAPTER

1. Eve chose to eat the forbidden fruit in the Garden of Eden.

2. Civilizations were affected because of Noah's wine-induced sleep.

3. All the world's languages evolved from building the *wrong* kind of tower.

Imagine a world without laws, a world in which everybody does whatever he or she pleases. No guilt! No punishment! Want a new car? Steal it. A new house? Kick the current residents out and move right in. Need money? Rob a bank or mug a little old lady. But what if *your* new car gets stolen? *you* get kicked out of your house? *your* bank account gets zapped? *your* mother or grandmother gets mugged? You get the message: Life without laws would be pretty frightening and downright chaotic. Before long civilization would collapse. Knowing that a sin-plagued human race could not survive without laws, God wrote a code of laws in the first section of the Bible, called the "Books of the Law."

A fancy name for the Books of the Law is the *Pentateuch*. Not to be confused with the Pentagon, so named for its five-sided configuration, *Pentateuch* simply means "five books." They are Genesis, Exodus, Leviticus, Numbers, and Deuteronomy, and they unfold the laws God gave to the ancient nation of Israel. Many of these laws establish moral and ethical principles on which the Western world's

19

WHO, TELL ME, WHO WROTE THE BOOKS OF THE LAW?

Traditional biblical scholarship attributes the writing of the books of the Law to Moses. Statements in these books affirm Moses' authorship (see Exodus 17:14; Numbers 33:1-2; Deuteronomy 31:9). Other books of the Bible refer to Moses as the author (see Joshua 1:7-8; 1 Kings 2:3; 2 Kings 14:6; Ezra 6:18; Daniel 9:11-13; Malachi 4:4; Mark 12:26; John 5:46-47; and Romans 10:5). Jesus Himself credited Moses with the writing of the books of the Law (Matthew 19:7-8). The account of Moses' death (Deuteronomy 34) must have been written by someone else.

system of justice rests. The Pentateuch describes the human condition that prompted God to give His laws, the benefits of heeding them, and the consequences of disobeying them.

The first book of the Law, Genesis, is the "Book of Beginnings." As you read it, you may want to jot down every beginning you find in it. There are quite a few, but for our study we will divide Genesis into three broad categories of beginnings:

1. The Beginning of Creation (Genesis 1–2)
2. The Beginning of Sin and Judgment (Genesis 3:1–11:26)
3. The Beginning of Israel's History (Genesis 11:27–50:26)

The Beginning of Creation (Genesis 1–2)

The United States has invested millions of dollars in the space program. One scientific goal of this remarkable and highly successful enterprise is to gain clues about the origin of life. But at no cost, except perhaps the purchase price of a Bible, you can find out how life began. The first chapter of Genesis holds the answer.

The Beginning of Everything Except the Beginner of Everything (Genesis 1:1-31)

The first verse of the Bible affirms the existence of God and identifies Him as the Creator of everything. Hebrews 11:3 states that God spoke everything into existence out of nothing. Matter is not eternal, but God is (see Deuteronomy 33:27). He created matter, as well as space and time and every living thing, including human beings—and He did so *par excellence!* He looked at what He had created and saw that it was good, very good (Genesis 1:4, 10, 12, 18, 21, 25, 31).

In creating all things, God followed an order that prepared everything for the benefit of us humans. If human life had been brought into existence before light, water, dry ground, and a food source, none of us would be alive to appreciate God's creation.

Here's a day-by-day record of God's creative work:

Day 1: Light is created to designate day and night (Genesis 1:3-5).
Day 2: Our atmosphere is created. Sky divides water on earth from water above the earth (Genesis 1:6-8).

Day 3: Water on earth forms seas. Vegetation covers the earth (Genesis 1:9-13).

Day 4: Sun, moon, and stars light up the sky and provide light for the earth (Genesis 1:14-19).

Day 5: Birds and sea creatures populate their designated environments (Genesis 1:20-23).

Day 6: Land creatures and human beings are created (Genesis 1:24–2:1).

Day 7: God rests from His perfect work of creation (Genesis 2:2-3).

Mr. and Mrs. Universe in Paradise (Genesis 1:27–2:25)

After creating a perfect world, God created a perfect couple and charged them with the tasks of populating the earth and exercising dominion over it (Genesis 1:27-28). Looking at a photo of your great-grandparents, you may find yourself thinking, *I'm glad I didn't inherit his nose or her ears.* Genesis 1:27 doesn't tell us a thing about the first couple's noses or ears, but we may safely assume they were perfect. After all, when God looked at everything He had created, He pronounced it "excellent in every way" (1:31). However, the most important facet of the first couple's perfection was their relationship to God. The man and the woman were stamped with the image of God (1:27).

Having the image of God, the first couple reflected God's personality, spirituality, morality, emotions, and rationality. The fact that they were physical beings does not mean God is a physical being. As Jesus once stated, "God is Spirit" (John 4:24). Mr. and Mrs. Universe each possessed a spirit and a soul as well as a body. Their bodies connected them to the material world. Their souls gave them a consciousness of their own identity. Their spirits related them to the Creator so they could know Him, enjoy Him, worship Him, talk with Him, and serve Him. The fact that they bore the image of God set them and all their offspring apart from everything else in God's creation.

Genesis 2 gives "birth" descriptions of the arrival of the first man and woman. Scooping up a handful of soil, the Creator sculpted a

IN CASE YOU'RE WONDERING
WHAT'S IN A DAY?

Some students of the Bible believe that each day of creation was a literal 24-hour day. Others insist the term *day* refers to a long period of time. The former group regards the earth and universe as young. The second group views the earth and universe as possibly billions of years old. The 24-hour-day group insists that the Hebrew word for "day" written elsewhere in the Bible normally means a 24-hour day. The day-age group asks how there could be 24-hour days before the creation of the sun on the fourth day. The 24-hour-day group counters by asking whether God's day of rest lasted an entire age of undetermined years. Further, they point out that each day had an evening and a morning—familiar components of 24-hour days.

man's body. Then He breathed into the man's nostrils, and man
sprang to life (2:7).

Home, sweet home for this man named Adam was a lush garden
paradise, situated in Eden, where four rivers met. It would be
Adam's divinely charged responsibility to take care of this choice
property.

After putting Adam to work, God put him to sleep and performed
the world's first surgery of a person under anesthesia. He extracted
one of Adam's ribs, fashioned the first woman from it, and presented
her to Adam as his lifelong companion, sweetheart, and wife. It was a
match made in heaven!

It All Began with a Piece of Fruit
(Genesis 3:1–11:26)

According to Genesis 2:16-17, God tested Adam's will. Would
Adam freely obey God if God prohibited him from eating of one
tree—the tree of the knowledge of good and evil? Surrounded by
trees producing delectable fruit, Adam surely wouldn't miss sampling the fruit of just one tree, would he? Besides, God warned
Adam that he would surely die if he ate from the tree of the knowledge of good and evil. Would Adam heed the warning and obey
God? We shall see.

Trouble in Paradise (Genesis 3:1-7)

If you think a snake talked Adam into eating a forbidden apple,
think again. It didn't work quite that way. Taking the form of a beautiful and extremely crafty creature, called "the serpent," Satan—the
former highest-ranking angel who rebelled against God—approached
Adam's wife, Eve, and duped her into three things:

- doubting God's word,
- doubting God's fairness, and
- desiring the forbidden.

Eve fell for Satan's tempting lies. The tree looked good. Its fruit
would taste so good! And hadn't the serpent said the tree would
make her as wise as God? What did she have to lose? She picked the

fruit, ate it, and gave some of it to Adam. He willingly joined her in violating God's will. Eve was deceived, but Adam sinned with his eyes wide open. They flunked the only test God had given them. Having lost their innocence, their eyes were opened to their nakedness, and they covered themselves with fig leaves sewn together. Guilt and shame replaced feelings of peace and confidence in God's presence.

Passing the Buck behind the Bushes (Genesis 3:8-24)

The consequences of Adam and Eve's sinning were swift and long lasting. They lost their innocence. The image of God in them was tarnished. They died spiritually; sin had disconnected them from fellowship with God. They no longer felt comfortable in God's presence, just as a criminal would feel uncomfortable at a cops' picnic. So they hid from God behind some bushes.

But God called to Adam, perhaps to give Adam a chance to admit his wrongdoing and seek forgiveness. However, instead of "'fessing up," Adam passed the buck and blamed God for giving him the woman who led him into sin.

Eve, too, passed the buck by blaming the serpent. "He tricked me, and I fell for it," she offered in her defense.

Those feeble excuses didn't cut it with God. He sentenced the serpent to the lowly existence of a reptile crawling on its belly. Satan, who had assumed the form of the serpent, would suffer a decisive and deadly defeat at the hands of the "seed" of the woman (most likely a prediction of the victory Jesus would achieve over Satan at the Cross). Eve and every childbearing woman after her would experience birthing pain. Adam was sentenced to hard labor for the rest of his life—now a human existence of a limited number of years. The good days of tending paradise were over. From that day on, Adam would sweat to earn a living. A divine curse on nature would cause weeds and thorns to infest the ground. (Next time you pull weeds or grab a bag of fertilizer with weed control, think about Genesis 3.) Furthermore, Adam and Eve were expelled from Paradise, and God placed flaming-sword-bearing angels at the Garden's entrance to keep out Adam and Eve and their future descendants.

INFO BYTE
SERPENT ON THE LOOSE!

The serpent mentioned in Genesis 3 walked upright until God sentenced this crafty creature to crawl on its belly. The devil, who used the serpent to tempt Eve, is called "that old serpent, the Devil" in Revelation 20:2. He is on the loose now, leading a powerful force of evil spirits and tempting humans to believe his lies and follow him instead of believing the truth and following God. Revelation 20:10 predicts that at the end of time, God will execute a fiery, eternal judgment on the serpent.

HUMANITY'S CORE PROBLEM

The Bible doesn't say Adam sinned because he ate an apple. An apple isn't even mentioned in the account of the temptation, but sin is described as humanity's "core" problem. Sin entered the human race through Adam (Romans 5:12), and the human record since is not pleasant. The Bible identifies and describes our sin as missing the mark, iniquity, perversity, unrighteousness, wickedness, transgression, unjustness, evil, rebellion, wrongdoing, unbelief, and lawlessness.

Fig Leaves: The First Fashion Craze (Genesis 3:21)

Before expelling Adam and Eve from the Garden, God showed love and mercy by giving them more comfortable and practical clothing than their fig "threads" offered. Because blood had to be shed to provide animal skins, we see in this action a mini-picture of the shedding of the blood of God's perfect Lamb, Jesus, to provide forgiveness for our sins (see John 1:29 and Ephesians 1:7).

The Rise and Erosion of Civilization (Genesis 4–5)

As human history progressed, it followed a downward spiral in terms of morality, ethics, and spiritual interest. Eventually, God would destroy this rebel civilization with the exception of Noah and his family.

One Meat Offering, Hold the Vegetables (Genesis 4:1-15)

Genesis 4:1-2 announce the births of Cain and Abel, baby boys born to Adam and Eve. As is the case in most families, the two boys had distinctly different interests. Abel became a shepherd. Cain became a farmer. Their parents must have taught them to worship God, because one day Cain and Abel brought offerings to Him. Cain's was a veggie offering, whereas Abel's was an animal sacrifice. When God accepted Abel's offering but not Cain's, Cain burned with rage and later murdered his brother Abel. His vicious crime did not escape God's notice, however. God banished him from home to roam the earth as a fugitive and a tramp.

Chips off the Old Block (Genesis 4:16-24)

After reaching the land of Nod, east of Eden, Cain married and fathered a son, Enoch. Cain's posterity increased not only in numbers but also in offensive behavior. The description in Genesis 4:18-24 argues for a highly developed civilization with an underdeveloped conscience. Bigamy, murder, and egomania characterized a civilization on the skids.

Meanwhile, Back at the Old Homestead (Genesis 4:25-26)

Again, Eve gave birth to a boy, whom she named Seth. She believed God had given him to her in place of righteous Abel. The new posterity that began with Seth was different from Cain's posterity, for Seth called on the name of the Lord. But would it be too little too late?

The Bible's Obituary Column (Genesis 5)

The older a person becomes, the faster he or she turns to the obituary section of the daily newspaper. Maybe it's a therapeutic exercise. Not finding one's name there sure makes the morning coffee taste better. But as we all know, everyone must die sooner or later. Death, after all, is a toll exacted by sin. When we read Genesis 5, we see the words "he died" repeatedly, but we get zapped by the realization that people who lived back then celebrated amazingly old birthdays. Today's centenarians are just kids by comparison.

Just look at the ages recorded in Genesis 5:

Life Spans in Genesis 5

Person	Years Lived
Adam	930
Seth	912
Enosh	905
Kenan	910
Mahalalel	895
Jared	962
Enoch	365
Methuselah	969
Lamech	777

Your observant eye picked out the longest and shortest life spans, didn't it? Methuselah holds the record for the longest life, at 969. Enoch's life was the shortest, at 365. So what happened to Enoch? The average life span of the others listed was 907.5. Did Enoch fall victim to the Old World Flu?

No way! Enoch didn't die. He was an exception to the rule that everyone must die. Enoch maintained a close friendship with God, and one day he was transported to heaven without dying (Genesis 5:24).

IN CASE YOU'RE WONDERING
CAN YOU DIRECT ME TO THE GARDEN OF EDEN?

Why can't we find the Garden of Eden? Knowing its proximity to four rivers, two of which are identifiable today, why can't we find a tour group that's going there? As we'll see a bit later in this study, God destroyed the Earth with a Flood. The Garden of Eden must have been wiped out by the Flood and/or undergone vast ecological changes caused by enormous alterations in the climate after the Flood.

IN CASE YOU'RE WONDERING
WHERE DID CAIN GET HIS WIFE?

Likely, Adam and Eve had many children between the births of Cain and Seth, fulfilling God's prediction that Eve would have numerous conceptions (Genesis 3:16). We know that Adam was 130 years old when Seth was born (Genesis 5:3). So there were likely several generations of people on earth by the time Cain killed Abel. The genealogy of Cain is given because he was the eldest son, and because it traces the escalation of sin in humanity—but there must have been other genealogies as well. These multiple generations would explain Cain's concern that people were out there who might kill him. So Cain likely married a relative, perhaps a distant relative, and took her with him when he became a vagabond.

The obituary column ends with Genesis 5:32, and the next verse introduces us to Noah, one of the most fascinating men of faith mentioned in the Bible.

Civilization Lost at Sea, but Noah Sails On
(Genesis 6–7)

As Earth's population boomed, sin boomed right along with it. "The sons of God saw the beautiful women of the human race and took any they wanted as their wives" (Genesis 6:2). Who were the "sons of God"? Some teach that they were fallen angels—angels who joined Lucifer, the devil, in his rebellion against God and were subsequently banished from heaven. Others believe they were descendants of Seth. Whoever they were, they surely didn't contribute any morality to the world. Their offspring became legendary heroes, but God considered them infamous, not famous. The human condition was so appalling that God shortened human life to 120 years. Corruption, violence, and depravity abounded. Even people's thoughts were continually and absolutely wicked. God grieved that He had created the human race and prepared to destroy both humans and animals from the face of the earth. But one man, Noah, found grace in God's sight. This man of faith led a righteous life and worshiped God. He would be spared!

What's a Boat? (Genesis 6:1-22)

Noah had never attended a boat show, but he was about to host one. God told him to build a boat—an ark—because He planned to cover the earth with a flood and drown every living thing. Not leaving anything to Noah's own designing, God delivered the construction plans. Noah was told to make the boat from resinous wood and seal it inside and out with tar. It would stand three decks tall and contain stalls throughout the interior. It was to be 450 feet long, 75 feet wide, and 45 feet high. An 18-inch opening was to be built below the roof and extend all the way around the boat. Noah was also told to place one door in the boat's side.

God promised to keep Noah and his family safe in the boat while every other living thing was dying in the Flood. God further instructed Noah to take his wife, sons, and daughters-in-law on board as well as pairs of each kind of bird and animal. And yes, he was to stock enough food on the boat to feed his family and the menagerie.

Obediently, Noah followed God's plans.

Water, Water Everywhere (Genesis 7)

Noah and his boat-building project must have been entertaining news in his community. Can you imagine the hee-haws and belly laughs he must have heard as he built and preached for 120 years? How could a flood occur? This must have been the leading question hurled at Noah. Noah would be proven right, but it would be too late for the skeptics to do anything but tread water.

Finally, the Lord announced that it was time to board. Obediently, Noah escorted his family, animals, and birds onto the boat—animals approved for eating and sacrifice by sevens, the other animals and birds by twos. Then God shut the door!

We don't know that Noah threw a party on his 600th birthday, but we do know it rained that day! That was the day God unleashed Earth's subterranean reservoirs and opened the floodgates of heaven. The waters rose higher and higher, the boat bobbed, and Captain Noah, his crew, and the floating zoo were riding out the storm.

Rain cascaded down continuously for 40 days, merging with the waters gushing from below. The Flood reached its highest point 150 days after the rain began to fall, covering even the highest mountain peaks. The enormous water pressure exerted on the earth by the Flood must have changed the topography dramatically and permanently. And every person, animal, and bird outside the boat perished. Noah would celebrate his 601st birthday on board before disembarking.

Dry Land, Ahoy (Genesis 8–9)

When the floodwater receded, Noah's boat touched down high in the Ararat mountain range, about 500 miles from its departure point. In order to get current reports on the drying process, Noah released a

IT'S A PROMISE!

"The Lord is faithful; he will make you strong and guard you from the evil one." (2 Thessalonians 3:3)

INFO BYTE

NOW, THAT'S A BIG BOAT!

Noah's ark was big enough to hold more than 43,000 tons. Each deck was about the size of one and a half football fields. Its capacity to house animals was that of over 500 railroad cattle cars. Plenty of room on board for passengers and animals!

HOW DID THE ANIMALS HAVE ENOUGH TO EAT?

Noah took enough food on board to last the voyage. Also, many of the animals may have hibernated for long periods.

raven. It flew around until it found a landing spot. It did not return to the boat. Next, he released a dove, but the dove soon returned because it didn't find a place to land. Seven days later, he released the dove again. This time it returned with an olive leaf in its beak—a positive sign that Earth was rejuvenating. Noah waited another seven days and released the dove again. This time the dove did not return to him. Noah lifted the boat's cover and looked out on dry land.

At God's command, Noah and his family left the ark and released all the animals and birds. It was a brand-new day for planet Earth!

To Noah's credit, upon leaving the boat he built an altar and offered approved animals as sacrifices to the Lord. This thanksgiving ceremony pleased the Lord and brought His promise that He would never again curse the earth and destroy all living things. For the life of the earth there would be a spring and fall, summer and winter.

God blessed Noah and his sons and charged them with the responsibility to repopulate the earth. He put the fear of humans into wild animals and gave humans permission to eat meat and to execute murderers. Then He promised that He would never again destroy the earth with a flood. A rainbow would serve as the sign of this pledge (Genesis 9:13-17).

Sleeping *au Naturel* (Genesis 9:18-32)

Maybe Noah should have stayed in the shipbuilding industry. In the new world he turned his interests to farming. He planted a vineyard, made wine, and got drunk. Instead of slipping into his pj's, he lay down *au naturel* in his tent and drifted into a deep, wine-induced sleep. His son Ham found him naked and reported the incident to his brothers Shem and Japheth. Out of respect for their dad, Shem and Japheth walked backwards to Dad and draped a robe over his nude body.

When Noah awoke and learned what his sons had done, he cursed the descendants of Ham but blessed the descendants of the other two. Ham's descendants, the Canaanites, would be reduced to the role of servants.

History records the fulfillments of Noah's curse and blessing. Centuries later in the land of Canaan, the Canaanites were dominated by the Hebrews, who descended from Shem. Joshua 9:23 reports that the Gibeonites, a Canaanite tribe, were forced to chop wood and haul water for the Israelites. The descendants of Japheth pushed westward and became prominent among the nations of the world. Genesis 10 reports the rise and migration of the world's people groups, all of whom descended from Noah's sons.

Sprechen Sie Français, Amigo?
(Genesis 10–11:26)

Suppose you were a construction worker involved in building a structure to rival the Sears Tower in Chicago. How successful would you be if you and your coworkers could not communicate? After several frustrating attempts to understand one another and be understood, you might just blow the whistle, grab your lunch bucket, and write off the project as a colossal waste of time.

That's kind of what happened when the new earth became heavily populated. Everybody spoke just one language, and a large population settled in Babylonia. The people decided to construct a brick tower that would reach to the skies. Their skyscraper would give them a sense of pride as well as a place to worship. Of course, they weren't interested in worshiping God. Why not? Maybe they didn't see any need for God. After all, weren't they self-reliant, united, and capable? Perhaps they had chosen gods more to their liking. Or they may have believed they could be guided by the planets and stars. A tower that reached into the skies would certainly put them in closer touch with those heavenly bodies (11:1-4).

But in spite of their inflated egos and apparent success in getting the tower well on its way to completion, they could not reject God and get off scot-free. Their highest construction platform was still far below God's lofty dwelling. He came down, looked at the tower, and halted the construction. How did He do it? He confused their speech by giving them many languages. The confusion ended the

INFO BYTE
COVENANTS

God's promises to Noah comprise the Noahic Covenant. The word translated "covenant" in the English Bible occurs over 300 times. The Old Testament word comes from a root word meaning "to bind." A covenant, then, binds two parties together. The New Testament word translated "covenant" or "testament" refers to a will rather than an agreement between two parties.

God's covenants were either unconditional or conditional. His covenant with Noah was unconditional. He did not attach any conditions to His promises.

INFO BYTE
THE TOWER OF BABEL
(GENESIS 11:9)

This notorious tower's name, *Babel*, derives from tweaking a Hebrew word meaning "to confuse." The Tower of Babel was probably a prototype for smaller towers called *ziggurats*, which had square foundations and steps up the sides. Usually a shrine occupied the top of a *ziggurat*. There, the people worshiped their gods.

project and sent the people in different directions (11:5-9). We can almost hear them shout farewells to one another as they left the tower. *"Au revoir!" "Auf Wiedersehen!" "So long!" "Adios!" "Arrivederci!"*

The scattering of these people far and wide led to the forming of people groups and nations (11:10-26).

The entire human race had failed repeatedly to love, respect, and obey God. So God turned next to one man, Abraham, through whom He would communicate His character and fulfill His will.

LET'S GET TESTY!

Complete the following multiple choice quiz by guessing what the Bible indicates was the reason or reasons why the people listed in Genesis 5 lived so long.

A. They were not exposed to harmful rays emitted by computers and TVs.
B. Health care was better in those days.
C. The climate was ideal.
D. Sin's effects had not yet shortened human life.
E. There was something in the water.
F. Nursing homes dispensed terrific vitamins.
G. Later, God restricted human life to 120 years.

(If you answered C, D, and G (see Genesis 6:3), take a break and grab a treat. Make sure it's low in sugar and fat, though. You just might live longer!)

Now, fill in the blanks:

1. God promised He would never again destroy the earth with a _____.
2. A _____ carrying an olive branch returned to the ark.
3. Noah built the ark in _____ years.
4. _____ is considered the author of the Books of the Law.

5. _____ was God's last work of creation.
6. In Genesis 5, _____ holds the record for living the longest.
7. The Garden of _____ was home to _____ and Eve.
8. After sinning, Adam and Eve tried to _____ from God.
9. _____ offered vegetables to the Lord.
10. Noah's three sons were Ham, Shem, and _____.

(Answers: 1. flood; 2. dove; 3. 120; 4. Moses; 5. Eve; 6. Methuselah; 7. Eden, Adam; 8. hide; 9. Cain; 10. Japheth.)

SUPPORT GROUP FOR MEN

"THIS IS ESAU'S FIRST TIME HERE. LET'S ALL TELL HIM THAT IT'S OK TO LOSE A BIRTHRIGHT."

One Man's Family: From Abraham to Joseph (Genesis 12–50)

Based on United States census data, you can expect that by the end of this year about 16 percent of Americans will have gathered up their possessions and changed residences.

Every move, of course, is an adventure—one that could rank high on the list of stress-producing events. That makes sense. After all, being surrounded by piles of boxes doesn't exactly bathe the soul in euphoria. And it's no fun looking for that unmarked box that holds your toaster.

In this chapter we'll meet Abraham, a person who wasn't planning to move until that life-changing day he received a call from God to do so. Abraham's response to that call led to one of the greatest adventures in history, not only for him but also for his posterity, the nation of Israel.

Now we are ready to survey the third category of beginnings in Genesis.

SOME THINGS YOU'LL DISCOVER IN THIS CHAPTER

1. Abraham, a pious man, was willing to sacrifice his own son on an altar.

2. God got into a wrestling match with Jacob, and both of them gained something.

3. A dream about fat and skinny cows was linked to the fate of Egypt and Joseph for seven years.

ABRAHAM AND SARAH

Abraham is called Abram when he is first introduced in Genesis. Later, God changed his name to Abraham. We will avoid confusion by referring to him only by the name Abraham. Because Sarai was later renamed Sarah, we will call her Sarah.

UR

Ur was an attractive and comfortable city boasting a huge library, exquisite buildings, an impressive, terraced temple in honor of the moon god, a sunny climate, a beautiful harbor, good fishing, and a highly developed culture. It would not have been easy to leave Ur. The ancient site lies about 225 miles southeast of Baghdad.

Leaving Beautiful Downtown Ur
(Genesis 11:27–50)

In these chapters we will read brief profiles of Abraham, Isaac, Jacob, and Joseph—all esteemed forefathers of the Jews. Don't be surprised, though, to find that each of them was human and messed up occasionally.

Abraham wasn't a believer in the true God when God called upon him to leave his hometown. Abraham lived in the beautiful city of Ur, situated on the Euphrates River in southern Babylonia, a land now occupied by Iraq. Like the rest of Ur's citizens, Abraham worshiped pagan gods, probably Nanna, the moon god. However, he showed a newfound faith in God by pulling up stakes at the age of 75 and leaving for an undisclosed destination. He believed that God would do what He promised and make him the father of a great nation through which God would bless the whole world.

Westward, Ho (Genesis 12:1-9)

Abraham, his wife Sarah, his father, his nephew Lot, his servants, and his flocks followed the Euphrates River about 200 miles north to Haran, where they took an extensive break. While there, Abraham's father died. Abraham then led his group southwest for 400 miles to Canaan, the land that includes modern Israel. In Canaan, Abraham received another promise from the Lord: He would give Canaan to Abraham and his descendants. Abraham responded by building an altar at Bethel and worshiping God.

The rest of Abraham's life was spent "on the road." He lived in tents, but later in the New Testament we read that Abraham, by faith, anticipated a city designed and constructed by God. If anyone deserved the title "king of the road," it was Abraham.

Take My Sister, Please! (Genesis 12:10-20)

When famine struck Canaan, Abraham and his beautiful wife, Sarah (a 65-year-old Barbie?), headed south to Egypt in search of food. Fearing that some womanizing Egyptians might knock him off in order to get to Sarah, Abraham asked her to identify herself as his sister. The ploy worked but nearly got Abraham killed anyway. Thinking Sarah was Abraham's sister, Pharaoh traded livestock and servants for her. Abraham got richer, but Pharaoh, who was smitten with love, got smitten with plagues from the Lord. So Pharaoh "read the riot act" to Abraham and expelled him and Sarah from Egypt.

INFO BYTE
RIVER ROAD OR DESERT TRAIL?

If Abraham had chosen the direct route to Canaan, he would have crossed 600 miles of desert—not a good plan for someone who had to feed and water livestock. The river route to Haran and southwest from there skirted the barren Arabian desert.

Range Wars (Genesis 13–14)

As in the days of the Old West, the land wasn't big enough for both Abraham and his nephew Lot. Their herds and flocks had become enormous, grazing land was scarce, and the cowpokes were restless. Fights broke out between Abraham's men and Lot's men. Abraham suggested that he and Lot divide the land, and he gave Lot first choice.

Crafty, but sometimes dumb, Lot chose the greenest pastureland in the vicinity of cities flanking the Jordan River. But again the Lord promised to give all the land to Abraham. And as things worked out, Lot lost big time. He moved into the wicked city of Sodom and settled down there, but then he and a few others were taken hostage by marauding warriors. Showing no ill will toward Lot, Abraham led 318 "commandos" in a daring and successful rescue of Lot and the rest of the hostages.

IN CASE YOU'RE WONDERING
HOW COULD A MAN OF FAITH "BLOW IT"?

Faith in God doesn't make anyone perfect. Every believer is capable of sinning, but God doesn't give up on any believer. His work in us, which we'll talk about later, guarantees heaven, and he uses our weaknesses and mistakes in the perfection process. As the bumper sticker claims, "Christians aren't perfect; they're just forgiven!"

Abraham's Not-So-Apparent Heir
(Genesis 15–21)

Abraham and Sarah were getting old, and the nursery section of their tent was still empty. Nevertheless, they would have a son—and descendants numbering as many millions as the stars. The Lord gave Abraham His word on this (Genesis 15). As the years rolled on with no baby, however, it became harder and harder for Sarah to believe God's promise.

So Sarah suggested that Abraham and Sarah's servant girl, Hagar,

INFO BYTES

ISH! WHAT'S THE BIG DEAL OVER ISHMAEL?

The clash over Ishmael has continued for centuries. Many Arabs consider him their forefather and therefore believe they have a legitimate claim to Palestine.

MRS. LOT'S SALT BATH

Asphalt pits, sulfur hills, and salt hills once ringed the area in which Sodom was located. Likely an earthquake caused sulfur, salt, and asphalt to mix and explode. Winds might have blown the burning sulfur skyward, causing it to fall on Sodom and its twin city, Gomorrah. Lot's wife hesitated too long; the blowing chemicals covered her.

THE NAME ISAAC—THAT'S A LAUGH

Isaac means "laughter." Abraham laughed when he heard that he would be a daddy at the age of one hundred. Later, Sarah laughed when she overheard the Lord promise once again that she and Abraham would have a baby boy. As it turned out, the Lord had the last laugh, because Isaac was born right on schedule as He had promised.

team up to produce a child (Genesis 16:4). The plan worked. At the age of 86, Abraham was bouncing the baby Ishmael on his knee, but Sarah was jealous and hopping mad. Eventually, Hagar grabbed Ishmael and fled for her life.

Once again, the Lord appeared to Abraham. Identifying Himself as the Almighty (it wouldn't be too hard for the Almighty to give Abraham and Sarah a son), He again promised that Abraham and Sarah would have a son whose descendants would possess Canaan. He affirmed that this promise would never expire. As a sign of this promise, Abraham and all the males in his household were circumcised. Abraham was then 99 years old (Genesis 17). Ouch!

That same year the Lord told Abraham that Sarah would have a baby boy. Sarah was eavesdropping and laughed out loud when she heard this news. After all, she was a barren 89 year old. The Lord also told Abraham that he would destroy wicked Sodom, the city Lot lived in (Genesis 18).

Just before the Lord nuked Sodom, angels yanked Lot, his wife, and his two daughters from Sodom. (Lot's two sons-in-law stayed in Sodom, thinking the warning was just a big joke.) The fleeing family was told not to look back, but Mrs. Lot turned her head and immediately turned into a pillar of salt (Genesis 19:1-29).

Seeing God's judgment didn't do much for Lot and his daughters' morality or good judgment. In a cave, Lot's daughters got him drunk and had sex with him. Two boys were born, Moab and Ben-ammi (Genesis 19:30-38).

Getting back to Abraham, we find that he lied a second time about Sarah. This time Abraham told the king of Gerar, a country to the south of Canaan, that Sarah was his sister. Fortunately, the Lord warned the king that he would be "dead meat" if he touched Sarah. Showing integrity and fear of the Lord, the king returned Sarah to Abraham. In addition, he gave Abraham oxen, sheep, female servants, and the offer to settle anywhere he chose to in the king's land (Genesis 20).

Finally, baby Isaac was born. He was truly a miracle baby, because Abraham was 100 years old and Sarah was 90 (Genesis

21:1-8). When Hagar's teenage son, Ishmael, picked on little Isaac, Abraham packed some provisions for him and his mother and sent them away. The two would have died in the desert, but God spared their lives and promised to build a great nation out of Ishmael's posterity (21:9-21).

Take Isaac on a Mountain Hike (Genesis 22)

After settling down at Beersheba in southern Canaan and watching Isaac grow up, Abraham was instructed by God to sacrifice Isaac as a burnt offering. Unbeknownst to Abraham, this was a test and only a test. Was he willing to obey God at any cost?

Abraham was willing. He prepared an altar on Mount Moriah, the place God had designated, and laid Isaac on the altar. But just as he was ready to plunge a knife into his son, he was stopped from doing so. God directed him to a ram caught by the horns in a thicket. The ram, God said, would take Isaac's place (Genesis 22).

Courting by Proxy (Genesis 23–25)

Sarah didn't live to be the mother of the groom at Isaac's wedding. She died and was buried in the cave of Machpelah. Perhaps knowing that he would die soon and wanting to see Isaac marry the right girl, Abraham charged a reliable servant to go to his old homeland and bring back a perfect bride for Isaac.

If the servant thought about contacting Mesopotamia Matchmakers, we'll never know. We do know, however, that he found just the right woman, thanks to the Lord's guidance. Her name was Rebekah. Abraham's loyal servant persuaded her and her family that getting married to Isaac would be the best thing that ever happened to her.

Abraham married again and had more children, but old age finally caught up with him. He died at the age of 175 and was buried by Ishmael and Isaac alongside Sarah.

INFO BYTES
CIRCUMCISION

Abraham circumcised Isaac when he was eight days old (Genesis 21:4). This circumcision was the sign that Abraham and his descendants were recipients of the promise God had given Abraham. Abraham's descendants, the Jews, have continued the practice of circumcision to this day.

MOUNT MORIAH

Today, the Dome of the Rock stands on the ancient site of Mount Moriah.

HE'S NOT TOAST

It took tremendous faith for Abraham to offer his son Isaac. After all, all the promises about millions of descendants and blessings to the entire world rested on Isaac staying alive and becoming a father. How could God keep His word to Abraham if Isaac ended up as burnt offering? Hebrews 11:19 reports that Abraham believed that if he sacrificed Isaac, God would raise Isaac from the dead. Now that's faith!

INFO BYTE
A FRIEND IN HIGH PLACES

The Bible calls Abraham God's friend (2 Chronicles 20:7; Isaiah 41:8; James 2:23). That's quite a tribute to a man who obeyed God's command to leave his homeland, trusted God to give him and his barren wife a son in their old age, and was willing to sacrifice that son in response to an incredibly difficult test of faith in God and love for him.

Like Father, Like Son (Genesis 26)

As an old saying claims, "An apple doesn't fall far from the tree." Isaac mirrored his father, Abraham, by hitting the road when famine struck. And of all places, he and Rebekah ended up in Gerar. Only the Lord stopped them from going farther south to Egypt.

History repeated itself in Gerar. Isaac tried to pass his wife off as his sister, but Abimelech, king of the Philistines, caught the two in a romantic mood and blew the whistle on them. Showing integrity, Abimelech ordered all the males in his country not to touch Rebekah. Failure to comply would carry the death penalty.

While in Gerar, Isaac became richer and richer because God blessed him.

Mom Always Liked You Best: The Story of Jacob and Esau (Genesis 27–36)

Isaac and Rebekah had twin sons, Jacob and Esau, but the two were totally different. Jacob was the stay-at-home type. Esau was the outdoors type. Jacob was smooth-skinned; Esau was hairy. Jacob was the younger by moments; Esau was the firstborn. Jacob seemed to be his mother's favorite, but Isaac seemed to prefer Esau. The way to Isaac's heart was his stomach, which Esau kept well supplied with game meat he had brought home from hunting expeditions.

When Isaac was old and nearly blind, he was tricked by Rebekah and Jacob into blessing Jacob instead of the elder son, Esau. This meant Jacob, not Esau, would receive a double portion of their dad's estate. Thinking that Esau would retaliate against her favored son, Rebekah persuaded Isaac to send Jacob to Uncle Laban's home in Haran (Genesis 27–28:5).

One night, while on his way to Haran, Jacob dreamed about a stairway reaching from earth to heaven, with angels climbing and descending it. At the top of the stairway stood the Lord, who gave Jacob the same promises He had made to Abraham, He also promised to keep Jacob safe, prosper him, and bring him home again (Genesis 28:10-20).

Jacob did prosper in Uncle Laban's country, where he married 2 of Laban's daughters, Leah and Rachel, and fathered 13 children: 6 sons and a daughter by Leah, 2 sons by Rachel, and 4 sons by 2 servant women. Later, when Jacob was back in his homeland, his dear wife Rachel died in childbirth after presenting him with her second baby, Benjamin, a brother for her first baby, Joseph. Jacob's 12 sons became the fathers of Israel's 12 tribes. However, Jacob fell out of favor with Uncle Laban and decided it was time to hit the road and return home (Genesis 29–31).

Wrestling for a Blessing (Genesis 32)

On the way home, Jacob was chased down by Laban, confronted by God, and reconciled to Esau. When he encountered God, he lost a wrestling match to Him, admitted that his name was Jacob, meaning "deceiver," and received a blessing and a new name—Israel (Genesis 32–33).

When Isaac died at the age of 180, Esau and Jacob buried him.

IN CASE YOU'RE WONDERING
A RAW DEAL

Why didn't Isaac undo Jacob's blessing when he discovered he had been deceived? Hebrews 11:20 reports that Isaac blessed his sons by faith. Apparently, he believed that, in spite of the deception, God had determined that Jacob, not Esau, would inherit the promises handed down to Abraham and Isaac. Abraham's physical and spiritual lineage would passs down through Jacob.

He Lived His Dream! The Story of Joseph (Genesis 37–50)

Jacob settled in Canaan, and his sons, who eventually became the founding ancestors of the 12 tribes of Israel, continued to grow and mature. But one son in particular would play a very significant role in Jacob's family. His name was Joseph.

Playing Favorites

As Jacob's family grew, he favored Joseph, who was born to Jacob when he was an old man. Also, Joseph was the firstborn son of Jacob's favorite wife, Rachel. To show his doting love for Joseph, Jacob gave him a really hot-looking robe. But it seems *Joseph* also favored Joseph. He had two dreams predicting his rise to prominence over his father and siblings, and he shared these dreams with them. The dreams and the "hot" robe made Joseph's brothers hot, too— really hot. Their opportunity for revenge came when Joseph brought

homemade goodies to them at Dad's request. They jumped him, ripped off his robe, threw him into a cistern, and later sold him as a slave to traders on their way to Egypt. As a cover-up, they soaked Joseph's robe in goat's blood and later showed it to their dad as evidence that a wild animal had ripped Joseph to pieces (Genesis 37).

Harassment in the Workplace

Down in Egypt, Joseph became a servant to Potiphar, the Pharaoh's captain of the guard. Things went fine until Potiphar's wife tried, and tried, and tried to seduce good-looking Joseph. But Joseph just said no. Then, one fateful day, "Mrs. Perversity Potiphar" grabbed Joseph by his cloak and tried to force him into bed. But the strong arm of morality had a tighter hold on Joseph. He fled while he still had his dignity. Unfortunately, he didn't have his cloak. *Femme fatale* had it, and she showed it to her husband as evidence of a sexual assault perpetrated by Joseph. Before long, Joseph was a jailbird (Genesis 39).

Because he was a model prisoner, Joseph was made a supervisor. Two of his fellow inmates had been servants to Pharaoh: one, Pharaoh's chief cupbearer; the other, Pharaoh's chief baker. What had they done, served Pharaoh day-old bread or cheap, warm Egyptian beer? The two had dreams in prison, which God enabled Joseph to interpret. The baker got bad news. His dream was a nightmare. Within three days, Pharaoh would hang him. But the cupbearer got good news. Within three days he would get his old job back (Genesis 40).

You've Changed after All These Years

Finally, Joseph got out of prison. Pharaoh called for him because he needed a dream interpreter, and Joseph had been highly recommended for the job. Joseph interpreted Pharaoh's weird dreams about seven fat and seven skinny cows and seven full heads of grain and seven empty heads of grain. Egypt, Joseph said, should store up food for seven years to prepare for seven years of famine. Pharaoh rewarded Joseph by making him his right-hand man in charge of saving the land from the predicted disaster (Genesis 41).

When the famine struck, it devastated countries near and far. Genesis 42–50 reports how a search for food by Joseph's brothers brought them to Egypt. Mystery and intrigue surround their visit, but ultimately Joseph—who was older and looked and talked like an Egyptian—disclosed his identity to them. It was a tearful reunion, as Joseph inquired about his father and younger brother, Benjamin, back in Canaan. Joseph made it clear that he harbored no ill will against his brothers, for he knew God had planned the whole adventure in order to keep alive the people to whom He had promised worldwide status and blessing.

The brothers returned home to bring back Jacob and Benjamin to Egypt, where they recognized Joseph and lived under his rule.

Eventually both Jacob and Joseph died in Egypt. Jacob's body was taken to Machpelah and buried alongside his ancestors in a cave there. Before dying, Joseph commanded his brothers to carry his remains to Canaan for burial there. He died at the age of 110. His body was embalmed and placed in a coffin in Egypt.

INFO BYTE
LAND OF GOSHEN

Joseph gave his family choice land in Egypt—the fertile land of Goshen—the northeastern section of the Egyptian Delta region. It is also called "the land of Rameses" (see Genesis 47:11 and Exodus 12:37).

LET'S GET TESTY

(Part 1): What was the main reason Abraham wanted a son?

A. He'd have to pay a dowry for a daughter when she wanted to get married.

B. He could use a set of muscles for heavy chores around the tent.

C. God promised him descendants as numerous as the stars in the sky.

D. He didn't want to give his inheritance to his nephew Lot.

(Part 2): Circle the correct multiple choice answer.

1. He was Jacob's favorite son.

   A. Beersheba

   B. Pharaoh

   C. Reuben

IN CASE YOU'RE WONDERING
WHY BURY JOSEPH IN CANAAN?

Hebrews 11:22 reports that Joseph's request to be buried in Canaan was an expression of faith. He believed that Canaan was the land God had promised to Abraham and his descendants. He fully expected his descendants to move back to Canaan, and perhaps he looked forward to being resurrected there one day. According to Exodus 13:19 and Joshua 24:32, Joseph's remains were carried to Canaan as he requested.

    D. Joseph

    E. None of the above

2. **He was prepared to sacrifice his son.**

    A. Abraham

    B. Esau

    C. Laban

    D. Pharaoh's chief baker

    E. None of the above

3. **He was Jacob's twin brother.**

    A. Benjamin

    B. Laban

    C. Esau

    D. Isaac

    E. None of the above

4. **Isaac married**

    A. Leah

    B. Rebekah

    C. Rachel

    D. Potiphar's wife

    E. None of the above

5. **Sarah's husband was**

    A. Abimelech

    B. Sodom

    C. Lot

    D. None of the above

(Answers: Part 1: C is the best answer. Part 2: 1. D; 2. A; 3. C; 4. B; 5. D)

CHAPTER FIVE

"NOW IF A WOMAN WERE LEADING THIS EXODUS, SHE'D STOP AND ASK FOR DIRECTIONS. BUT NO, WE HAVE TO WANDER."

Your Second and Third "Law" Books (Exodus and Leviticus)

It's time to meet Moses, revered by the Jews as their deliverer and lawgiver. In this chapter we'll learn how God saved Moses from infanticide and elevated him to the position of prince of Egypt. We will also see how God used him to rescue His chosen people from Egyptian bondage, to give them His laws, and to guide them to the border of the Promised Land. As you read about Moses, you will discover that his life fell into three distinct 40-year periods: 40 years in Egypt, 40 years in Midian, and 40 years in the wilderness.

The book of Exodus begins by introducing us to . . .

A New Sheriff in Town (Exodus 1)

Maybe you know what it is like to have a really nasty boss after having a really nice boss. The "new sheriff in town" is a slave driver, making you work your fingers to the bone. The first chapter of Exodus describes "a new sheriff" on the throne of Egypt. Unlike the pharaoh (many pharaohs ago) who was kind to Joseph and Joseph's people, the Israelites, the new pharaoh treated the Israelites

SOME THINGS YOU'LL DISCOVER IN THIS CHAPTER

1. The reason the Egyptian Pharaoh set free two million Hebrew slaves

2. The reason the Hebrews worshiped a golden calf even though they had received the Ten Commandments

3. The important purpose of the Day of Atonement in the life of Israel

WHAT'S IN A NAME?

Abraham's descendants through Isaac and Jacob are known by such names as Hebrews, Israelites, the children of Israel, the children of the covenant, God's chosen people, and the Jews. We will refer to them most often as Hebrews, Israelites, or the Jews.

IN CASE YOU'RE WONDERING
SWIFTLY FLY THE YEARS

Exodus 12:40 tells us the Israelites had been in Egypt 430 years by the time they left for the Promised Land. Because Moses was eighty at that time, we know the Israelites had been in Egypt 350 years by the time Moses was born.

like dirt. Why? He felt threatened by them. Their numbers had increased from the original 70 who moved there at Joseph's invitation to approximately 2 million people 350 years later. So Pharaoh tried to work them to death, forcing them to build cities as weapons-and-supply centers. Next, he ordered the Hebrew midwives to kill every newborn boy. But the midwives let the bouncing baby boys live because the midwives feared God more than Pharaoh. Finally, Pharaoh ordered his people to throw all the Hebrew baby boys into the Nile River (Exodus 1).

Hush Now, Baby; Don't You Cry (Exodus 2)

How do you keep a baby boy quiet for the first three months of his life? If you can answer that question, millions of sleep-deprived parents would like to hear from you. You can appreciate, then, how hard it must have been for Baby Moses' parents to keep him quiet and secluded for three months. The Egyptians didn't have a clue that little Moses existed. But his parents knew they couldn't keep their secret much longer, so Mom put Moses in a waterproof (at least on the outside) basket made of papyrus reeds and floated him along the edge of the Nile River among some reeds.

Pharaoh's daughter found Moses, took him home, and raised him in the Egyptian palace. Eventually, Moses became prince of Egypt. However, one day he saw an Egyptian beating up a Hebrew. Thinking there were no witnesses, Moses killed the Egyptian and buried him in the sand. The next day, when Moses tried to stop a Hebrew from decking a fellow Hebrew, the aggressor questioned Moses' right to judge, recalling that Moses had killed an Egyptian. The word was out. Soon Pharaoh wanted Moses dead (Exodus 2:15). Fearing for his life, Moses fled to Midian, where he married and tended sheep and goats for his father-in-law. Meanwhile, back in Egypt the Hebrews were crying their hearts out to God and pleading with Him to deliver them from their bondage. He paid attention and prepared to deliver them (2:23-25).

"You Da Man!" (Exodus 3–4)

Candles that keep relighting no matter how often they are puffed out are one thing, but how about a burning bush that stays intact? Moses saw such a bush in Midian and heard God speak from it. God told Moses to return to Pharaoh and demand that Pharaoh let the Hebrews depart for the Promised Land. Moses protested that God had picked the wrong man, insisting that he wasn't much of a speaker. But God assured Moses that He was eternal and all-powerful. God would perform miracles to persuade Pharaoh to let the Hebrews go. Further, He would appoint Moses' brother, Aaron, to do the talking. So Moses returned to Egypt for the greatest showdown on earth.

IT'S A PROMISE!

"But the person who loves God is the one God knows and cares for." (1 Corinthians 8:3)

The Bricklayers Are Restless (Exodus 5–6)

The Hebrews were encouraged by Moses' report of his encounter with God, but their mood soon changed. The demand to let God's people go infuriated Pharaoh so much that he cut off the supply of straw to the Hebrew slaves while ordering increased production under harsher working conditions. The Hebrews blamed Moses for the rotten mess they were in, and Moses passed along their complaint to the Lord. Once again, the Lord mentioned His promises and sent Moses back to Pharaoh.

WHAT'S UP WITH THE GOOD BOOK?

"The books of the Bible were written over a long period of time. It took God longer to write the Bible than it has taken him to build the British Empire."
—William C. MacDonald

Plagued with Problems! (Exodus 7:1–12:36)

Pharaoh was as stubborn as a mule. Whenever Moses and Aaron demanded that he set the Hebrews free, Pharaoh hardened his heart against God and said no. That's when the Lord put Pharaoh's feet to the fire. He used ten plagues to force Pharaoh to cry "uncle" and release his hold on the Hebrews. The gods of the Egyptians were powerless to withstand Him and save the Egyptians. The plagues showed Moses that God is all-powerful and merciful. The Egyptians felt the brunt of God's judgment, but the Hebrews were kept safe through the ordeal. Moses would need to rely on God's power later, when he led two million Hebrews on their desert trek to the Promised

INFO BYTE

EATING ON THE RUN: THE PASSOVER

The Passover meal, so named because the Lord passed over every house displaying the blood of an unblemished lamb, was to be eaten quickly. Those who ate it were to wear sandals and a cloak and have a staff in hand. This was not an occasion for casual Hebrew dining; the people would quickly exit Egypt, their land of bondage.

IT'S A PROMISE!

"But I lavish my love on those who love me and obey my commands, even for a thousand generations." (Exodus 20:6)

46

Land. Also, crises would occur in the desert when Moses would need to draw upon God's mercy.

The Ten Plagues

Plague	Result
First plague	Nile River turned to blood (Exodus 7:14-25)
Second plague	Frogs everywhere (Exodus 8:1-15)
Third plague	Gnats blanketing humans and animals (Exodus 8:16-19)
Fourth plague	Flies swarming everywhere (Exodus 8:20-32)
Fifth plague	Deadly disease strikes Egyptian livestock (Exodus 9:1-7)
Sixth plague	Boils cover humans and animals (Exodus 9:8-12)
Seventh plague	Devastating hail (Exodus 9:13-35)
Eighth plague	Infestation of voracious locusts (Exodus 10:1-20)
Ninth plague	Thick darkness (Exodus 10:21-29)
Tenth plague	Death of every firstborn human and animal (Exodus 11:1–12:30)

Hitting the Road with a Lot of Gold

The last plague was the clincher. Grieving over the loss of all the firstborn sons was heard in homes across Egypt, including the palace. Pharaoh's firstborn son was among those slain when the Lord passed over the land by night. Only the Hebrew families were spared because they obeyed the Lord's instructions to kill an unblemished lamb, smear its blood on their doorposts, and eat a special meal prescribed by the Lord. This meal would become an annual celebration called the Passover.

Pharaoh called for Moses and Aaron in the dead of night and told them, in effect, "Hit the road! Get out of here! And take the rest of the children of Israel with you." The Hebrews were glad to leave, of course. Freedom beats slavery any day of the week. But they didn't leave empty-handed. The fear of the Lord was so strong among the Egyptians that they gave the Hebrews provisions for the journey—plus gold and silver jewelry.

Parting Ways with Egypt (Exodus 12:37–18:27)

The first leg of the Israelites' journey took them to the edge of the Red Sea. The Lord provided a cloud by day and a pillar of fire by night to guide them (Exodus 12:37–13:22). Having reached the Red Sea, the escaping multitude looked back and saw Pharaoh's elite cavalry closing in on them. Another fine mess Moses had gotten the Israelites into! How could they cross the Red Sea? How could they elude Pharaoh's cavalry?

Resolutely, Moses assured the people that the Lord would handle the situation. And He did. He made a dry path through the sea for the Hebrews and then collapsed the heaps of water down on the pursuing Egyptians. The enemy and their horses drowned in the swirling water (Exodus 14).

A desert can be a hot, dry, thirsty place. People can also get hungry in a desert. (If they see lemonade stands and burger places there, they are probably looking at mirages.) By the time the Israelites reached Mount Sinai, almost three months after leaving Egypt, their tongues were hanging out and their stomachs were growling. They complained, whined, and talked about the good old days back in Egypt, where water and food weren't so scarce. Mercifully, the Lord answered each grumble with water and food (manna) air-dropped from heaven (Exodus 15:23–17:16). News of the Lord's miracles on behalf of His people reached Moses' father-in-law, Jethro, and persuaded him to join Moses' tour group (Exodus 18).

It's Lonely at the Top (Exodus 19–31)

From Mount Sinai the Lord told Moses what He wanted him to convey to the Israelites. He would make them a kingdom of priests and a holy nation if they would obey Him. When he passed along this message, the people agreed to obey the Lord. Three days later the Lord summoned Moses to climb the mountain. Alone on Mount Sinai, Moses received the Ten Commandments from the Lord. He then returned to tell the people what the Commandments were and what impact they were to have on Israel's relationship with the Lord and their interpersonal relationships. After calling Moses a second

INFO BYTE
THIS FOOD IS HEAVENLY!

Manna means "What is it?" The Lord sent the Israelites manna from heaven in the second month of their journey from Egypt to the Promised Land. The supply continued for 40 years, stopping only when the Israelites entered Canaan, their destination. The manna tasted like wafers made with honey or oil (Exodus 16:31; Numbers 11:8). Each household was to gather about 6 pints every day except the Sabbath. A double quota of manna was prescribed for the day before the Sabbath. The manna was supposed to be eaten in a day. Leftover manna spoiled the following day. Many Bible teachers believe the manna pictures Jesus, the Bread of Life, who came down from heaven to bring us life (see John 6:47-51).

time to climb the mountain, the Lord gave him plans for building a tabernacle, or tent, where He would meet with His chosen people. He also gave detailed instructions for the tabernacle's furnishings, the priesthood, and Sabbath observance.

IN CASE YOU'RE WONDERING
WHY A GOLDEN CALF?

The Egyptians worshiped Apis, a god in the form of a bull. It symbolized strength and vitality. Aaron and his fellow Hebrews would have been familiar with such worship in Egypt, so accepting a young bull sculpted from gold was a natural, but wicked, regression to the culture from which God had freed them.

Don't Have a Cow, Israel! (Exodus 32)

It was a clear case of "out of sight, out of mind." Moses had been at the top of Mount Sinai 40 days and 40 nights, and the Israelites had grown tired of waiting for him to return. So they stormed Aaron's "office" and demanded that he make gods for them. He caved in to their demand, asked for their gold earrings, melted them, and fashioned the melted gold into a golden calf for them to worship. Then, when a naked, wild celebration was under way, Moses arrived, carrying two tablets of stone on which God had engraved His laws.

Infuriated, Moses broke the tablets by throwing them to the ground. Later, heavy punishment fell upon the Israelites, and only Moses' pleading with the Lord to forgive Israel ended that dark day in Israel's history.

Back to the Drawing Board (Exodus 33–40)

The closing chapters of Exodus reaffirm the Lord's promise to give Israel the Promised Land, His instructions to Moses to prepare two new stone tablets like the first ones, and the people's construction of the tabernacle and furnishings. All the plans, including the materials to be used and the most minute production details, came from the Lord and were to be followed precisely by the builders He had gifted for the work. Then as now, God set the terms for approaching Him.

Everything from Diets to Ethics
(Leviticus 1–27)

With a house of worship in place (the tabernacle), Israel was ready to learn from the Lord how to worship Him properly. The third book of the Law, Leviticus, provides those instructions. Taking its name from the tribe of Levi, Leviticus focuses on the laws that related to Israel's priests and their ministry on behalf of Israel. In Leviticus we read about offerings and sacrifices (Leviticus 1–7); the preparation and performance of the priests' duties (Leviticus 8–10); dietary and medical laws (Leviticus 11–15); the Day of Atonement, Israel's holiest day of the year (Leviticus 16); rituals and ethics (Leviticus 17–25); and the need to obey the Lord and value what is dedicated to Him (Leviticus 26–27).

Before you read about the book of Numbers in our next chapter, think back to the numbers you came across in this chapter.

Crunching the Numbers in Exodus

- Moses lived in Egypt **40** years before fleeing to Midian.
- He fled after killing **1** Egyptian and then trying to break up a fight between **2** Hebrews.
- He lived in Midian **40** years before returning to Egypt.
- The Lord struck Egypt with **10** plagues, the last of which took the life of every firstborn Egyptian son.
- After **430** years in Egypt, about **2** million Hebrews departed.
- The Red Sea claimed the lives of **0** Hebrews but all the pursuing Egyptians.
- Manna was to be gathered only **6** days per week, because the **7**th day was the Sabbath.
- After leaving Egypt, the Hebrews reached Mount Sinai almost **3** months later.
- The Lord delivered **10** Commandments to Moses.
- In a fit of rage, Moses broke **2** stone tablets containing God's laws for Israel.
- The Lord gave Moses plans for constructing the tabernacle, leaving **0** to human ingenuity.

INFO BYTE
THE DAY OF ATONEMENT

The Day of Atonement, Yom Kippur, was to be held annually on the tenth day of the seventh month of the Hebrew calendar (which begins in spring). This holiest of Israel's holy days was marked by fasting, repentance, and sacrifice. Its purpose was to find, in God's mercy, a covering for the nation's sin. The highlight of the day occurred when the high priest entered the Most Holy Place in the tabernacle. He first entered carrying the blood of a young bull (a sin offering), which he sprinkled on the lid (the mercy seat) of the ark of the covenant. He entered a second time with the blood of a ram (a burnt offering) and sprinkled it, too, on the lid of the ark of the covenant. Only the high priest was allowed to enter the Most Holy Place, and only on the Day of Atonement. Read Leviticus 16 for complete details surrounding this special day.

LET'S GET TESTY

SAYS WHO?

Which of the following commands are not included in the Ten Commandments? If you wish, you may approach this exercise as an open book test. Reading Exodus 20:1-17 will help you get a perfect score.

1. Do not steal.
2. Do not borrow.
3. Love your neighbor as yourself.
4. Honor your mother and father.
5. Do not covet.
6. Be poor.
7. Do not worship any other god but the Lord.
8. Do not misuse the Lord's name.
9. Work only five days a week.
10. Eat your veggies.

(Answers: 2, 3, 6, 9, 10.)

CHAPTER SIX

"CAPTAIN, THIS MAN IS UNDER ARREST FOR DEFYING THE LAW OF GRAVITY."

Your Fourth and Fifth "Law" Books (Numbers and Deuteronomy)

Just two more books to read and you will graduate from Moses' Law School. Congratulations! Your final two law books are Numbers and Deuteronomy.

The Numbers Game

If you sometimes feel like a statistic—merely a number in the world's 6 billion-plus population figure, it may help to know that census-taking helps us understand what's happening in our nation so citizens and the government can plan better for the future. Back in the early 1600s, England conducted a census in Virginia, a British colony at the time. Following independence, America conducted its first census in 1790, counting 3.9 million inhabitants. No traffic gridlock back then! The activity of taking a census is at least as old as the period described in the book of Numbers. As a matter of fact, Numbers got its name from the census recorded at the beginning of the book and another recorded near the end (chapters 1 and 26).

SOME THINGS YOU'LL DISCOVER IN THIS CHAPTER

1. The Hebrews would have rather stayed in the desert than gone into the Promised Land.

2. There are a lot more laws than just the Ten Commandments, many having to do with purity.

3. Seeking water, Moses struck a rock one too many times.

INFO BYTE
DESERT CAMP

The Levites encamped around the tabernacle, which stood at the center of Israel's camp. The other tribes formed the perimeter: three to the north, three to the south, three to the east, and three to the west. Ephraim and Manasseh were half tribes (the names of Joseph's sons). The circumference of the camp has been estimated at 12 miles.

Not Countless but Pretty Close
(Numbers 1:1–10:10)

After a year at Mount Sinai, the Israelites prepared to continue their journey to Canaan, the Promised Land. It was not supposed to be a long journey, but by the time the book of Numbers closes, Israel will have wandered in the desert from Sinai to Canaan. Before Moses led the Israelites from Sinai, he received a command from the Lord to take a census of all the males who were at least 20 years old and able to go to war. Every tribe except the tribe of Levi underwent a head count (1:49). The Levites were charged with tabernacle duty. They would take down the tabernacle, transport it, set it up, and assist Aaron and his sons with their priestly duties (1:50-51; 3:6-9). The census totaled 603,550—a sizable but untested army (2:32).

Preparations for Israel's march to Canaan included the tribes' camp assignments (2:1-34), instructions concerning the priests and Levites (3–8), the observance of the first Passover in the desert (9:1-14), and instructions about trumpet signals (10:1-10).

How Grumpy Can You Get? (Numbers 11–25)

The grumpy Israelites didn't improve with age; they just got grumpier. You would think they would have learned from past experiences that God would take care of them and that grumbling just brings trouble. But as you read Numbers 11–25, you will find them whining about the daily menu. They missed Egyptian cuisine: cucumbers, melons, onions, garlic, and . . . leeks? (Numbers 11). Moses' brother, Aaron, and sister, Miriam, complained about Moses (Numbers 12). When 12 spies dispatched by Moses to Canaan returned and reported on both Canaan's bounty and military strength, the people shuddered and sobbed all night. Although two spies, Joshua and Caleb, had encouraged the Israelites to enter and possess Canaan, believing the Lord's promise to give them the land, the people wanted to recall Moses and Aaron and appoint someone to lead them back to Egypt (Numbers 13–14). Consequently, the Lord announced that of that generation only Joshua and Caleb would live to enter Canaan.

Numbers 16 reports a rebellion by more than 250 men against

Moses and Aaron. Their complaint? They felt Moses and Aaron held too much authority. Numbers 20 drops in on the Israelites as they whine again about a lack of water. Once again, Moses struck a rock (see Exodus 17:6), and water gushed out. However, the Lord had directed him to only speak to the rock. Later, as recorded in Numbers 21, the Israelites complained about the food. Then to top off their rebellion against the Lord they committed adultery with the Moabites and worshiped the Moabites' false gods (Numbers 25).

IN CASE YOU'RE WONDERING
WHAT'S THE BIG DEAL ABOUT STRIKING THE ROCK?

The Lord told Moses to speak to the rock and water would gush from it (Numbers 20:8). By striking the rock, Moses disobeyed the Lord's command. Also, the rock pictured Christ, who was struck on the cross so we might receive the water of life. Now, spiritual refreshing comes by speaking to Christ, who lives forevermore. He does not have to be struck again (see 1 Corinthians 10:4 and Hebrews 4:14-16). By striking the rock once again, Moses marred the spiritual symbolism portrayed by the rock.

Planning in the Plains of Moab (Numbers 26–36)

Chapters 26 through 36 of Numbers report another census of Israel, some civil and ceremonial laws, assignment of land in Canaan, the death of Aaron at the age of 123, and reminders to expel the Canaanites and reject their false gods.

Deuteronomy: Preparing for the Promised Land

Deuteronomy, meaning "second law," contains Moses' final address to Israel, which he delivered east of the Jordan River. The new generation of Israelites about to enter Canaan, the Promised Land, needed a refresher course on laws that would govern their civil, social, and religious life in the new land.

History Lessons (Deuteronomy 1–3)

Moses began his speech by recounting the Lord's faithfulness to Israel during the trek through the desert. Moses was now 120 years old, but his memory was sharp and his voice was clear.

Law Lessons (Deuteronomy 4–26)

Israel received a crash course on the Law, including reasons for obeying it. No one could break the Law and plead ignorance as an excuse.

IT'S A PROMISE!

"God is our refuge and strength, always ready to help in times of trouble."
(Psalm 46:1)

Covenant Restrictions (Deuteronomy 27–30)

Moving into a new neighborhood may introduce you to covenant restrictions—a list of what you can and can't do. If you do what you can't do, you can expect to hear about it. You know how it goes: You can't build a ten-foot fence around your property; you can't keep a boat or a camper in the driveway; you can't construct a storage shed in an area visible from the street; you can't rent out parts of your dwelling to several families; you can't paint your house any color that sticks out like a sore thumb! Moses passed along covenant restrictions to Israel. As God's covenant people, they could rely on God to keep His promises. If they kept their promise to obey God's laws, they would enjoy blessings. However, if they disobeyed His laws, they would face His judgment. The covenant had restrictions!

And in Conclusion (Deuteronomy 31–34)

Moses appointed Joshua as his successor, taught Israel a song about the Lord and His ways, and pronounced the benediction. Then he ascended Mount Nebo, from which the Lord gave him a panoramic view of Canaan. Moses died there at the age of 120.

LET'S GET TESTY

YES, I REMEMBER IT WELL!

Underline the correct word or words in the following statements.

1. Numbers gives one/two/three/four census reports.
2. At Sinai the Israelites observed their first desert Dust Bowl/Thanksgiving Day/Passover/Independence Day/Communion.
3. The Israelites complained about dogs barking/tight camping spaces/food/Moses' leadership/cold nights.
4. Moses struck/bulldozed/painted/wrote his name on the rock that gave forth water.

5. It took Israel 40 years/20 years/60 months/120 days to go from Egypt to Syria/Canaan/Spain/Babylon.

6. Joshua/Jonah/Josiah/Jeremiah became Moses' successor.

7. Moses taught Israel a card game/rock hunting/a song/calculus.

8. Moses died at the age of 100/120/139/140.

(Answers: 1. two; 2. Passover; 3. food, Moses' leadership; 4. struck; 5. 40 years, Canaan; 6. Joshua; 7. a song; 8. 120.)

WHAT'S UP WITH THE GOOD BOOK?

"When you read God's Word, you must constantly be saying to yourself, 'It is talking to me, and about me.'"
—*Søren Kierkegaard*

CHAPTER SEVEN

JOSHUA QUICKLY SPREAD THE WORD TO THE TROOPS . . .
"HORNS UP FOR BATTLE."

Conquest, Failed History Lessons, and a Love Story (From Joshua to Ruth)

You've probably heard someone ask, "Who died and made you king?" When we read Israel's history from the book of Joshua to the book of Ruth, we find out that Israel slid from the superb leadership of Joshua to a period that can be described best as "the pits." The nation started out well in Canaan with Joshua as its divinely appointed general and successor to Moses. However, in the period of the judges, everyone thought of himself as a king with the right to do whatever he wanted (see Judges 17:6; 21:25). The book of Joshua reports how the Israelites, under the command of Joshua, conquered their enemies. Judges, the book that follows Joshua, reports that the Israelites failed to conquer their own egos and therefore became slaves to their enemies.

Joshua: Conquest

If you enjoy military strategy and supporting the good guys—the troops with the right stuff—the book of Joshua is tailor-made for you.

SOME THINGS YOU'LL DISCOVER IN THIS CHAPTER

1. Joshua conquered Jericho the easy way.

2. Achan stashed away the spoils of battle and paid a heavy price for his thievery.

3. The Gibeonites played a game of masquerade in front of Joshua and succeeded in their deception.

INFO BYTES
GEOMETRY LESSON

Canaan was 180 miles long and about 40 miles wide. It extended north to Lebanon, south to the Sinai desert, west to the Mediterranean Sea, and east to the Euphrates. It lay at the center of powerful nations that made a great impact on history: Egypt to the south, Syria to the north, Babylon and Persia to the east, Greece and Rome to the northwest.

A GOOD NAME

The name *Joshua* means "The Lord is salvation." What a good name for the person appointed by the Lord to lead Israel from aimless wandering in the desert to a new and better life in the Promised Land. Israel's success depended upon their trust in the Lord for salvation.

Follow the Leader (Joshua 1)

The Lord appointed Joshua as Moses' successor and the one who would lead the Israelites into Canaan. With the appointment came assurance from the Lord that He would give him the land, invincibility, and His presence. The Lord challenged Joshua to be strong, courageous, and a devoted adherent to the law handed down by Moses.

I Spy Something That Is Red (Joshua 2–6)

Joshua selected his first Canaanite target, the thick-walled city of Jericho. Then he sent two spies there on a fact-finding mission. After traveling about six miles, the spies crossed the Jordan River. Another six miles brought them to Jericho, where they entered the prostitute Rahab's house, situated on one of the city's walls. Having already become a believer in Israel's God after hearing about His mighty deeds on Israel's behalf, Rahab hid the spies. Later, she assisted in their escape from Jericho by lowering them to the ground with a rope. However, first she requested that Israel spare her life and the lives of her family members in the impending assault on Jericho. The spies agreed but instructed her to hang a scarlet rope from her window to signify that the people inside were to be spared.

Soon it was time for Israel to cross Jordan and enter the Promised Land (Joshua 3). The priests carrying the ark of the covenant went first.

When the priests set foot in the Jordan River, the waters parted, allowing them and the people to cross on dry land. Next, Joshua ordered the tribes to select 12 men who would use 12 stones from the Jordan to build a monument commemorating the miraculous crossing (Joshua 4). Chapter 5 records the circumcising of Israel's males, a Passover observance, and the end of the provision of manna. The time had come to claim Canaan and to live off the fat of that good land.

The old song "Joshua fought the battle of Jericho" seems to have missed an important point. Joshua did not have to fight his way into Jericho. The Lord delivered it into his hands. All Joshua and the Israelites did was circle Jericho once a day for six days, then circle it seven times on the seventh day. On the seventh trip on the seventh day, when the priests blew their rams' horns, the people shouted, and "the walls came a-tumblin' down!" Everything and everyone inside the city was destroyed except Rahab and her family. Her faith, evidenced by the scarlet rope hanging from her window, had saved her.

INFO BYTE
AMAZING GRACE!

Not only did the Lord spare Rahab because of her faith, He included her in the genealogy of Jesus. She became one of Jesus' ancestors (see Matthew 1:1-5).

Something's Rotten in the State of Israel
(Joshua 7–8)

Joshua had ordered that no one take anything from Jericho for his or her own use. Everything was supposed to be destroyed. When Israel's next battle—the battle for the small town of Ai—went haywire and 36 Israelite soldiers returned in body bags, Joshua asked the Lord what went wrong. Joshua learned that Achan had disobeyed the hands-off-the-spoils order and had buried some valuables (a stylish robe and five or six pounds of silver and gold) under his tent. The Lord had withdrawn His blessing from Israel because of Achan's sin. But after Joshua put Achan and his family to death, the Lord enabled Israel to take Ai.

IN CASE YOU'RE WONDERING
JUST ACHAN FOR PUNISHMENT

Achan's tent was anything but a spacious, multiroom condo. It was a tent. Surely his family members knew what he had done and where he had stashed the loot. They may have helped him hide it, and they certainly assisted in the cover-up. As accomplices, they fell party to the same punishment Achan received. Further, the punishment made clear to Israel that God expected obedience. A casual approach to sinning would eventually take Israel down the road to the same immoral, lawless lifestyle practiced by the pagan Canaanites.

Who Were Those Masked Men? (Joshua 9)

Well, they weren't clones of the Lone Ranger. And they didn't wear masks, but they certainly masked their appearance. They were Gibeonites, a Canaanite tribe. Upon hearing what happened to Jericho and Ai, they hatched a plan to con Joshua into thinking they had just arrived in Canaan after a long journey. They put worn-out sacks on their donkeys, carried worn-out wineskins, dressed in worn-out clothes, wore old sandals on their feet, and carried dry, crumbly bread. When they met Joshua, they told him they were

INFO BYTE
WE TOLD YOU SO

Almost forty years before the battle of Jericho, Joshua and Caleb had spied out Canaan and advised the Israelites to enter it without delay. They believed the land was ripe for the picking (Numbers 14:6-9). Rahab's story about the inhabitants' fear of Israel and the ease with which Jericho fell supported Joshua and Caleb's counsel. Of course, the generation that had rejected their counsel died in the desert, so they weren't around to acknowledge that Caleb and Joshua were right.

from a faraway country, and they requested a peace treaty. Joshua agreed but later found out their true identity. He honored the treaty but made the Gibeonites Israel's servants.

Fight On to Victory! (Joshua 10–13)

These chapters highlight crucial victories Joshua and the Israelites achieved in Canaan with the Lord's help. Five Amorite kings fell to Joshua as the Lord hurled crushing hailstones on them and extended daylight to Joshua's advantage. Also, other kings, cities, and massive armies buckled under the power of the Lord resting on Joshua and his soldiers.

This Land Is Your Land (Joshua 13–22)

Joshua had reached old age, but he still had more to give to Israel. As directed by the Lord, he gave the tribes of Israel their respective shares of Canaan. The tribes still had to drive out the remaining Canaanites from those areas.

Caleb, Joshua's old spy buddy, requested and received the hill country of Hebron, which the Lord had promised to him 45 years earlier.

Unfortunately, the Israelites failed to expel all the Canaanites from the Promised Land and simply coexisted with many of them.

Who Says Old Soldiers Never Die? (Joshua 23–24)

Joshua gathered the rulers and people of Israel together. He reminded them of the Lord's mighty deeds on their behalf, challenged them to drive out the Canaanites, and urged them to serve and obey the Lord exclusively and to stay true to their covenant with Him. Joshua wrote in a book the people's pledge to do so, and then he dismissed the tribes to settle their territories. His life work having ended, he died at the age of 110.

Judges: Failed History Lessons

How well did you do in History? The Israelites flunked! The book of Judges is an open report card showing this sad fact to everyone who reads it.

Judah, You Go First (Judges 1–2)

The people of Israel asked the Lord which tribe should go first into its assigned territory. The Lord answered, "Judah." So Judah marched into its territory, soundly defeated the Canaanites living there, and captured the strategic city of Jerusalem.

The other tribes weren't as successful. When the smoke of battle cleared, significant numbers of Canaanites were still entrenched in the territories.

INFO BYTE
THE HIGH COURT OF JUDGES

Not to be confused with courtroom judges, most of the judges we read about in the book of Judges served as military leaders, rulers, and champions of justice. Deborah, the only female judge, was also a prophet.

Support Your Local Judges (Judges 3–12)

Coexisting with their pagan neighbors spelled trouble with a capital T. Before long, the Israelites were marrying pagans and worshiping their false gods. This spiritual decline brought divine judgment. The Lord gave the Israelites over to their enemies as a wake-up call. The people responded by repenting and calling on the Lord to deliver them. Subsequently, He raised up judges, who led the Israelites to victory over their enemies. However, not long after each taste of freedom, the Israelites fell back into their old pagan practices. This cycle of departure from righteousness, followed by judgment, followed by repentance, followed by deliverance recurs often in Judges.

The following chart summarizes the period of the judges:

The Period of the Judges

Biblical Account	Enemies	Period of Oppression	Judges	Period of Rest
Judges 3:5-11	Mesopotamians	8 years	Othniel	40 years

IN CASE YOU'RE WONDERING

DO MORALS AFFECT POLITICAL LEADERSHIP?

Big question! Look for an answer to this question as you read Joshua and Judges. For now, zip on over to the Proverbs and read Proverbs 14:34. Also, stop by 1 Timothy 2:1-2 to discover how believers can assist their government leaders.

Judges 3:12-30	Moabites Ammonites Amalekites	18 years	Ehud	80 years
Judges 3:31	Philistines?		Shamgar?	
Judges 4-5	Canaanites	20 years	Deborah Barak	40 years
Judges 6:1-8:32	Midianites	7 years	Gideon	40 years
Judges 8:33-9:57	Abimelech	3 years		
Judges 10:1-2			Tola	23 years
Judges 10:3-5			Jair	22 years
Judges 10:6-12:7	Ammonites	18 years	Jephthah	6 years
Judges 12:8-10			Ibzan	7 years
Judges 12:11-12			Elon	10 years
Judges 12:13-15			Abdon	8 years
Judges 13-16	Philistines	40 years	Samson	20 years

Samson: Is There a Cure for Hair Loss?
(Judges 13–16)

One of Israel's judges was Samson, who was extraordinarily strong before he lost his hair in Delilah's "Hair Salon." Afterwards, he was easily captured and imprisoned by his enemies, the Philistines. But was Samson's strength "rooted" solely in his hair? No. From the time of his birth Samson was separated to the Lord as a Nazirite—someone who pledged not to cut his hair, touch a dead body, or partake of any grapevine product (Numbers 6:1-6; Judges 13:5). But Samson derived his strength from the Holy Spirit, who came upon him at various times (Judges 14:6; 15:14). The haircut marked a low point in Samson's life. He had become disobedient, self-reliant, and unaware that the Lord had withdrawn from him. Without the Lord's presence and power, Samson was easy prey for the Philistines. When his hair grew back, his strength also returned. Having repented, he brought the house down, killing all the Philistines in the building.

Rogues Gallery (Judges 17–21)

The closing chapters of the book of Judges hang portraits of immoral rogues who reflected the times in which they lived—a period in which everyone rejected moral absolutes (Judges 21:25). Theft, rape, deviant sexual behavior, and kidnapping are just a few of the despicable deeds we read about in these chapters. The indictments stand as a warning to any society that opts to live without moral laws.

Ruth: A Love Story

Reading the book of Ruth after the book of Judges is like breathing clear, crisp, refreshing mountain air after leaving the choking air pollution of a big city far below. It's like finding a richly scented and exquisitely beautiful rose in a thorny thicket. The history recorded in the book of Judges depicts a people defiant toward God, but the history recorded in the book of Ruth portrays a woman devoted Him.

A Widows' Conference (Ruth 1)

Elimelech and his wife, Naomi, chose to leave Bethlehem in Judah during a famine. Believing a better life awaited them in the neighboring land of Moab, they and their sons, Mahlon and Kilion, moved there. During their stay Elimelech died, and their sons married Moabite women. Ten years later both sons died. Naomi decided to put Moab and the grief associated with it behind her and return to Judah. She suggested that her daughters-in-law return home to their mothers.

After the three widows conferred, one daughter-in-law, Orpah, decided to stay in Moab. However, the other daughter-in-law, Ruth, decided to accompany Naomi, choosing to identify with Naomi's homeland, people, and God.

Beauty and the Boss (Ruth 2)

After arriving in Judah, Ruth went into a farmer's fields to pick barley left behind by the harvesters. As it turned out, the farmer, Boaz, noticed this Moabite beauty and asked his workers who she was.

Romance began to blossom in the barley fields. Boaz instructed

INFO BYTE
WHAT'S IN A NAME?

The name Ruth means "beauty." This Moabitess was not only beautiful on the outside but on the inside as well.

Ruth to keep returning to his farm and to join his workers at break times. Beverages and food would be on the house! He explained how pleased he was that she had come not only to his farm but also to faith in the God of Israel.

The Farmer Takes a Wife (Ruth 3–4)

You just knew Boaz and Ruth would get married, didn't you? But tying the knot wasn't easy. Knowing that Boaz was a relative, Naomi coached Ruth to take a bath, splash on some perfume, and sleep at Boaz's feet one night. This strange scenario was actually an honorable custom that worked well for Ruth. She explained to Boaz, when he awoke in the night, that he was related to Naomi and that she—Ruth—wanted to marry him. Boaz was flattered but acknowledged that he knew of an even closer relative who was entitled to marry her. When Boaz notified the other relative of Ruth's situation, the man was interested in buying the property that had belonged to Naomi's husband. But when he learned that he would also have to marry and support Ruth, the relative forfeited his right to the property. This left the door open for Boaz to buy the property and marry Ruth.

It was a marriage made in heaven. Boaz, the son of Rahab (remember her from Jericho?), and Ruth, the beauty from Moab, became parents of a baby boy. They named him Obed, and he was destined to become the grandfather of King David. And Ruth would be the second Gentile woman in the genealogy of someone even greater than King David. King Jesus would be born someday as the family's greatest descendant!

LET'S GET TESTY

How Well Do You Know Your Judges?

After reading Judges 3–16, name the judges who match the following descriptions:

1. Brought the house down
2. Composed a song to commemorate a victory
3. Led an "army" of 300 and defeated the Midianites
4. Caleb's son-in-law
5. Left-handed assassin
6. Lost his hair, his strength, and his eyes
7. A combat-ready female
8. Her co-general
9. Used an ox goad to kill Philistines
10. Made a regrettable vow to the Lord

Answers: 1. Samson; 2. Deborah; 3. Gideon; 4. Othniel; 5. Ehud; 6. Samson; 7. Deborah; 8. Barak; 9. Shamgar; 10. Jephthah

IN CASE YOU'RE WONDERING

WASN'T RUTH NERVY TO PICK BARLEY IN BOAZ'S FIELDS?

Not at all. In the law of Moses, God had instructed His people not to pick their fields clean. They were told to leave some of the harvest for the poor (Leviticus 19:9-10; 23:22).

Answer yes or no.
1. Ruth lived in the time of the judges. _____
2. Barak was a female judge. _____
3. The Israelites lived by a strong set of absolutes in the time of the judges. _____
4. Samson was a Nazarene. _____
5. Naomi had three sons. _____
6. Boaz was Rahab's son. _____

(Answers: 1. Yes; 2. No; 3. No; 4. No; 5. No; 6. Yes.)

Three Men and a Kingdom (1 and 2 Samuel)

1. The unusual calling of Samuel to be a prophet

2. Why the prophet Samuel warned the Israelites about the dangers of having a king

3. The major negative consequences of David's watching another man's wife take a bath on a rooftop

First Samuel and 2 Samuel comprise one book in the Hebrew Bible. So we will treat them as one in our study. The history covered by the Samuel account stretches from the closing period of the judges through the last years of Israel's renowned King David. Hang on to your hat as we fly through this section of the Bible. The ride will take us on an emotional roller coaster to high points in Israel's history, then drop us suddenly to incredibly low points. We will read about the ministry of Samuel, one of Israel's finest prophets. Also, we will read about the rise and fall of Israel's first king, Saul. Then we will read about Israel's most famous king, David, who subdued powerful enemies but failed to subdue his own sexual lust.

The prophet Samuel is credited with writing part of the Samuel account, but his death, recorded in 1 Samuel 25:1, leads us to believe another person compiled the complete record.

As you read 1 and 2 Samuel, look for Israel's transition from rule by the judges to a monarchical form of government. Expect to see the royal crown move from Saul's head to David's. Anticipate bumping into the giant Goliath. Gasp when you watch David commit adultery, and empathize with him as he loses a baby boy and is later opposed by an egomaniacal, power-hungry adult son.

ABANDONED BABY AT THE TABERNACLE DOORSTEP?

Nursing children doesn't last very long today, but it continued quite a while in Old Testament times. Samuel may have been four or five years old when his mother stopped nursing him. So he wasn't wearing a little blue blanket when he became Eli's assistant.

IT'S A PROMISE!

"Trust in the Lord with all your heart; do not depend on your own understanding. Seek his will in all you do, and he will direct your paths."
(Proverbs 3:5-6)

You Saw Me Crying in the "Chapel" (1 Samuel 1–7)

No house is big enough for one man and two wives. Although Elkanah showed that he loved his wife, Hannah, deeply, he could not heal the hurt she felt as a barren woman. That hurt only intensified as Elkanah's other wife, who had children, ridiculed Hannah's barrenness (1 Samuel 1:1-8). So when Hannah visited the tabernacle in Shiloh, she prayed and wept, pleading silently with the Lord to give her a son and promising to dedicate the boy to the Lord as a Nazirite (remember Samson the Nazirite?).

Noticing Hannah's lips moving as she mouthed her silent prayer, Eli the priest accused her of being drunk. However, upon learning what was really going on, he assured her that the Lord would answer her prayer (1 Samuel 1:9-18).

True to her vow, after weaning her bundle of joy, whom she named Samuel, Hannah gave him to Eli to assist him in the tabernacle (1:19-28). Although Eli had two sons, they were scoundrels and, therefore, totally unqualified for ministry (see 1 Samuel 2:12-17). So the Lord called Samuel to be Israel's prophet and judge (1 Samuel 3). Later, the Philistines won a decisive victory over the Israelites. They captured the ark of the covenant and killed thirty thousand Israelites, including Eli's sons. When the tragic news reached old Eli, he fell backwards from his seat, sustained a broken neck, and died (1 Samuel 4). Eventually, though, with the Lord's intervention and Samuel's spiritual support, the ark was returned to Israel, and the Israelites devastated the Philistines (1 Samuel 5–7).

"We Want a King! We Want a King!" (1 Samuel 8–15)

Have you noticed how TV commercials make you feel underprivileged—even "out of it"—if you don't have what everybody else seems to have? "*All* the kids have the 'what's hot' toy!" "*All* the young professionals are driving our car!" "You owe it to yourself to discover what millions of successful men and women have discovered by using our product!" The Israelites didn't watch TV, but they had their eyes glued to the nations around them, and they saw that *all* those nations had kings. So they demanded that Samuel give them a king (1 Samuel 8:20).

The Lord told Samuel to warn the people about the consequences of having a king, but He permitted them to have their way. The king they got was Saul, a tall, handsome young man. He looked like the ideal king, and he seemed to be just what Israel needed when he rallied 330,000 men to fight and defeat the Ammonites (1 Samuel 11). But Saul became too big for his royal britches. He took upon himself Samuel's prerogative by presenting a burnt offering instead of waiting for Samuel to arrive and do it (1 Samuel 13:8-10). As a result of his disobedience, the Lord pledged to end Saul's kingship and give the crown to another (1 Samuel 13:11-14). On another occasion, Saul vowed to put to death any soldier who ate before the enemy was routed. But Jonathan, Saul's son, hadn't heard about this vow, so he ate (1 Samuel 14). When Saul found out that Jonathan had eaten, he planned to kill him. Fortunately, the Israelites esteemed Jonathan as a national hero and persuaded Saul to withdraw his son's death sentence. Later, Saul disobeyed the Lord's command to destroy the Amalekites and all their possessions and animals. He spared the Amalekites' king and the best livestock. When Samuel arrived at the end of the battle, he exposed Saul's disobedience and told him the crown would fall from his "big" head (1 Samuel 15).

INFO BYTE
THOSE PESKY AMALEKITES

The Amalekites had descended from Esau (Genesis 36:12). When the Israelites were traveling through the desert on their way to Canaan, the Amalekites launched a rear attack, assaulting the weak and faint stragglers (Exodus 17:8-16; Deuteronomy 25:17-18). So the Lord commanded Israel to annihilate the Amalekites (Deuteronomy 25:19).

From Shepherd's Rod to Sovereign Rule; Here Comes David (1 Samuel 16–2 Samuel 10:19)

These chapters introduce Israel's greatest king, David, whom the Bible identifies as a man after God's own heart (1 Samuel 13:14; Acts 13:22). Samuel privately anointed David king over Israel when David was a shepherd boy. David was clearly the Lord's choice, although Samuel had first guessed that David's big brother Eliab was the logical choice. After all, David was the youngest of Jesse's eight sons (1 Samuel 16:1-13).

Although David's anointing threatened Saul's grip on Israel, David actually consoled Saul in times of distress by playing sweet

INFO BYTE

THE BOAZ-DAVID CONNECTION

David's father was Jesse. His great-grandfather was Boaz. This significant family lived in Bethlehem where, centuries later, Jesus, "the son of David," was born.

harp music (1 Samuel 16:14-23). He also became a champion for Israel's army when he stared down the giant Goliath, who had defied and terrified Saul's soldiers. Trusting in the Lord for strength and eager to exalt the Lord's name, David took nine-foot, heavily armed Goliath down with a well-placed slingshot stone to the forehead. When the dust settled after Goliath's fall to the ground, David finished the big-mouthed giant off by whacking off his head with the giant's own sword (1 Samuel 17).

Watch Your Back!

At times Saul loved David. Other times, he became extremely jealous of him and tried to pin him to the wall with his spear. Eventually, David became a fugitive, hiding in caves with a small, but fiercely loyal, band of outlaws, while Saul pursued him relentlessly (1 Samuel 18–30). Ironically, Jonathan, Saul's son, helped David escape Saul's fury.

Finally, the all-clear signal sounded for David. The Philistines had killed Saul, but they had also killed Jonathan, David's best friend (1 Samuel 31–2 Samuel 1). David became king over Judah (2 Samuel 2), but ultimately all the tribes of Israel proclaimed him king (2 Samuel 5:1-5). David conquered and established Jerusalem as his capital city. He received a promise from God through the prophet Nathan that his lineage would produce an everlasting kingdom (2 Samuel 5:6–7:29).

David's early years as king were marked by military successes, stability, and justice. Everything was going well, but something bad—really bad—was about to happen!

Bathsheba Takes a Bath, and David Gets into Hot Water (2 Samuel 11–20)

Maybe looks *can* kill. One spring night, from his rooftop, King David looked at a beautiful neighbor woman who was taking a bath. If he had been out of town and fighting alongside his soldiers, what happened next would not have happened. But idleness often leads a person straight to the devil's workshop! David found out that the

gorgeous neighbor was Bathsheba, whose husband, Uriah, just happened to be an officer in David's army—and out of town on a military assignment.

The plot thickened.

David sent for Bathsheba, committed adultery with her, and got her pregnant.

The plot got thicker.

David ordered Uriah home from the battlefield, hoping Uriah and Bathsheba would sleep together. Uriah would have no reason to suspect that Bathsheba's pregnancy was due to anyone but himself. But the scheme didn't work. While home, Uriah's mind was exclusively on the war.

The plot got as thick as it could get.

So, David arranged to have Uriah killed on the front lines so he could marry Bathsheba. Amazing, isn't it, how David could fall from devotion to God to such a low-level life of lust, adultery, treachery, deception, and murder!

David repented and confessed his sin (Psalm 51), and God forgave him (Psalm 32), but nothing could turn back the tide of severe consequences launched by his sins. David was disgraced publicly. Bathsheba's baby died. One of David's sons, Amnon, raped his sister, Tamar. Another son, Absalom, arranged the murder of Amnon and rebelled against David. Civil war followed, and David became a fugitive. But proud, handsome, long-haired Absalom was eventually killed by David's general, Joab. Absalom's hair had become tangled in a low tree, and he was left dangling in midair when his mule kept going. Joab found him and hurled three spears through Absalom's heart.

Fading Glory (2 Samuel 21–24)

These concluding chapters tie up some loose ends of David's story in 2 Samuel. They recount an act of vengeance against Saul's survivors, a psalm David wrote, a report of the heroics of David's fighting men, and a census (taken for less than noble motives) that cost David much more than he bargained for—a pestilence spread across the land.

INFO BYTE
A ROOF WITH A VIEW

Houses in Bible times had flat roofs that afforded extra space for storage and/or living. Usually, outside stairs led to the roof. David had probably gone to his rooftop to relax and catch some cool breezes. Unfortunately, no cool breezes chilled his hot passion that night.

IN CASE YOU'RE WONDERING
NOT EXACTLY KING OF HIS CASTLE

Why did David's kids turn out so bad? We can only conjecture, but it does seem probable that David's immoral behavior gave his children an excuse to disregard God's laws and decency. Nonetheless, we can't directly link one person's behavior with someone else's sin.

LET'S GET TESTY

ON THE WAY TO THE KINGDOM

Cross out the wrong word(s) in the following sentences.

1. Elkanah/Elimelech was married to a barren woman.
2. Her name was Hagar/Hannah.
3. She prayed for a son, and Elijah/Eli assured her that God would grant her request.
4. She had a baby and named him Samson/Samuel.
5. The boy devoted himself to tabernacle/postal service.
6. Eventually, he became a king/prophet.
7. He anointed Solomon/Saul as Israel's first king.
8. But Saul disobeyed the Lord by sparing the Ammonites'/Amalekites' king and some of their livestock.
9. So Samuel anointed Daniel/David as the next king of Israel.
10. This new king had distinguished himself by killing the Philistine giant Gomer/Goliath.
11. Jonathan/Jesse and David were best friends.
12. David's great-grandfather was Jesse/Boaz.
13. David lusted for Bathsheba when he saw her walking her dog/taking a bath.
14. Bathsheba's husband was Uzzah/Uriah.
15. David had Bathsheba's husband decorated/killed on the battlefield.
16. Absalom, David's nephew/son, rebelled against him.
17. Absalom was known for his beautiful, long mosaics/hair.
18. David's son Amnon/Abner raped his own sister.
19. Her name was Tammy/Tamar.
20. Joab/Jonah killed Absalom.

(Answers: The wrong words are 1. Elimelech; 2. Hagar; 3. Elijah; 4. Samson; 5. postal; 6. king; 7. Solomon; 8. Ammonites; 9. Daniel; 10. Gomer; 11. Jesse; 12. Jesse; 13. walking her dog; 14. Uzzah; 15. decorated; 16. nephew; 17. mosaics; 18. Abner; 19. Tammy; 20. Jonah)

CHAPTER NINE

The Divided Kingdom
(1 and 2 Kings, 1 and 2 Chronicles)

Chances are, world geography has changed significantly since you last looked at a world atlas. The breakup of the Soviet Union is just one indication that nations can break apart almost overnight. First and 2 Kings, organized as one book in the Hebrew Bible, outdistance our evening news programs with the breaking story of ancient Israel's dividing into two kingdoms. Subsequent news from 1 and 2 Kings traces the decline of both kingdoms to their respective collapses, and we receive updated reports of what caused such calamity as we read these fast-paced books.

Wise King Solomon and his Dumb Marriages
(1 Kings 1–11)

King David had grown old and feeble, and his oldest son, Adonijah, added to his misery by trying to take over the throne. However, the prophet Nathan told David that the Lord had selected Solomon to be David's successor. So David ordered a swift coronation ceremony for Solomon. Seeing that Solomon had been crowned king to the

SOME THINGS YOU'LL DISCOVER IN THIS CHAPTER

1. What King Solomon's 300 concubines ultimately cost the kingdom of Israel

2. The many kings of Israel and Judah and their numerous exploits

3. How one woman scared Elijah more than all the opposing prophets of Baal

INFO BYTE
SOL WHO?

Solomon, whose name means "peaceable," was David's son by Bathsheba (2 Samuel 12:24; 1 Chronicles 3:5). His empire enjoyed peace, productivity, and prosperity unmatched in the history of Israel. During his reign, the magnificent temple bearing his name was constructed. He is listed in Matthew 1:6-7 in the lineage of Israel's greatest king, Jesus. As a wise king whose rule was characterized by peace, Solomon pictures, in part, the infinite wisdom King Jesus possesses and the perfect peace He gives to His subjects.

overwhelming delight of the people, Adonijah withdrew his claim and begged for mercy (1 Kings 1).

Here are some dates to sweeten your knowledge of the time of the kings in the Old Testament.

The United Kingdom (1050–930 B.C.)
Saul's reign (1050–1010 B.C.)
David's reign (1010–970 B.C.)
Solomon's reign (970–930 B.C.)

The Divided Kingdom (930 B.C.–)

Israel (Northern Kingdom)	Judah (Southern Kingdom)
First king: Jeroboam (930–913 B.C.	First king: Rehoboam (930–909 B.C.)
Last King: Hoshea (732–722 B.C.)	Last king: Zedekiah (597–586 B.C.)
Years as a nation: slightly over 200	Years as a nation: nearly 350

Just before he died, David encouraged young King Solomon to be strong in character and conduct by obeying God's law (1 Kings 2:1-9). The fatherly advice was not wasted, for Solomon showed early in his reign that he wanted to honor the Lord. Given opportunity to request whatever he wanted from the Lord, the young king asked for wisdom to discern between good and evil for Israel's benefit. The Lord was pleased to grant this request and give, as a bonus, riches and honor—and longevity, too, if Solomon would continue to honor Him (1 Kings 3). First Kings 4 describes Solomon's kingdom as extensive, prosperous, and peaceful. Solomon had 40,000 stalls of horses for his chariots and 12,000 horsemen. His wisdom was unmatched anywhere, and he was credited with 3,000 proverbs and 1,005 songs. He was also an outstanding botanist and zoologist.

Perhaps Solomon is best remembered for building and dedicating a temple—a house for God—in Jerusalem (1 Kings 5–8). Workers and materials for the construction came from as far away as Lebanon. When the ark of the covenant was set up in the temple's Most Holy Place, the glory of the Lord filled the temple.

But wise Solomon was really dumb in the love department! He made 700 trips to the altar and also took 300 concubines. Just try to picture his royal closet littered with thousands of women's sandals. And think what Solomon had to endure with thousands of unmentionables hanging in the royal bathroom! We can only guess how exhausting shopping trips were for Solomon. Do you wonder how deafening it must have been for Solomon when a trip to the kitchen was met with the roar of 1,000 voices shouting, "Stay out of my kitchen!" Eventually, Solomon's wives persuaded him to worship their false gods—an act of idolatry that incurred the Lord's anger. As punishment for his waywardness, Solomon's kingdom would be divided in the days of his son Rehoboam (1 Kings 9–11).

The Not-So-Great Divide (1 Kings 12–17)

Raising taxes has never made any leader popular, so we shouldn't be surprised that King Rehoboam's popularity rating fell lower than a rock dropped into the Jordan. Ten of Israel's 12 tribes seceded from the United Kingdom, proclaimed Jeroboam king, and called their kingdom "Israel." The other two tribes, Judah and Benjamin (who lived in the southern part of Israel), remained loyal to Rehoboam and became known as the kingdom of Judah. Because Jeroboam didn't want his followers returning to Jerusalem (which was controlled by the kingdom of Judah) to worship at the temple, he set up two worship centers in Israel—one at Bethel and the other at Dan. A golden calf at each place would serve as Israel's gods! This defiant act of idolatry launched Israel on a downward course that ultimately destroyed the nation.

Meanwhile, Judah, too, was sliding into idolatry—even to the point of employing male cult prostitutes. Fortunately, Judah would experience revival from time to time, which restored the Lord's blessing temporarily and prolonged its life.

Reign, Reign, Go Away! A Brief History of Israel's Kings
(1 Kings 12–2 Kings 17)
Scan the following list of Israel's kings, and you will begin to see how evil they were and what happened to them.

Jeroboam. He split the kingdom, initiated idol worship, and ended up with a withered arm and a dead son, Abijah (1 Kings 12:1–14:20).

WHAT'S UP WITH THE GOOD BOOK?

"Scripture has been, and can be the most dangerous weapon in the world unless it is carefully read and understood in full context."—*Sidney J. Harris*

INFO BYTE
NAME THAT KINGDOM!

As we proceed through 1 and 2 Kings and 1 and 2 Chronicles, we will sometimes refer to Israel as the "northern kingdom" and Judah as the "southern kingdom." Occasionally, Scripture calls the northern kingdom "Samaria."

INFO BYTE
BAAL

Archaeology has uncovered a white lime-stone slab depicting Baal with a club in his right hand and a lance in his left hand. The lance is decorated with branches, perhaps representing lightning. On his helmet are bull's horns. He was regarded by the Canaanites and Phoenicians as the god of fertility and rain. The worship of Baal included prostitution and occasionally child sacrifice.

Nadab. A chip off the old block, this son of Jeroboam committed evil and was killed by a conspirator named Baasha (1 Kings 15:25-31).

Baasha. Another wicked, idolatrous king, he fell under God's judgment (1 Kings 15:33-16:7).

Elah. A son of Baasha, Elah got drunk and was assassinated. His whole family was wiped out (1 Kings 16:8-14).

Zimri. The victim of a coup, Zimri burned down a section of his palace on himself. He ended up as toast (1 Kings 16:15-20)!

Omri. He had to fend off a rival "king," Timri. Omri built the city of Samaria, but he also built a wretched reputation as Israel's most wicked king (1 Kings 16:21-28).

Ahab. This king married the infamous Jezebel. Together, they instituted Baal worship, killed prophets, tried to kill the prophet Elijah, and experienced violent deaths. They both went to the dogs, literally (1 Kings 16:29-22:40; 2 Kings 9:30-37)!

Ahaziah. Ahab's son Ahaziah served Baal. He fell as Israel's king—right through his upper room's lattice. He never recovered from this violent fall (1 Kings 22:51—2 Kings 1:18).

Joram. During his reign, the Arameans besieged the city of Samaria (2 Kings 3; 6:24-7:20).

Jehu. Commissioned by the prophet Elisha to punish Ahab's descendants, Jehu killed more than 70 of Ahab's sons and relatives and also their priests. But Jehu failed to obey God's laws, preferring idol worship over the worship of God. Incidentally, Jehu drove the fastest chariot in Israel (2 Kings 9-10).

Jehoahaz. He practiced idol worship, as his father, Jehu, had done, and was assaulted by the Arameans (2 Kings 13:1-9).

Jehoash. A good fighter but a terrible spiritual leader, Jehoash gained a military victory over Judah's King Amaziah. He followed the idolatrous ways of the kings before him (2 Kings 13:10-14:16).

Jeroboam II. He regained some lost territory, but he, too, was a wicked king (2 Kings 14:23-29).

Zechariah. The son of Jeroboam II, Zechariah reigned only six

months, but he crammed a lot of evil into his brief reign. He was assassinated by Shallum (2 Kings 15:8-12).

Shallum. What goes around comes around. Shallum was assassinated after reigning only one month (2 Kings 15:13-15).

Menahem. This extremely evil man raised taxes on the rich in order to give Assyria protection money (2 Kings 15:16-22).

Pekahiah. Another wicked king, Pekahiah, was taken down by the assassin Pekah (2 Kings 15:23-26).

Pekah. Here we go again. The Assyrians assaulted Israel, and Pekah was eventually removed from the throne by Hoshea, who assassinated him (2 Kings 15:27-31).

Hoshea. Israel's last king, Hoshea, paid protection money to Assyria but tried to enlist Egypt's military help. The scheme failed. The Assyrians overran Israel, threw Hoshea into prison, carted off most of the Israelites in 722 B.C., and repopulated the land with foreigners (2 Kings 17).

INFO BYTE
A SERIOUS DROUGHT

The Lord had plagued Israel with a three-year drought, but rain finally came when Elijah's faith triumphed over the prophets of Baal in the altar contest. Then Elijah had them put to death (1 Kings 18:41-45).

Israel's Twin Towers of Faith: Elijah and Elisha (1 Kings 17—2 Kings 13)

Elijah and his successor, Elisha, stood against Israel's corrupt kings and wicked ways like twin towers of faith. Much of Elijah's ministry took place during Ahab's reign. After seeing God perform miracles, Elijah rebuked Ahab for rejecting the Lord and worshiping Baal, and he called for a showdown on Mount Carmel between himself and hundreds of false prophets. If Baal sent fire from the sky to consume the false prophets' sacrifice, he would be declared worthy of worship, but if the Lord sent fire down to consume Elijah's sacrifice, He would be declared the true God.

You might think that Baal, who held a lightning rod, could have struck the sacrifice and set it ablaze, but nothing happened because he was a phony. However, in response to Elijah's faith and prayer, the fire of the Lord consumed Elijah's sacrifice, the wood, the stones, and the dirt. It even licked up all the water in the ditch! This miracle turned the hearts of the Israelites back to the Lord temporarily.

IN CASE YOU'RE WONDERING
SWING LOW, SWEET CHARIOT!

Yes, that old spiritual recalls what happened to Elijah. God sent a chariot and horses of fire in a whirlwind to pick up Elijah and taxi him live to heaven (2 Kings 2:11). Centuries earlier, Enoch had also been taken to heaven without dying (Genesis 5:24).

IT'S A PROMISE!

"So you see, the Lord knows how to rescue godly people from their trials, even while punishing the wicked right up until the day of judgment." (2 Peter 2:9)

Life's high points are sometimes followed by low points. After the exhilaration of defeating the false prophets on Mount Carmel, Elijah learned that Ahab's strong-willed, diabolical wife, Jezebel, had put out a contract on his life. So Elijah dropped his faith, feared for his life, and ran for cover—clear out of Israel, south through Judah, and far into the desert. Taking refuge under a broom tree, he asked the Lord to end his life. (If he had really wanted to die, he could have stayed in Israel. Jezebel would have granted his request.) Nevertheless, the Lord revived Elijah, assured him that He had everything under control, and commissioned him to go to Damascus and anoint two new kings and a new prophet, Elisha.

The story of Elisha can be found in 2 Kings 2–13. This prophet asked for a double portion of Elijah's spirit, and it seems he received it. He performed twice as many miracles as Elijah. His prophetic career involved kings and leaders of Israel, Syria, and Judah, but neither he nor Elijah before him was able to stop Israel from sliding into disaster.

National Decline, Southern Style
(2 Kings 18–25)

Judah, the southern kingdom, enjoyed some periods of revival, but it, too, declined and ultimately collapsed. The following list includes the kings and one queen of Judah, but only a few will be reviewed after the listing.

- **Rehoboam** (1 Kings 14:21-31)
- **Abijam** (1 Kings 15:1-8)
- **Asa** (1 Kings 15:9-24; 2 Chronicles 14–16)
- **Jehoshaphat** (1 Kings 22:41-50; 2 Chronicles 17–21:3)
- **Jehoram** (2 Kings 8:16-24; 2 Chronicles 21)
- **Ahaziah** (2 Kings 8:25-29; 9:14-29; 2 Chronicles 22:1-9)
- **Queen Athaliah** (2 Kings 11; 2 Chronicles 22:10–23:15)
- **Joash** (2 Kings 12; 2 Chronicles 24:1-27)
- **Amaziah** (2 Kings 14:1-22; 2 Chronicles 25)
- **Uzziah** (aka Azariah) (2 Kings 15:1-7; 2 Chronicles 26)

- Jotham (2 Kings 15:32-38; 2 Chronicles 27)
- Ahaz (2 Kings 16; 2 Chronicles 28)
- Hezekiah (2 Kings 18–20; 2 Chronicles 29-32)
- Manasseh (2 Kings 21:1-18; 2 Chronicles 33:1-20)
- Amon (2 Kings 21:19-26; 2 Chronicles 33:21-25)
- Josiah (2 Kings 22:1–23:30; 2 Chronicles 34–35)
- Jehoahaz (2 Kings 23:31-35; 2 Chronicles 36:1-4)
- Jehoiakim (2 Kings 23:34–24:7; 2 Chronicles 36:5-8)
- Jehoiachin (2 Kings 24:8-17; 25:27-30; 2 Chronicles 36:9-10)
- Zedekiah (2 Kings 24:18–25:26; 2 Chronicles 36:11-16)

Lots of Ups and Downs

Judah survived about a century and a half longer than Israel, but it didn't take full advantage of those extra years to turn its spiritual decline around. Hezekiah, a king of sound faith, began his rule in Judah shortly after Israel's collapse. He brought about a series of reforms to remove idol worship from the land, and God honored his devotion by keeping the Assyrians at bay. He even extended Hezekiah's life.

Hezekiah's son Manasseh walked a different road, however. He reversed his dad's reforms and even offered his son as a sacrifice to a pagan idol. During his 55-year reign, evil spread across Judah like a flood.

Josiah launched reforms after Manasseh died. He called for a restoration of the temple, which had fallen into disrepair. While the repairs were under way, a priest discovered a scroll with the law of Moses written on it. Perhaps, as some scholars insist, this scroll contained the book of Deuteronomy.

This remarkable discovery cut to Josiah's heart and subsequently to the hearts of Judah's leaders. Josiah expunged the land of foreign idols and did all he could to lead Judah into a life of obedience to the Law.

Then *wham!* Along came four evil kings in succession. Zedekiah, the last of these kings, witnessed the destruction of Jerusalem and the temple by the Babylonians in 586 B.C. One of the last scenes he saw before the enemy blinded him was that of his sons being killed.

IN CASE YOU'RE WONDERING
WHAT ARE 1 AND 2 CHRONICLES ALL ABOUT?

These two books were originally one book. They cover the same period of history reported in 2 Samuel through 2 Kings.

The fall of Judah was decisive and deadly; many of its people were dragged off to Babylon to live in exile there. It would be seventy long years before any exiles returned to Judah.

First Kings began with a united kingdom enjoying peace and prosperity. Second Kings ended with a divided kingdom plundered and pummeled. Wise King Solomon ruled Israel at the beginning of 1 Kings. Foreign kings ruled by the end of 2 Kings. A glorious temple arose at the beginning of the period of the kings, but that temple was in ruins at the end of the period. The people of Israel celebrated God's providence when the temple was dedicated but came under His punishment when the temple was destroyed. The nation was close to God at the beginning of 1 Kings but far from Him by the end of 2 Kings. The people of Israel were safe in their own land when the period of the kings began, but they were scattered to foreign lands when the period closed.

The book of 2 Kings ends with a sliver of hope, though. After 37 years of exile and imprisonment, King Jehoiachin of Judah was released to become a part of the court in Babylon. The royal line would not be destroyed.

LET'S GET TESTY

KINGS, KINGDOMS, AND KILLERS

Answer T for true or F for false.

____ 1. Solomon's mother was Bathsheba.

____ 2. Elijah ordered the killing of prophets of Babel.

____ 3. Jezebel put out a contract on Elijah's life.

____ 4. Israel lay to the south of Judah.

____ 5. Jehu was a super-fast chariot driver.

____ 6. Judah existed about 150 years longer than Israel.

____ 7. Zedekiah's sons were killed.

____ 8. Josiah initiated reforms in Judah.

____ 9. Omri was an extremely wicked king.

____10. Ahab was married to Jezebel.

___11. Athaliah was a queen in Judah.

___12. Israel's last king was Hoshea.

___13. Shallum assassinated Zechariah.

___14. Shallum was assassinated after ruling as king only one month.

___15. Hezekiah brought reforms to Israel.

(Answers: 1. T; 2. F; 3. T; 4. F; 5. T; 6. T; 7. T; 8. T; 9. T; 10. T; 11. T; 12. T; 13. T; 14. T; 15. F.)

CHAPTER TEN

To Babylon and Back
(Ezra, Nehemiah, and Esther)

For 70 years God's people, the Jews, were captives in Babylon. This period of their history, known as the Babylonian captivity, was hardly a vacation in paradise. They were foreigners in Babylon, a pagan country, and they pined for their homeland and the freedom to worship again the God whom they had offended (Psalm 137:1-6). They must have known that they had brought on the Captivity by violating the Sabbath and by worshiping false gods (Deuteronomy 28:58-65; 30:16-18; 2 Chronicles 36:20-21). But God had not forgotten or abandoned His people. Long before the people of Judah were dragged into captivity, God predicted through the prophet Jeremiah that the captivity would end after 70 years (Jeremiah 25:11). He even foretold which king—Cyrus—would permit the Jews to return to their homeland (Isaiah 44:28).

Pack Your Bags; We're Going Home
(Ezra 1–6)
Babylon, an extremely powerful nation, had deported the Jews from Judah to Babylon in three waves: 605 B.C., 597 B.C., and 586

SOME THINGS YOU'LL DISCOVER IN THIS CHAPTER

1. How the Israelites made it back home after being captives in Babylon

2. How the Jews rebuilt Jerusalem's city wall in only 52 days

3. How a beautiful young Jewish woman saved the Jews from extinction

83

INFO BYTE

TWO HUNDRED YEARS FROM NOW

The prediction that King Cyrus would permit the Jews to return to Judah from Babylon came through the prophet Isaiah, who lived about 200 years before Cyrus. No one can predict by name who a nation's top political leader will be and what he will do 200 years from now. Only God knows the future. The fact that God's prediction came true affirms the Bible as God's Word and not simply the product of keen human insight.

IN CASE YOU'RE WONDERING

WHAT IN THE WORLD?

In the time of Ezra, some big world events transpired. The battles of Salamis, Thermopylae, and Marathon were waged. Confucius and Buddha died. The Bible's focus, however, is on events of the time that affected God's people. Remember, the Bible is not a world history book but a book about the history of redemption.

84

B.C. But as powerful a nation as Babylon was, it met its match when the Medes and Persians, led by Cyrus, overthrew it in 539 B.C. Cyrus, a Persian, had conquered Media in 550 B.C. and formed the Medo-Persian Empire. Four years later he conquered Asia Minor. After conquering Babylon, he established Darius the Mede to rule in Babylon.

The book of Ezra records the favorable treatment the Jews in Babylon received at the hands of Cyrus and the adventures of Zerubbabel and Ezra in leading two separate expeditions from Babylon to Jerusalem. Zerubbabel, a direct descendant of King David, served as "general contractor" for the rebuilding of the temple in Jerusalem and as the Jews' political leader in their homeland. Ezra, a scribe from a priestly family, returned to Jerusalem to institute worship in the temple and to teach God's law to the returnees.

Cyrus of Persia offered the Jews the opportunity to go home, resettle Jerusalem, and rebuild the temple. Apparently, he wanted to gain the favor of as many gods as possible by allowing conquered people to resettle their lands and worship their regional gods. When he issued his charitable decree in 538 B.C. allowing the Jews to return home, about 50,000 of them took him up on his offer. Led by Zerubbabel, they went back to Jerusalem, rebuilt the altar at the temple site, and observed religious feasts before starting to rebuild the temple. The construction didn't go along without a hitch, though. A Persian governor named Tattenai led a delegation in opposition to what the Jews were doing. But after jumping through some substantial bureaucratic hoops, the beleaguered workers completed the temple and dedicated it to the Lord.

Give Us Another Wave (Ezra 7–10)

Ezra himself led a second wave of Jews from Babylon to Jerusalem about 80 years after the first group returned under the leadership of Zerubbabel. This second wave was much smaller, only about 1,800, but they displayed great faith by traveling the 900 miles to Jerusalem without an armed escort. However, they did carry a letter from the king Artaxerxes, instructing his territorial governors to give Ezra and his group whatever they needed for their journey and for worship in Jerusalem.

After reaching Jerusalem, Ezra led the Jews in a renewed commitment to God's law, even to the point that they willingly ended their unlawful marriages.

A Cluster of Dates

Some scholars suggest the 70 years of the Babylonian captivity may be counted from the third deportation of the Jews from Jerusalem to Babylon in 586 B.C. to the completion of the rebuilding of the temple in Jerusalem in 515 B.C. Other scholars count the 70 years from the beginning of the Captivity in 605 B.C. to 536 B.C., when the foundation of the temple was laid. Significant dates from this period of Israel's history, often called the "Times of Captivity and Return," appear below.

First Deportation to Babylon	605 B.C.
Second Deportation to Babylon	597 B.C.
Third Deportation to Babylon	586 B.C.
Babylon Falls to Cyrus	539 B.C.
Cyrus's Decree	538 B.C.
First Return to Jerusalem—Zerubbabel Arrives	536 B.C.
Temple's Foundation Laid	536 B.C.
Temple Completed	515 B.C.
Second Return to Jerusalem—Ezra Arrives	457 B.C.
Third Return to Jerusalem—Nehemiah Arrives	444 B.C.

Smile! You're in Artaxerxes' Courtroom
(Nehemiah 1:1–2:10)

Nehemiah, a devout Jew and the author of the book of Nehemiah, held a highly responsible position in the court of Artaxerxes I. He was the king's cupbearer, charged with the task of first tasting and then serving the king's wine. If anyone tried to poison the king's

INFO BYTE
THE ROAD HOME

The returnees' 900-mile journey from Babylon to Jerusalem would have taken more than four months—from March to July (Ezra 7:8-9).

IT'S A PROMISE!

"When they call on me, I will answer; I will be with them in trouble. I will rescue them and honor them. I will satisfy them with a long life and give them my salvation." (Psalm 91:15-16)

WHAT'S IN A NAME?

The name Nehemiah means "the Lord consoles." Truly the Lord consoled Nehemiah by replacing his sadness with joy. When Nehemiah heard that the wall of Jerusalem was broken down, he was deeply saddened. However, when the Lord enabled him and his countrymen to rebuild the wall, he experienced great joy (compare Nehemiah 1:4 and 12:43).

wine, Nehemiah would be the first to know. Theoretically, he would give the king a "drop-dead" hint not to drink the wine. Nehemiah had another responsibility—to look pleasant in the king's presence. Service with a smile was more than a motto in the king's courtroom; it was just plain smart to put on a happy face. A frown might win a free ticket to the gallows!

However, one day Nehemiah received sad news from a countryman that Jerusalem's wall was broken down and the gates were burned. So after four months of fasting, praying, and confessing Israel's waywardness, Nehemiah approached the king with a request in his heart but a sad look on his face. When the king noticed Nehemiah's down-in-the-dumps countenance, he asked the reason. Quickly, Nehemiah related the bad news he had received about Jerusalem, shot a silent prayer to heaven, and asked the king to authorize him to rebuild Jerusalem. The request was granted, and before long Nehemiah was on his way to Jerusalem, much to the displeasure of two governors—Sanballat of Samaria and Tobiah of Ammon.

No Place for Wallflowers (Nehemiah 2:11–7:73)

Three days after arriving in Jerusalem Nehemiah made a nighttime inspection of the city's wall. Then he met with the city fathers, related how God had given him the opportunity to rebuild the wall, and challenged them to join in the effort. Soon the enormous task was under way, but critics, hostile enemies, and conspirators tried to stop it. This was no time for wallflowers; the workers had to defend their work stations. Nevertheless, the project forged ahead as workers held a tool in one hand and a weapon in the other. In 52 days the city's wall was rebuilt.

It's Time to Build the People, Too
(Nehemiah 8–13)

The priest Ezra spearheaded events that led to another revival among the people in Jerusalem. Key among them was the reading

of the Law translated from Hebrew into Aramaic. When the people heard the Law, they confessed their sins and repented. Believing that reforms had taken hold in Jerusalem, Nehemiah returned to the Persian court. Seven years later, he returned to Jerusalem to further enforce the reforms set in motion by the revival.

Beauty and the Feast (Esther 1–2)

It was a long drunken feast in King Xerxes's (also called Ahasuerus) winter palace at Susa. The year was 482 B.C., about forty years before Nehemiah made his first trip to Jerusalem. The king had invited officials from throughout the empire to this party so he could show off his treasures, one of which was his wife, Vashti. But Vashti refused to play by the king's rules. On the final day of the feast, when he summoned Vashti to parade her beauty, he received an abrupt refusal. Infuriated, Xerxes held a contest to find a replacement for Vashti. A young, beautiful Jewish woman named Esther was chosen to succeed Vashti, but Esther's uncle, Mordecai, a member of the Persian bureaucracy, warned her not to reveal her nationality. Esther soon proved her worth by revealing an assassination plot against the king, which Mordecai had uncovered.

The Man Who Refused to Bow (Esther 3–4)

Four years earlier, an Amalekite named Haman had been appointed to a high position in Persia. As we have seen already in this study, Jews and Amalekites had been in bitter conflict for centuries. Now that conflict embroiled two men—Haman, an Amalekite, and Mordecai, a Jew. Mordecai refused to bow down to Haman according to the custom in honor of Haman's rank, so Haman blew an Amalekite gasket! He hatched a plot to kill all the Jews in Persia and seize their property. Mordecai heard of the plot, made official by royal decree, and appealed to Esther for help.

INFO BYTE
THE REST OF THE STORY

The Feast of Purim, an annual Jewish celebration held early in March, honors the story of Esther. Purim marks the day God rescued the Jews who lived in Persia at the time of King Xerxes from annihilation at the hands of Haman, a court official.

IN CASE YOU'RE WONDERING
WHAT'S THE MEANING OF *PUR?*

The word *pur* or *lot* (Esther 3:7) refers to a die that Haman cast to determine the best time to execute his plan against the Jews. Some scholars suggest that Haman may have rolled the die on a large calendar. Of course, what superstitious Haman failed to realize is that God is in control of time and destiny.

What's Cookin' Isn't to Haman's Liking (Esther 5–7)

Esther put her life on the line by arranging to see the king without an invitation. Then she arranged two banquets to gain Xerxes' approval, believing the best way to a man's heart is through his stomach. Her guests included not only Xerxes but also Haman. In the meantime, Haman built a gallows, thinking he would ask King Xerxes for permission to hang Mordecai. But Xerxes decided to reward Mordecai for revealing the assassination plot four years earlier, and he ordered Haman to carry out the reward. At the second banquet, Esther revealed her heritage and Haman's plot against the Jews. For a few moments Xerxes stepped outside to consider the plight of Esther and her people. Haman used this interval to beg Esther for his life, but he trembled so much that he fell on the couch where Esther was sitting. When the king returned and found Haman on the couch, he assumed the worst and ordered Haman to be hanged on the gallows prepared for Mordecai.

This Isn't Gallows Humor (Esther 8–10)

Once a Persian king issued an edict, it could not be reversed. So the Jews were still open to attack even while Haman was dangling from the gallows. However, Xerxes introduced another edict allowing the Jews to defend themselves if attacked. The Jews succeeded in warding off every attack, and they defeated their enemies. Esther persuaded the king to extend the Jews' efforts for another day and to hang Haman's ten sons. Mordecai was appointed second-in-command to the king, and the Jews were safe.

LET'S GET TESTY

HOW DO YOU SPELL RELIEF?

Circle the letter that indicates who brought relief to a difficult situation.

1. He uncovered a plot to assassinate Xerxes.

    A. Ezra

    B. Haman

    C. Mordecai

2. **He signed a decree allowing the Jews to return to Jerusalem.**

    A. Nehemiah

    B. Zerubbabel

    C. Cyrus

3. **He brought revival to Jerusalem.**

    A. Ezra

    B. Artaxerxes I

    C. Haman

4. **He ordered the execution of Mordecai's enemy, Haman.**

    A. Sanballat

    B. Sinbad

    C. Solomon

    D. Xerxes

5. **She saved the Jews from annihilation.**

    A. Ruth

    B. Esther

    C. Vashti

6. **He led the Jews to rebuild Jerusalem's broken-down wall.**

    A. Nebuchadnezzar

    B. Nadab

    C. Nehemiah

(Answers: 1. C; 2. C; 3. A; 4. D; 5. B; 6. C)

CHAPTER ELEVEN

Poetry in Motion (Job, Psalms, Proverbs, Ecclesiastes, and Song of Songs)

Do you like poetry? Even if you're not wild about sonnets or couplets or nursery rhymes or haiku, you will enjoy reading the Bible books classified as poetry. They express life's struggles, victories, wisdom, love, and lessons for everything from relationships to finances. From these books we learn: how to handle trials, how to choose our friends, how to avoid moral failure, how to succeed in business, how to experience joy, and how to empathize with those who hurt. So let's set the poetry in motion right now!

Job in the Crosshairs (Job 1–2)

The book of Job describes the sufferings of a man named Job, his patience, his triumphant faith, and the agelong conflict between good and evil, God and Satan. As the story of Job opens, we learn that Job was both righteous and rich. He worshiped God and avoided evil. He was also a family man, having a wife, seven sons, and three daughters. His livestock numbered 7,000 sheep, 3,000

SOME THINGS YOU'LL DISCOVER IN THIS CHAPTER

1. God took a lot away from Job even though Job didn't do anything wrong. (It's all explained at the end.)

2. The Psalms are not just poetry, but worship. Accompanied by music, they foster an intimate experience of God.

3. Proverbs gives us great advice for practical living.

91

camels, 500 yoke of oxen, and 500 female donkeys. In addition, he had numerous servants.

But Satan accused Job before God, claiming that Job wouldn't serve God if God took away everything Job had. In other words, Satan suggested Job played up to God for what he could get from God. Showing confidence in Job's integrity, God permitted Satan to test Job. Satan would learn that Job's faith was genuine; he wasn't a gold digger.

Relentlessly, Satan struck Job with severe trials. In quick succession Job lost his livestock, his servants, his sons and daughters, and his health. But Job's faith remained strong. Even when his wife advised him to curse God and die, Job refused to abandon his faith in God. Satan inflicted Job with severe disease and illness. A look at Job's medical records reveals that he suffered massive boils (Job 2:7-8), extreme pain (Job 2:13), parched, infected skin that was covered with worms (7:5), and perhaps bone cancer (30:30).

Job must have lived around the time of Abraham, nearly 2,000 years before the birth of Jesus. He lived 140 years, a life span that matches that of Abraham's era. Livestock was an indicator of Job's wealth, as it was in Abraham's time. Like Abraham, Job served as the priest for his family. Of course, Job may have lived before Abraham, but it is unlikely that he lived at a later time.

Mouths in Overdrive, Brains in Neutral
(Job 3–37)

Hearing about Job's misfortunes, three of his "friends" showed up to comfort him. To their credit, they stuck with him through his suffering. However, they debated Job's insistence that he had done nothing amiss to bring on his troubles. The friends argued that the troubles must have been caused by some sin Job had committed. In fact, they put Job so much on the defensive that he began to sound self-righteous. It took a younger man, Elihu, to bring perspective to the situation for both Job and his friends.

Now That's Character

Scripture honors Job as a man of outstanding moral and spiritual character. Referring to His intention to send judgment to Judah, the Lord mentioned Job, along with Noah and Daniel, as a man whose righteousness stood out from the crowd (Ezekiel 14:14, 20). James 5:11 cites Job as an example of patience. In one of his answers to his friends, Job assured them that he would come through his trials as pure as gold tested by fire.

INFO BYTE
THE TITLE OF PSALMS

The Hebrew title is "Praise" or "Book of Praises." The "Psalms" title derives from the Greek. The early Christian fathers referred to this book as the Psalter.

Who's in Charge, Job? (Job 38–42)

After listening patiently to his friends, Job received a revelation from God. God spoke to him from a whirlwind. He reminded Job that Job could not unlock the mysteries of the created universe. How, then, could Job possibly understand spiritual mysteries? Confessing his pride and finiteness, Job acknowledged God's sovereignty and repented.

God corrected Job's friends and restored Job's fortunes, actually doubling all of Job's assets from what they had been before the trials began. Although Job had experienced many severe trials, he emerged from them with a clearer picture of God's faithfulness. The trials had refined Job's righteousness and deepened his relationship with God. Perhaps the story of Job demonstrates that it is easier to look up when we are flat on our backs!

Poetry Set to Music (The Book of Psalms)

Psalms are all about worship. When you read Psalms, you will feel that you are reading an ancient book filled with a variety of sacred songs. Some psalms celebrate God's majesty. Others dedicate the worshiper to God's service. Still others thank Him for His creation, for His faithfulness, and for His Scriptures. Joy spills over from some psalms. Others communicate the hush of contemplation. A few open the door to the confessional of the heart. Some reveal a

INFO BYTE
NO KIDDING; IT'S THE TRUTH!

Taken together, Job, Psalms, and Proverbs are sometimes called "the Books of Truth," because the first letters of these books together spell the Hebrew word for truth.

depressed human spirit. But all the psalms reflect the process of working out a lifelong relationship with God.

Some 73 psalms are attributed to David, the shepherd and king of Israel. Fifty psalms are anonymous. Asaph, a worship leader and prophet, wrote 12 psalms. Ten others were composed by the sons of Korah, a music guild. Solomon wrote two psalms, and even Moses wrote a psalm. Heman and Than are credited with one psalm each.

This guide will review only 10 of the 150 psalms. But make a point of reading all 150 sometime. You just might find yourself singing as you commute to the workplace.

The Composition of the Songs We Call Psalms

The book of Psalms is comprised of five sections, each with a prominent theme that relates it to one of the first five books of the Bible (the Law or Pentateuch).

Division	Theme	Related Book
Psalms 1–41	Creation	Genesis
Psalms 42–72	Redemption	Exodus
Psalms 73–89	Worship	Leviticus
Psalms 90–106	Israel's Wanderings	Numbers
Psalms 107–150	God's Word	Deuteronomy

The longest psalm is Psalm 119 (176 verses). The shortest is Psalm 117 (2 verses). Psalm 117 is also the middle chapter of the Bible.

A Psalm about Successful Living (Psalm 1)

This psalm of David offers practical counsel for living a successful life. The tips are: (1) Don't hang with a bad crowd, and (2) meditate daily on God's Word. Whoever follows this advice will thrive like a fruit tree planted by streams of water.

A Psalm about Self-Worth (Psalm 8)

The psalmist looked at God's majestic creation—the heavens, sun, moon, and stars—and would have felt insignificant except he knew that God has crowned human beings with great honor and put them

94

in charge of His creation. Reading this psalm should give you a sense of both humility and self-worth.

A Psalm of the Singing Creation (Psalm 19)

Most human beings have enjoyed the opportunity to marvel at some of God's creation—a sky washed with stars, a breathtaking mountaintop view, an intricate and beautiful flower, or a cellular structure under a microscope. According to this psalm, all creation sings to us the message that God is alive, well, and worthy of worship.

A Psalm of the Shepherd (Psalm 23)

A favorite of many people, Psalm 23 compares the Lord to a shepherd who protects and provides for his sheep. When you read this psalm, notice how the personal pronoun representing the Lord changes from third person, *He,* to second person, *You,* when the scene shifts from pleasant pastures to the valley of the shadow of death. Trials do have a way of making the Shepherd's sheep more aware of how close the Shepherd is.

A Psalm of Reassurance (Psalm 42)

The sons of Korah captured the feelings of those who sometimes wonder why God seems so distant. The directive here is to reassure oneself that God is near even when He seems distant.

A Psalm of a Repentant King (Psalm 51)

This psalm lays bare the heart and soul of David as he confesses his sin of adultery with Bathsheba. He doesn't rationalize his sin but simply repents and asks for forgiveness and restoration.

A Psalm of Moses (Psalm 90)

Moses wrote this psalm to emphasize the fleeting nature of life and the importance of learning from God how to make the most of it.

A Psalm of the Word (Psalm 119)

This lengthy psalm extols the Scriptures and relates the benefits of making the Scriptures an integral part of one's life.

WHAT'S UP WITH THE
GOOD BOOK?

"God's Book is packed full of overwhelming riches; they are unsearchable—the more we have the more there is to have."
—Oswald Chambers

A Psalm of Worship (Psalm 150)

This short psalm summons everyone to praise the Lord joyfully with music, remembering who He is and what He has done.

Now Listen Up, and Listen Up Good!
(Proverbs 1–9)

The book of Proverbs is a collection of "wisdom sayings," most of which are attributed to Solomon. Here is just a sampling of what you will find in Proverbs. Knowledge and wisdom are rooted in the fear of the Lord. Just as a wise father passes along advice to his children, so Proverbs 1–9 read like a father-to-son-or-daughter heart-to-to-heart talk. Among the topics discussed are the value of wisdom, the dangers of immorality, the importance of fidelity, and the virtue of honesty.

A Potpourri of Proverbs (Proverbs 10–24)

Solomon was responsible for 3,000 proverbs. You will find 375 of them in this section of Proverbs, but they don't follow any particular order. Just navigate through them, and you will find more than enough wisdom to keep your life on *terra firma* for a long time.

Solomon's Supporting Cast (Proverbs 25–29)

Judah's King Hezekiah sponsored this collection of Solomon's proverbs. It's possible, then, that the prophets Isaiah and Micah from Hezekiah's era might have helped put this section together.

Tips from a Couple of "Wise Guys"
(Proverbs 30–31)

Proverbs 30 was written by Agur. He taught that no one can probe the nature and ways of God by human intellect. He stressed the importance of good character and listed four kinds of evil men:

the disrespectful, the hypocritical, the arrogant, and the person who preys on the needy. Agur also extolled the practical wisdom of four small creatures, and wrote of the consequences of acting foolishly.

Proverbs 31 was written by Lemuel, but he credits his mother with the teaching he was passing along to others. The advice warned against immorality and the irresponsible use of alcohol. The chapter also praises women of noble character as excellent role models for marriage and parenting.

Ecclesiastes, "The Street-Smart Teacher"

The Hebrew title for this book is Koheleth, meaning "teacher" or "one who calls an assembly together and speaks." Most likely, Solomon was the Teacher who wrote this book to express his philosophy of life. He may have written it in his old age, having "been around the block" and aware of how empty life is apart from a commitment to the Creator.

Lookin' for Meaning in All the Wrong Places (Ecclesiastes 1–2)

From a strictly human perspective, the Teacher concluded that life is meaningless. He had tried unsuccessfully to find significance in human wisdom, pleasure, wealth, houses and property, and possessions. All of his pursuits seemed to him to be nothing more than a chasing after the wind.

Lookin' for Meaning in All God's Appointments (Ecclesiastes 3–4)

The Teacher sensed that God controls human destiny. He has appointed the times of our lives, and it is futile for us to do less than enjoy God's gifts, including the gift of companionship.

IN CASE YOU'RE WONDERING
ECCLESIASTES ON THE MENU

The Feast of Tabernacles, an early autumn Jewish festival, commemorated Israel's wanderings in the desert between Egypt and the Promised Land. Ecclesiastes was read at this feast to remind the faithful how empty life can be for anyone who wanders from God's pathway.

Look Out for the Money Trap
(Ecclesiastes 5–6)

The Teacher warned about the futility of riches. Life is too short to spend in the pursuit of riches. You can't take it with you, the Teacher cautioned.

Look at Life around You (Ecclesiastes 7–11)

Chunks of life are dissected by the Teacher, and counsel for dealing with life is dispensed. He advised that a good reputation and good listening skills are valuable assets. It is important not to believe everything one hears. Obeying the law keeps people out of trouble. Appreciate your spouse. Work diligently. Keep your composure. Be generous. Applying this ancient counsel today would reduce stress, crime, and blood pressure, save marriages, and equip people with the skills to detect and reject scams.

IN CASE YOU'RE WONDERING

SEX IN THE BIBLE?

The Bible condemns illicit sex but depicts sex between husband and wife as ordained of God and honorable (see Hebrews 13:4).

You're Not As Young As You Used to Be
(Ecclesiastes 12)

The Teacher's conclusion points us to God, whom we should remember in our youth. Old age with its debilitating effects arrives sooner than we anticipate. At the end of a brief life, each person's deeds will be judged by God, who sees and knows everything.

The Song of Songs: The Greatest Love Song of All Time

The Song of Songs is read at Passover, a Jewish festival held in the spring. The song celebrates the love between Solomon and one of his brides. At that time his harem consisted of 60 queens and 80 concubines (Song of Songs 6:8). This special bride is described as a Shulamite woman who worked in her family's vineyards. Many of Solomon's marriages, in accordance with the times, were arranged for political purposes.

A Perfect Match (Song of Songs 1:1–3:5)

The Song of Songs records the decision of two lovers to get married. It celebrates their love for each other. Solomon sings the praises of his sweetheart. She is beautiful. In detail, Solomon describes her physical attributes and confesses that even the sound of her voice attracts him to her. She in turn sings his praises. Solomon is everything a woman would want in a man—strong, protective, handsome—the kind of guy a woman would be proud to introduce to her mother. He was literally the man of her dreams (3:1-5), her sweetheart. The lovers experience the joy of consummating their relationship.

Marching to the Altar
(Song of Songs 3:6–8:14)

Solomon describes the marriage procession. Like any eager groom, he anticipated receiving his beautiful bride. On his wedding day, he extolled her charms and told his bride that he was eager to consummate the marriage. She responded by inviting him to do so. Sometime after their wedding, however, the marriage was in trouble; Solomon had left home without saying where he was going. But love overcame this challenge. The two were reconciled and retired to his princely bed (6:11-12). The final chapters of the Song of Songs focus on the joy of the sexual relationship between Solomon and his wife.

LET'S GET TESTY

DID SOLOMON SAY THAT?

Place a check-mark beside each of the following proverbs that are based on the book of Proverbs. You may need to guess now but find out for sure when you read Proverbs.

1. "Cleanliness is next to godliness." _____
2. "The Lord helps those who help themselves." _____
3. "A rolling stone gathers no moss." _____
4. "A bird in the hand is worth two in the bush." _____
5. "If you want to have friends, be a friend." _____
6. "Smile, and the world smiles with you." _____
7. "An apple a day keeps the doctor away." _____
8. "A cheerful heart is good medicine." _____

(Answers: 5 and 8 should be checked; see Proverbs 17:22 and 18:24.)

CHAPTER TWELVE

"DANIEL IN THE LIONS' DEN"

Prophets and Losses
(From Isaiah to Malachi)

Driving in the mountains can be scary; a wrong turn or excessive speed can send a car hurtling into a steep canyon. That's why warning signs are posted on mountain roads: "Reduce Speed. Dangerous Curve Ahead"; "Steep Grade. Use Lower Gear"; "No Passing Zone"; "Stay in Your Lane." Cars coming down Pike's Peak must have their brakes checked. Overheated brakes are just as dangerous as overheated drivers. Like road signs, the Old Testament prophets delivered warnings to Israel, Judah, and the Gentile nations. Their messages carried divine authority and told of impending danger. The prophets urged their audiences to heed God's warnings. If they continued on their reckless, downhill course, they would suffer enormous losses. The exile of the northern kingdom at the hands of the Assyrians in 722 B.C. was one such loss. When the prophets Isaiah and Jeremiah addressed the southern kingdom (Judah), it was on the skids and drawing closer and closer to destruction and loss.

SOME THINGS YOU'LL DISCOVER IN THIS CHAPTER

1. Isaiah spoke very clearly of the coming Messiah and how He would suffer on our behalf.

2. Jeremiah had the unenviable role of preaching the fall of Jerusalem and appearing as a traitor.

3. Hosea married a prostitute at God's command to prove a point to the nation of Israel.

WHAT'S IN A NAME?

The Hebrew word for *prophet* means "declarer" or "announcer." The Greek word for *prophet* means "one who speaks for another." The Old Testament prophets spoke and wrote for God, declaring His messages.

IN CASE YOU'RE WONDERING
WHAT RAYS OF HOPE?

Isaiah wrote of hope by predicting the coming of the Messiah in 7:14; 9:6-7; and 11:1-5. In the second half of his book, Isaiah devoted an entire chapter (53) to hope found in the Messiah.

Big and Small Prophets

The prophets who wrote Old Testament books are classified as Major Prophets and Minor Prophets. The words *major* and *minor* have nothing to do with the importance of the prophets. They refer only to the length of the books they wrote. The books classified as Major Prophets are Isaiah, Jeremiah, Lamentations (part of Jeremiah's message), Ezekiel, and Daniel. Twelve books comprise the Minor Prophets: Hosea, Joel, Amos, Obadiah, Jonah, Micah, Nahum, Habakkuk, Zephaniah, Haggai, Zechariah, and Malachi.

These prophets can also be arranged according to when they prophesied, whether before the Exile, during the Exile, or after the Exile. Those who prophesied before the Exile were Joel, Jonah, Amos, Hosea, Micah, Isaiah, Nahum, Zephaniah, Habakkuk, and Jeremiah. Prophesying during the Exile were Ezekiel, Daniel, and Obadiah. Those who prophesied after the Exile were Haggai, Zechariah, and Malachi.

First, the Bad News (Isaiah 1–39)

The prophet Isaiah ministered in Judah for almost six decades—from about 740 B.C. to 680 B.C. His prophetic career spanned the reigns of four kings: Uzziah, Jotham, Ahaz, and Hezekiah. Isaiah's message didn't win him any accolades. The people of Jerusalem and Judah preferred to follow their own sinful course rather than heed Isaiah's warning that unrepentance would bring on a fate similar to what Israel had met at the hands of the Assyrians. Tradition holds that Isaiah met a martyr's death, being sawed in half by King Manasseh.

Isaiah 6 records Isaiah's call to prophetic ministry. It came in the year that King Uzziah died. Isaiah entered the temple and saw a far more important king than the one the nation had just lost. He saw the King Eternal, the Lord of Hosts, and after getting cleansed from his sin, Isaiah volunteered to serve as the spokesman for the King Eternal. The Lord responded by commissioning Isaiah to prophesy for Him.

Often called "the Evangelist of the Old Testament," Isaiah thundered against injustice and immorality and proclaimed judgment for Judah and surrounding nations if they failed to abandon their wickedness and turn to the Lord. However, through the dark clouds of judgment portrayed in chapters 1 through 39, rays of hope appear. Isaiah predicted the coming of the Messiah, a Savior who would make possible forgiveness and reconciliation.

Now the Good News (Isaiah 40–66)

The first verse of this section of Isaiah offers comfort for God's people. Indeed, comfort is the theme that runs to the end of the book of Isaiah. God's people could take comfort because the enemy Babylon would fall, Judah and Israel would be restored, the Messiah would someday come, and the earth itself would be restored to be what God intended.

I'm No Public Speaker (Jeremiah 1)

Jeremiah must have been fairly young when God called him to declare His messages. Jeremiah protested at first, claiming he was no public speaker and was too young for the job. Nevertheless, the Lord told Jeremiah not to be afraid of the audience's faces. Also, the Lord promised to put His words into Jeremiah's mouth.

Cryin' Out Loud! (Jeremiah 2–45)

Known as "the weeping prophet," Jeremiah endured tons of grief and sadness in his lifetime. He lived when Israel had been taken into captivity and Judah was declining rapidly. He began his ministry 60 years after Isaiah's death and declared a highly unpopular message for more than 40 years (627–580 B.C.). Jeremiah insisted that Judah would fall to Babylon and go into exile because of its disregard for God and His laws. He advised the leaders to surrender to Babylon.

INFO BYTES

WHAT'S IT LIKE HALFWAY THROUGH?

Isaiah 53 commands the center position in the second half of the book of Isaiah (chapters 40–66). This chapter graphically describes the trial and suffering that Jesus, the Messiah, endured to provide salvation and comfort for all who believe in Him. Significantly, the middle verse of chapter 53, verse 6, identifies the Messiah as the One who would bear our iniquity. This prophecy was fulfilled when Jesus died on the cross in our place.

JEREMIAH, THE LONER

Jeremiah must have been lonely. He was not permitted to marry (Jeremiah 16:1-2). He was ridiculed, considered a traitor, put on trial, thrown into a well, and generally mistreated.

IT'S A PROMISE!

"Ask me and I will tell you some remarkable secrets about what is going to happen here." (Jeremiah 33:3)

Spreading the Doom and Gloom Around
(Jeremiah 46–51)

Judah would not be the only nation to smart under God's judgment. Jeremiah prophesied doom and gloom for nine Gentile nations in the Near East. However, he held out the hope of restoration to four of the nine.

Thud! (Jeremiah 52)

The fall of Jerusalem is recorded in chapter 52. Judah's leaders were killed, their houses were torched, the walls of Jerusalem were broken down, the temple was plundered and burned, and a number of Jewish captives were dragged off to Babylon. Zedekiah, Judah's king, was forced to watch his sons be killed. Then the Babylonians plucked out his eyes, tied him with chains, and carted him off to Babylon.

Sad! So Sad! (The Book of Lamentations)

This brief book records Jeremiah's deep sadness over the fall of Jerusalem. However, hope shines through the darkness in 3:22-24. Jeremiah expressed the truth that God is merciful, faithful, and compassionate. In the midst of what seemed like a hopeless situation, Jeremiah hoped in God.

Ezekiel's Big Wheels (Ezekiel 1-3)

Ezekiel was around 25 years old when the Babylonians took him captive in 597 B.C. His early prophecies fell between his own captivity and the third stage of Babylon's assault on Jerusalem in 586 B.C. After the fall of Jerusalem, Ezekiel prophesied for another two decades.

In the first three chapters of his book, Ezekiel described his call to be a prophet. This call included a vision of living beings and wheels alongside them. Likely, these big wheels symbolized God's glory and sovereignty.

A Captive Audience for a Long Time to Come
(Ezekiel 4–24)

If the Jews hoped for a brief stay in Babylon, they were mistaken. The captivity had just begun in the early days of Ezekiel's ministry. He informed his fellow Jews that Jerusalem would collapse and the captivity would drag on. Decades of warnings had gone unheeded; it was time now to reap the consequences.

There Goes the Neighborhood (Ezekiel 25–32)

Thanks to Babylon, most of Judah's neighbors were also on the brink of destruction. In this section, Ezekiel pronounced judgment on Ammon, Moab, Philistia, and Tyre at the hands of the Babylonian king Nebuchadnezzar. Egypt would simply decline in power. History affirms what Ezekiel predicted.

It Ain't Over 'Til It's Over (Ezekiel 33–44)

Babylon could not overturn God's promises. Nor could that mighty nation crush God's people. Ezekiel prophesied spiritual renewal for the people of Judah and restoration for Judah and Jerusalem. Eventually, there would be a new temple filled with the glory of God. This was a message of hope that would carry the Jews through the dark days of captivity.

Bones of Contention

In one of his visions, Ezekiel saw himself looking over a valley filled with dry bones. He heard the Lord tell him to prophesy to those bones, and he obeyed. Suddenly, the bones moved and came together to form skeletons. Next, the skeletons received tendons, flesh, and skin. When Ezekiel prophesied again, breath entered the bodies. The resuscitated bodies became a huge army (Ezekiel 37:1–14). God gave this vision as an object lesson of the revival He would bring to His people.

BABYLONIAN BRAINWASHING

Daniel and his friends were given new names in Babylon, names referring to Babylonian gods. This was just part of Babylon's effort to erase Jewish faith and culture from the Hebrew captives and to immerse them into Babylonian religion and culture.

Just Say No (Daniel 1–6)

Picture four devout young men uprooted from their homeland to a place where no one worships God or cares about His laws. What chance of retaining their faith and morals would you give them? Daniel and three of his friends—Hananiah, Mishael, and Azariah—found themselves in that challenging situation, having been uprooted from Jerusalem to Babylon. Because the four were outstanding specimens of young manhood, they were placed in King Nebuchadnezzar's palace and destined for government roles. However, their faith was tested when they refused to drink the king's wine and eat food disallowed under levitical dietary laws.

At the end of ten days, after receiving permission to follow a diet of water and vegetables, the four young men appeared healthier than all who drank the wine and ate the Babylonian food. In time, all four entered the king's personal service (Daniel 1).

One night the king tossed and turned in his bed. He could not rid his mind of a troublesome dream. So he summoned his top advisers and demanded that they tell him what the dream was and what it meant. When they failed the assignment, the king executed an order that all his wise men should be killed. But Daniel asked his friends to pray. Then God revealed the dream and its meaning to Daniel, who later passed along the information to the king, giving due credit to the true God.

The dream featured a tall statue with a head of gold, silver chest and arms, bronze belly and thighs, and feet of iron and clay mixed together. A massive rock cut from a mountain rolled into the statue, crushing its feet and collapsing the statue. Daniel reported that each part of the statue represented a kingdom. Nebuchadnezzar and his kingdom of Babylon were the head of gold. Three kingdoms would succeed Babylon (probably Persia, Greece, and Rome). The rock pictured God's destroying the Gentile kingdoms and establishing His own kingdom (Daniel 2).

Later, Nebuchadnezzar showed his pride by setting up a 90-foot statue in his own honor on a high plain and commanding everyone to bow before it when the king's musicians began to play music. Daniel's friends refused to bow down to the statue, because God's law forbade idol worship. Their penalty was death by fire in a furnace heated seven times beyond its usual temperature. The flames were so hot they consumed the guards who threw the tethered friends into the furnace. Nebuchadnezzar peered in and saw a fourth figure who appeared to him to be a supernatural being. When Nebuchadnezzar called them to come out of the furnace, the three exited. There wasn't a trace of smoke on their clothes or hair, and the fire had simply burned off their ropes. The king was so impressed that he ordered his subjects everywhere to honor the God of Shadrach, Meshach, and Abednego (the new names of Daniel's friends; see Daniel 3).

Daniel, too, would shortly face a crisis—a test of his faith. Daniel's enemies persuaded Darius, a successor to proud Nebuchadnezzar, to prohibit his subjects from praying to any god or person other than himself for 30 days. When Daniel was discovered praying to his God (Daniel was open about doing so), he was tossed into a lions' den, and a stone was rolled over the opening. However, Darius worried all night about Daniel, and in the morning he hurried to the lions' den. Daniel shouted that God had sent His angel to protect him. Daniel emerged from the lions' den without so much as a tooth mark on him. His conspirators learned by firsthand experience that Daniel's experience was supernatural. They were thrown into the den and devoured (Daniel 6).

Whatever Happened to Nebuchadnezzar?

God judged Nebuchadnezzar's pride by turning him into a wild thing for seven years. After his seven-year wildness, Nebuchadnezzar admitted that God is all-powerful and gives kingdoms to whomever He chooses. Check it out in Daniel 4.

The Handwriting's on the Wall

Another Babylonian king, Belshazzar, threw a wild party and violated the sacred gold and silver vessels that had been taken from the temple in Jerusalem. Suddenly, he saw fingers write a message of doom on a wall. His wise men could not interpret the writing, but Daniel could. Basically, the writing spelled "finished" for the

IN CASE YOU'RE WONDERING
WHERE WAS DANIEL WHEN HIS FRIENDS WERE IN THE FURNACE?

Daniel was a high-ranking government official. Likely, he was out of the country on state business when this crisis occurred.

IN CASE YOU'RE WONDERING
THE FOURTH FIGURE IN THE FURNACE

Who was the fourth person in the furnace? Who was the angel among the lions? We can't say for sure, but many Bible teachers believe that Jesus in a preincarnate form filled both roles.

Babylonian Empire and a successful strike by its conquerors, the Medes and the Persians. That same night Belshazzar was killed (Daniel 5).

Visions for the Future (Daniel 7–12)

The closing chapters of the book of Daniel report his visions concerning a line of future empires and their leaders. The book closes with optimism: God's people will experience intense trials, but the angel Michael will guard them.

Twelve Minor Prophets Who Majored on the Majors

Clustered together at the end of the Old Testament are twelve prophetic books called the Minor Prophets. Named "minor" because of their brevity, these prophetic books communicate major truths and major motivation for their audiences to obey the Lord. Major losses would befall the disobedient.

Who Wants to Marry a Prostitute? (Hosea 1–3)

Hosea's prophetic ministry took place during the final generation before Israel fell to Assyria. His message summoned both Israel and Judah to abandon idol worship and turn back to the Lord. Both Israel and Judah had trusted in political alliances to enhance their roles, but Hosea pointed out that they needed to trust in the Lord.

By joining hands with pagan nations and ignoring the Lord, Israel and Judah had prostituted themselves. So the Lord commanded Hosea to marry a prostitute. Television has demonstrated that eligible women will line up for the opportunity to marry a multimillionaire, but the line of men wanting to marry a prostitute would probably be as long as a chalk mark on a sidewalk after a driving rainstorm. Nevertheless Hosea obeyed the Lord and married a prostitute named Gomer. The marriage would serve as a vivid object lesson for God's wayward people.

In time, the preacher and the prostitute had three children: a son, a daughter, and another son. Hosea and Gomer didn't have to check out any baby name books from the library, because the Lord told Hosea what to name each baby. No Tom, Jane, and Harry on the list; the first son was named Jezreel, the daughter was named Lo-ruhamah, and the second son was named Lo-ammi. Strange names, but each held a significant message for the Lord's rebellious people.

- Jezreel: "God sows"
- Lo-ruhamah: "unpitied"
- Lo-ammi: "not my people"

The Lord would uproot Israel and sow her in a foreign land (Assyria). He would show no pity, because the nation had deliberately rejected His many offers of reconciliation and forgiveness. He would treat them as though they were not His people.

Gomer proved to be like Israel, determined to chase after new lovers. She left Hosea and the children to pursue an adulterous course (2:5). At the Lord's command, Hosea went looking for Gomer. He found her in slavery and redeemed her. It cost him 15 pieces of silver and 50 pecks of grain (3:1). The Lord, too, would redeem His adulterous people in the last days and restore them to Himself (3:4-5).

Israel's Criminal Record (Hosea 4–10)
These chapters catalog Israel's crimes against the Lord. The people were guilty of swearing, deception, murder, stealing, adultery, violence, idolatry, breaking their covenant with the Lord, and pride. Yet through the prophet Hosea, the Lord urged His wayward people to return to Him.

Hey, There's Hope (Hosea 11–14)
If Israel would repent and Judah would reject idols, the Lord would show them mercy. He loved them too deeply to give up on

THE DAY OF THE LORD

The term "day of the Lord" (Joel 1:15; 2:1, 11) refers to a time of severe trials for Israel followed by restoration and the coming of the Messiah to rule the earth.

them. But judgment would surely come if they rejected His offer of mercy. The book ends with the promise that someday the Lord's people will be restored to a loving and trusting relationship with the Lord.

Squeeze Play

Instead of trusting in the Lord for protection and power, Israel trusted in foreign governments. She made a treaty with Assyria but exported oil to Egypt, Assyria's enemy (Hosea 12:1). By doing so, Israel had put herself right in the middle of a feud between two superpowers.

How Brown Is My Valley! (Joel 1:1–2:11)

Joel, whose name means "The Lord is God," prophesied in Judah around 835 B.C., about the time Elisha was a prophet in Israel. Joel wrote about the devastation caused by a plague of locusts in a time of famine. The pesky invaders ate everything in sight, leaving the land stripped bare of vegetation. Joel used the plague to call Judah's attention to a future judgment at the hands of a voracious and destructive military power in the Day of the Lord.

How Beautiful Is God's Mercy (Joel 2:12–3:21)

God promised to restore and protect His people if they turned to Him. He also promised future deliverance, predicting that Judah would experience revival. God would pour out His Spirit on the nation and punish her enemies.

Down on the Farm (Amos 1–2)

Amos worked on a farm in Tekoa, about ten miles south of Jerusalem, when the Lord gave him prophetic duties. Amos's ministry involved a series of warnings for Israel, Judah, and the surrounding nations. He made clear to the nations that the Lord controls their destinies and holds them accountable for their actions.

Nobody to Blame but Themselves (Amos 3–6)

Passing the buck is as old as the Garden of Eden. But Amos assured Israel and Judah that they deserved the judgment the Lord had brought on them in the past and the judgment He would execute in the future.

CITY CENSUS

If Nineveh had 120,000 children, its total population may have been around half a million. Obviously, Jonah needed a lesson on values. He seemed to value his shade from the sun far more than he valued God's forgiveness of all the residents of a heavily populated metropolis.

All Shook Up (Amos 7–9)

Amos received five visions signifying Israel's coming judgment. They featured locusts, fire, a plumb line, ripe fruit, and shattered temple columns. The Lord promised to shake Israel among the nations as grain is shaken in a sieve (9:9), but He also promised to restore His people to their land.

The Last Laugh (Obadiah)

Obadiah is the shortest book in the Old Testament, but it is long on judgment. Many think Obadiah's message of judgment, aimed at Edom (Esau's descendants), should be dated around 840 B.C. Others argue for 586 B.C.

Edom was marked for judgment because it gloated over Jerusalem's destruction. The Lord promised to obliterate Edom and give the land to His people.

You Should Have Seen the One I Got Away From (Jonah)

You've heard about Jonah being swallowed by a whale, haven't you? Well, here's the rest of the story. Actually, the Bible says he was swallowed by a great fish. It may have been a whale or some other enormous sea creature. At any rate, the Lord had commissioned Jonah to preach in Nineveh, the capital of Assyria, against its wickedness. But Jonah went AWOL. Not only was Nineveh an

INFO BYTE
OH, LITTLE TOWN OF BETHLEHEM

Micah 5:2 predicts that the Messiah would come from the little town of Bethlehem. Quite a prediction, made around 700 years before the birth of Jesus!

enemy city, but Jonah reasoned that the Lord would forgive the people of Nineveh if they repented. That was something Jonah didn't want to see. His prejudice just would not tolerate it.

Jonah's plan to go west aboard a ship instead of northeast to Nineveh didn't work out. When a raging storm arose, Jonah interpreted it as divine judgment because of his disobedience and told the sailors to toss him overboard. They did, and that's when the great fish swallowed Jonah. Later, it upchucked him onto dry land.

Once again, the Lord commanded Jonah to go to Nineveh. This time Jonah obeyed. Nineveh repented, and Jonah pouted in the shade of a vine. When a worm destroyed the vine and Jonah sweltered in the heat of the day, he despaired and begged to die. The Lord rebuked him, pointing out that Jonah cared more about the vine and himself than about all the people of Nineveh, including its 120,000 children.

Crooked Politicians and Corrupt Prophets
(Micah 1–5)

Micah prophesied in Judah in the time of Isaiah, when Hosea prophesied in Israel. He targeted corruption and injustice in Judah and Israel. Prophets and princes alike were guilty of such sins as ripping people off and being indifferent to the needs of the poor. Judgment would surely come upon them.

In spite of judgment, hope lay ahead. A time of restoration would follow the judgment, for the Lord would send the Messiah to shepherd His people.

Courtroom Drama (Micah 6–7)

These closing chapters present Micah's message in a courtroom setting. The Lord presents His case, and Micah responds. By arguments' end, it is crystal clear that Israel and Judah are guilty as charged and ought to be punished. Still, Micah's message ends with the good news that the Lord will ultimately restore His people.

Some People Never Learn (Nahum)

Nahum prophesied about 100 years after Jonah's visit to Nineveh. In spite of its repentance when Jonah preached there, Nineveh fell back into its wicked ways and would experience divine judgment. This well-fortified city would fall hard. Fifty years later, at the hands of the Babylonians, this prophecy was fulfilled.

Questioning God (Habakkuk)

Habakkuk prophesied in the early years of King Jehoiakim (around 607 B.C.), when Babylon was poised to invade Judah. He asked the Lord when Judah would be punished. The answer: Real soon! Next question: Why punish Judah at the hands of such a wicked nation as Babylon? Answer: Judah's sins are just as obnoxious as Babylon's.

Finally, Habakkuk turned from questioning God to praising Him and pleading for His mercy.

The End Is Near! (Zephaniah)

Zephaniah ministered during the reign of King Josiah of Judah (640–609 B.C.). He was Hezekiah's great-great grandson, the only "blue-blooded" prophet. Perhaps his ministry laid the groundwork for Josiah's reforms.

The prophet predicted the Day of the Lord, when the Lord would judge the nations and Jerusalem. However, Zephaniah also offered Jerusalem the Lord's promise of restoration and comfort.

Under Construction (Haggai)

Haggai prophesied when the Jews returned from Babylon. His mission was to encourage the people to finish rebuilding the temple, a task that had languished for 16 years. Zechariah, another prophet, teamed up with Haggai to encourage the construction.

Haggai reported the Lord's displeasure that the people had built

INFO BYTE
CAN YOU SEE JESUS?

Read Zechariah 11:12-13 and 12:10. Can you see in these verses the price Judas received for betraying Jesus and the piercing with nails Jesus received on the cross?

houses for themselves while His house—the temple—was unfinished. He had withheld material blessings from the people because of their failure to complete the temple project. Speaking through Haggai, the Lord promised to judge the nations and fill the temple with His glory in the latter days.

The King Is Coming (Zechariah)

Zechariah was from a family of priests. He delivered positive messages to the Jews to encourage them to change their behavior and rebuild the temple. He received visions of gold lampstands, soaring scrolls, four chariots, and a woman in a basket. He predicted judgment but also wrote about a glorious future involving the restoration of Israel and the coming of her Messiah-King.

Chiding Backsliding (Malachi)

The book of Malachi, the last book of the Old Testament, was written by the prophet Malachi around 425 B.C., about 100 years after the return of the Jews from Babylon to their homeland. Using a series of questions and answers, Malachi underscored the people's corruption and their failure to tithe (give a tenth of their income and possessions to the Lord). They had grown indifferent to the Law and doubted that the Lord cared about them. Malachi reminded them that God is faithful. He will remember those who honor Him, and someday the Messiah will arrive to heal and restore the nation.

LET'S GET TESTY

NAME THAT PROPHET

Whew! We've covered a lot of ground in this chapter—from Isaiah to Malachi—16 prophets in all. How well do you know your prophets? Identify the prophets who match the following descriptions by circling each correct answer:

1. After King Uzziah died, this prophet saw the Eternal King.
   A. Malachi   B. Jonah   C. Isaiah
2. He was King Hezekiah's great–great grandson.
   A. Zephaniah   B. Zechariah   C. Daniel
3. He is known as "the weeping prophet."
   A. Obadiah   B. Jeremiah   C. Ezekiel
4. He saw big wheels in the sky.
   A. Isaiah   B. Nahum   C. Ezekiel
5. He was a farmer.
   A. Zechariah   B. Amos   C. Jeremiah
6. The Babylonians tried to brainwash him and his friends.
   A. Daniel   B. Hosea   C. Jonah
7. He cared more about a vine than an entire city.
   A. Malachi   B. Joel   C. Jonah
8. He predicted Jesus' birthplace.
   A. Micah   B. Zephaniah   C. Isaiah
9. He deserted his post.
   A. Jeremiah   B. Joel   C. Jonah
10. He told the Jews to tithe.
    A. Malachi   B. Habakkuk   C. Zechariah
11. He encouraged the Jews to complete the rebuilding of the temple.
    A. Jeremiah   B. Jonah   C. Haggai
12. He predicted the destruction of Nineveh.
    A. Nahum   B. Ezekiel   C. Haggai
13. He wrote 39 chapters about judgment and 27 chapters about comfort.
    A. Micah   B. Habakkuk   C. Isaiah
14. He revealed King Nebuchadnezzar's dream and its interpretation.
    A. Jeremiah   B. Daniel   C. Obadiah
15. He prophesied against Edom.
    A. Malachi   B. Obadiah   C. Hosea

16. He married a prostitute.

   A. Hosea   B. Jeremiah   C. Zephaniah

17. He never married.

   A. Jonah   B. Obadiah   C. Jeremiah

18. He is sometimes called "the Evangelist of the Old Testament."

   A. Malachi   B. Isaiah   C. Zechariah

19. He was thrown into a den of lions.

   A. Isaiah   B. Nahum   C. Daniel

20. Tradition says that he was sawed in half.

   A. Isaiah   B. Obadiah   C. Jonah

(Answers: 1. C; 2. A; 3. B; 4. C; 5. B; 6. A; 7. C; 8. A; 9. C; 10. A; 11. C; 12. A; 13. C; 14. B; 15. B; 16. A; 17. C; 18. B; 19. C; 20. A.)

The Intertestamental Period

Between the last written word of Malachi and the first written word of the New Testament, four centuries intervened without a single recorded communication from God. Called "The 400 Silent Years," this period must have been excruciatingly painful for Israel. The final prophecy of the Old Testament had promised that a deliverer would heal and restore Israel and crush her enemies underfoot (Malachi 4:2-3), but Israel's enemies overran her land, Palestine, and ruled the Jews with a heavy hand throughout those four centuries.

First, Israel endured harassment from the Persians, including deportation. Next, the Greeks, under Alexander the Great, occupied the Jews' homeland, having defeated the Persians in 333 B.C. After the death of Alexander, Palestine came under the rule of Ptolemy, who had served as general to Alexander the Great. Later, Antiochus Epiphanes, king of Syria, grabbed Palestine by the throat. His hatred of the Jews knew no limits. He offered a pig on the temple's altar, commanded the Jews not to worship in the temple, and forced them to eat swine, which was forbidden by the Law (Leviticus 11:1-8). Any Jews who refused to comply with the Syrian king's rules were put to death.

How patient could Israel be? Would the promised deliverer ever arrive?

The antics of Antiochus Epiphanes kindled rage and a spirit of nationalism among the Jews. When Antiochus tried to persuade Mattathias, an old Jewish priest, to offer a pagan sacrifice as a goodwill gesture, Mattathias responded by killing a Syrian officer and a compromising Jew. Then he took to the hills, where, joined by his sons, he fought against the Syrians. When Mattathias died, his son Judas "the Maccabee" (meaning "the hammerer") led the Jewish guerrilla forces and carried on the struggle for independence. He managed to take possession of Jerusalem in 164 B.C. and reinstitute daily offerings in the temple. Although Antiochus died soon after, the Maccabees and the Syrian rulers continued to fight one another. There was no peace in Palestine.

How patient could Israel be? Would the deliverer ever arrive?

Rome took control of Palestine in 63 B.C., granting some freedoms to the Jews. They were allowed to practice their religion and uphold their traditional, religious laws, but the Jews were heavily taxed by the Roman authorities. It was into this milieu of Roman occupation and Jewish traditionalism that Jesus was born to bring spiritual liberty and eternal hope. Appropriately, the first books appearing in the English Bible are the Gospels: Matthew, Mark, Luke, and John, because *gospel* means "good news."

The promised deliverer had arrived!

PART THREE

The New Testament

"IN ADDITION TO WISE MEN FROM THE EAST, JOSEPH AND MARY WERE VISITED BY WISE GUYS FROM CLEVELAND."

Good News from the Tax Man (Matthew)

SOME THINGS YOU'LL DISCOVER IN THIS CHAPTER

1. The wise men may not have numbered three and were not at the manger scene at the birth of Jesus.

2. Jesus fed more than 5,000 people with only five bread rolls and two fish—and still had leftovers.

3. Jesus predicted His own death and His future return as well.

When tax day rolls around, groans emanate from offices, shops, factories, stores, houses, and numerous other places. Taxpayers can't think of a day they dread more, unless it's the day they "attend" their own funeral. On tax day they must dig deep into their pockets while the tax man whispers gently but firmly, "You can pay me now or pay me later—with interest." Of course, there's always somebody who receives good news on tax day, but why does it always have to be the other guy?

Now, this may surprise you: Matthew, the first book of the New Testament, was written by a tax man, yet it communicates good news to everyone. That's why it's called the Gospel of Matthew— the word *gospel* translates a Greek word meaning "good news." We don't have to wait until tax day to discover this good news; we can do so right now.

Sending Announcements before the Birth (Matthew 1)

Announcing Jesus' birth before it happened may seem odd, but the event was sure to take place. God Himself preserved the lineage

ISAIAH COULDN'T MISS!

Around 725 B.C. the prophet Isaiah predicted that the Messiah would be born of a virgin (Isaiah 7:14). Of course, Isaiah's chance of being right was 100 percent, because God inspired the book of Isaiah. Matthew wrote that the birth of Jesus fulfilled Isaiah's prediction (Matthew 1:22-23).

IN CASE YOU'RE WONDERING
DIDN'T THREE WISE MEN VISIT BABY JESUS IN A MANGER?

The Bible doesn't identify the number of wise men. Many have assumed three wise men arrived at Bethlehem, because they seem to have presented three gifts. Their visit to Jesus may have occurred up to two years after Jesus' birth. We don't know when the star appeared. The trip from the East may have taken months to complete. They entered a house, not a stable, in Bethlehem.

through which Jesus would be born and by which He would rightfully claim the throne of David. That lineage stretched all the way from Adam through David to Joseph, Jesus' adoptive father (1:1-17).

Mary wasn't surprised either. The angel Gabriel had told her she would become pregnant miraculously, by the agency of the Holy Spirit, and she would bear a son. His name would be Jesus. He would be God's Son, and He would become Israel's everlasting King (Luke 1:26-35). But Joseph was surprised to learn that Mary was pregnant. He did not know that Mary, to whom he was engaged, had become pregnant by the miraculous intervention of the Holy Spirit (Matthew 1:18). When he saw that she was pregnant, he considered breaking off the engagement, but an angel of the Lord visited him and explained what had happened and who the baby would be (1:19-22). The angel told Joseph to go through with the marriage and name the baby Jesus. Joseph followed instructions perfectly (1:24-25).

Follow That Star (Matthew 2)

You have probably looked at a manger scene and pointed to the three wise men beside baby Jesus' cradle. In chapter 2 of his Gospel, Matthew points to those wise men, too, but he doesn't tell us how many wise men visited Jesus. He also places them in a house, not a stable. According to Matthew, an undisclosed number of wise men—magi or astronomers—traveled to Jerusalem from the East because they had seen a special star announcing the birth of the King of the Jews. A troubled King Herod called on the Jewish priests and scribes to identify the birthplace of this new king and learned that the Scriptures predicted Bethlehem.

The wise men journeyed to Bethlehem and saw the star once again. Now it stood over a house. Upon entering the house, the wise men found Jesus, who was now a young child, and Mary. They worshiped Jesus and gave Him gifts of gold, frankincense, and myrrh. Later, they were warned by God to bypass Jerusalem and King Herod on their return trip home. Also, Joseph was warned to take

Jesus and Mary and escape to Egypt, because Herod was about to murder all the little boys two years old and younger in his attempt to eliminate any potential rivals to his throne.

Let Me Introduce My Friend (Matthew 3)

A man called John the Baptist (or, "the Baptizer") served as the messenger God had appointed to introduce Jesus to Israel. A no-nonsense kind of preacher, he resembled Elijah of the Old Testament calling the people of Israel to repentance so they would be ready to receive the Messiah. Crowds of repentant Jews came to John the Baptist at the Jordan River and were baptized by him as they confessed their sins. However, when Pharisees and Sadducees showed up, they found themselves on the receiving end of some hot words from John. He exposed them as hypocrites.

When Jesus asked John to baptize Him, John told Him that he should be baptized by Jesus. But Jesus insisted on being baptized. It was His way of showing compliance with God's will.

After Jesus' baptism, the Holy Spirit descended like a dove upon Him, and God the Father spoke His approval of His Son, Jesus.

IN CASE YOU'RE WONDERING
WHY ARE SOME STORIES REPEATED IN VARIOUS GOSPELS?

The Gospels of Matthew, Mark, and Luke are often referred to as the synoptic Gospels. *Synoptic* simply means "similar view." These three Gospels report the life and ministry of Jesus from a fairly similar perspective. John's Gospel took a different perspective, focusing on eight miracles that demonstrated Jesus' deity.

As you read the Gospel of Matthew, you will see many references to Jesus as King of the Jews and to His kingdom as well. Matthew wrote to present Jesus to Israel as its Messiah-King.

Three Strikes and You're Out (Matthew 4:1-11)

Immediately after Jesus' baptism, the Holy Spirit led him into the desert to fast for 40 days and 40 nights. At the end of this time—when Jesus was tired and hungry—the devil stalked Jesus and tempted Him to disobey God the Father. The devil pitched three temptations at Jesus: (1) turn stones into bread; (2) throw yourself down from the top of the temple; and (3) fall down and worship me. Jesus answered each temptation successfully by quoting Scripture. He refused to act in any way that contradicted what God the Father wanted Him to do!

The devil was called out on strikes. Jesus had won!

Fielding a Team and Coaching the Players
(Matthew 4:12–7:29)

After overcoming the devil's temptations, Jesus began to preach and select His disciples. The first four were fishermen who left their nets when Jesus called them to follow Him. Multitudes became enthralled with Jesus' teachings and tagged along behind Him and His disciples. Seeing the multitudes, Jesus went up a mountain, sat down, and delivered a series of teachings about the kind of values and practices that are descriptive of citizens of His kingdom. The famous Beatitudes (Matthew 5:3-11) are a part of this teaching called the Sermon on the Mount.

Power Surge (Matthew 8–9)

With crowds tagging along, Jesus performed miracles on behalf of desperately needy people, young and old alike. He healed a leper, a Roman military officer's servant, and His disciple Simon Peter's mother-in-law. During a raging storm at sea that threatened to capsize the boat and drown Jesus and the disciples, Jesus stood up and commanded the wind and waves to calm down. They did so immediately, much to the astonishment of the disciples.

When Jesus and His disciples docked, He healed two violent, demon-possessed men. Then Jesus and His disciples sailed back across the sea. Soon after that He forgave a paralyzed man's sins and empowered him to get up and walk. Not long after this miracle, Jesus added Matthew, the tax man and writer of the Gospel of Matthew, to His entourage. Matthew was so glad to leave his tax business behind and become one of Jesus' followers that He hosted a party so his cronies could meet Jesus. No, Matthew didn't write the party off as a business entertainment expense. It was totally a gift of love to Jesus.

After the party, while Jesus was on His way to a synagogue official's house to revive the ruler's dead daughter, He healed a woman who had had a hemorrhage for 12 years. Upon arriving at the official's house, Jesus was greeted by mocking laughs when He announced His mission. But He shooed the mockers away and raised the girl to life.

Others, too, experienced Jesus' healing power. A mute spoke, and every kind of disease and sickness released its hold on many as Jesus preached and healed.

Almost Like Flying Solo (Matthew 10)

By now Jesus had drafted 12 disciples, and it was time to send them out on their own to preach to the Jews that the kingdom of heaven was at hand. He instructed them to bless those who received the message but to pronounce judgment on those who rejected it. They should expect persecution, He told them; but He assured them that if they suffered, they would be rewarded.

It's a Jungle Out There! (Matthew 11–16)

Savage attacks against King Jesus and His kingdom sprang up from the religious leaders and from King Herod. John the Baptist, who had announced King Jesus' arrival and Israel's need to repent and welcome the King, had been thrown into prison and was pretty discouraged. But Jesus sent John assurances that He was alive and well. Then Jesus condemned cities that rejected Him but invited tired and burdened men and women to come to Him and find rest.

Those pesky, picky Pharisees found fault with Jesus and plotted to destroy Him. Nice bunch of religious do-gooders, weren't they? They wanted everybody to think they were so devoted to the Old Testament law, but they had murder on their minds! However, when they openly opposed Jesus, He exposed their hypocrisy and kept right on healing and teaching. Herod, too, showed his hatred of Jesus by cutting off the head of John the Baptist. His wife Herodias, whom he had stolen from his brother Philip, had told her daughter to request it. The daughter had danced and pleased Herod so well that he had invited her to ask of him whatever she wished. So Herod presented John's head to her on a platter.

INFO BYTE
WHAT'S IN A NAME?

Scribes were supposed to know the Scriptures very well. After all, scribes copied Old Testament writings by hand. In the first century, scribes were professional teachers and administrators of the Old Testament law. Some scribes served as judges in the Jews' highest court, the Sanhedrin.

WHO WERE THE PHARISEES AND SADDUCEES?

No, they weren't Jewish soccer teams. The Pharisees were a strict and powerful Jewish sect that enjoyed parading their self-righteousness and enforcing the Old Testament law and hundreds of additional laws they had created. The Sadducees were mostly made up of Jewish priests and members of Israel's upper class. They refused to believe in miracles or angels or a resurrection. Although their beliefs conflicted with those of the Pharisees, they often teamed up with the Pharisees to oppose Jesus.

In spite of all this opposition, Jesus continued to minister. He fed 5,000 people out of a supply of only five bread rolls and two fish, saved Simon Peter from drowning, healed a Gentile woman's demon-possessed daughter, and fed another huge crowd with only seven bread rolls and a few small fish. All the while, the Pharisees kept on attacking Him with savage fury. Jesus knew He would be put to death before long, and He told His disciples He would die and rise again. He also challenged them to deny themselves, take up their crosses, and follow Him.

A Huddle of "Offensive" Herods

King Herod the Great (Matthew 2:1-19). An Idumean (Edomite) by race and a Jew by religion; had nine or ten wives; put his favorite wife to death along with her brothers; ordered the execution of his own son; was responsible for the slaughter of the male infants after the birth of Jesus.

Herod Archelaus (Matthew 2:22). Succeeded Herod the Great; ruled Samaria, Judea, and Idumea; killed 3,000 Jews at Passover. Dead bodies filled the temple.

Herod Antipas. Archelaus's younger brother; Jesus called him a fox (Luke 13:32); tetrarch of Galilee and Perea; while married, took Herodias, his brother's wife; ordered the beheading of John the Baptist (Matthew 14:3-11); when Jesus was on trial, he mocked Him and returned Him to Pilate (Luke 23:6-11).

Herod Philip II. The son of Herod the Great and Cleopatra; married Herodias's daughter Salome; ruled Iturea; buried at a monument he had built for himself.

Herod Agrippa I. A grandson to Herod the Great; married a cousin; grew up in Rome but was a zealous Jew; ruled all Palestine; beheaded James, the brother of John, and incarcerated Simon Peter (see Acts 12); suffered a horrible death.

Herod Agrippa II. Called Herod Agrippa in Acts 25–26; ruled Palestine; joined forces with Rome in battling his own subjects; when Jerusalem fell to the Romans in A.D. 70, Agrippa settled in Rome, where he died in A.D. 100.

Mountaintop Experiences (Matthew 17–25)

This section begins on a mountaintop with a miraculous transformation of Jesus' outward appearance and God's voice booming from heaven and calling on the disciples, Peter, James, and John, to listen to Jesus. This was well-timed counsel, because Jesus was about to engage His followers in a series of life-related lessons. He would teach them how to deal with forgiveness and service on a personal level. He would also teach about humility and church discipline, and He would answer questions about marriage and divorce. He would speak about eternal rewards, the need to respect the temple as a holy place, and the cordial invitation God was extending to all people. Sharp opposition from the Pharisees and Sadducees provided occasions for Jesus to speak to the multitudes and the disciples about the religious leaders' hypocrisy and bloodthirsty intentions. Finally, Jesus taught about future events that would follow His crucifixion but precede His return to the earth in glory.

WHAT'S UP WITH THE GOOD BOOK?

"In the Bible there is no twilight, but intense light and intense darkness."
—Oswald Chambers

IT'S A PROMISE!

"If you believe, you will receive whatever you ask for in prayer." (Matthew 21:22)

The King on Calvary Road (Matthew 26–27)

After observing the Passover with His disciples (remember this meal from chapter 5?), Jesus predicted His death and resurrection. He also predicted that they would abandon Him and that Simon Peter would deny Him. Then Jesus led them to Gethsemane, a garden on the side of the Mount of Olives. There, He prayed and expressed to His heavenly Father His willingness to die on the cross. His disciples, however, were sleeping, not praying. So Jesus woke them and announced that His arrest was imminent.

Judas, one of Jesus' disciples, betrayed Jesus with a kiss, a sign to the arresting officers that this was indeed Jesus, whom the religious leaders had conspired against. Without a struggle or protest, Jesus allowed Himself to be arrested, unjustly tried, and sentenced to die by crucifixion. While the trial was under way, Peter denied Jesus. After the trial, Judas was filled with remorse, returned the money he had received to betray Jesus, and committed suicide.

Governor Pilate knew Jesus was innocent, but he was a political

INFO BYTE

JESUS' CHURCH PREDICTED

Jesus foretold that He would build His church and that Simon Peter would play a prominent role in it. The church would be built on the Rock—Jesus Himself. Not even hell itself would be able to destroy Jesus' church (Matthew 16:16–18).

INFO BYTE
PREDICTING THE FUTURE

Matthew 24–25 was delivered from the Mount of Olives. Some Bible teachers believe these events began after Jesus ascended to heaven. Others believe they will occur before Jesus returns. Whatever position a person takes, he or she should avoid setting actual dates (see Matthew 24:36).

IN CASE YOU'RE WONDERING
WHY WOULD ANYBODY BELIEVE THE GUARDS' PHONY STORY?

Good question. The disciples had already shown their cowardly side by abandoning Jesus. Even Simon Peter had denied Jesus when confronted by a young servant girl (Matthew 26:69-70). Why would they suddenly be courageous and powerful enough to confront and overpower the guards at the tomb, roll away the large stone, and carry off Jesus' body to a place where no one could have found it? The fact is, Jesus had risen! But lies are sometimes more attractive than truth.

ladder climber and saw that sentencing Jesus to death would gain the favor of the Jews. So he ordered Jesus' crucifixion.

On the cross Jesus suffered insults, accusations, loneliness, and excruciating pain before giving up His spirit to God the Father. He died, and a rich follower of Jesus wrapped His body in a clean linen cloth, laid it in his own family's tomb, and rolled a large stone against the opening. Later, remembering that Jesus had predicted His resurrection, the chief priests and scribes received Pilate's permission to post a guard at the tomb. Pilate consented, placed a seal on the stone, and posted a guard.

Up from the Grave He Arose (Matthew 28)

In a few days, just as Jesus had predicted, He arose from the dead. An angel rolled away the stone from the tomb's entrance and scared the guards half to death. He had rolled the stone away not to let Jesus out (He was already risen and out of there) but to let visitors in to see for themselves that Jesus wasn't there.

A group of women visited the empty tomb first, and they learned from the angel that Jesus had risen. They peered into the tomb and then rushed away to tell the disciples the wonderful news. On the way, they were met by the risen Jesus, who told them to instruct the disciples to meet Him in Galilee.

Bothered and bewildered by what had happened, the religious leaders who had planned Jesus' trial and crucifixion concocted a phony story and paid the guards to spread it. The fiction they passed along credited Jesus' disciples with stealing the body. In the meantime, Jesus met His disciples in Galilee and told them to make disciples throughout the world. He promised to be with them to the end of the age.

LET'S GET TESTY

Match the fol-
lowing correctly.

1. Matthew
2. He denied Jesus.
3. Pharisees
4. Sadducees
5. A rich follower
6. He almost drowned.
7. They were bribed to tell a phony story.
8. He betrayed Jesus.
9. Jesus fed 5,000 people with
10. She received the head of John the Baptist on a platter.
11. Wise men visited the baby Jesus in a
12. Herod ordered the death of infant boys
13. Jesus' sermon about future events is called
14. Before going to Gethsemane, Jesus and His disciples observed
15. The stone at the tomb's entrance was rolled away by

___ A. entombed Jesus' body
___ B. an angel
___ C. Peter
___ D. Judas
___ E. house
___ F. a temple
___ G. Mary Magdalene
___ H. Herodias's daughter
___ I. Philip
___ J. two years old and younger
___ K. the Passover
___ L. the Olivet discourse
___ M. the Sermon on the Mount
___ N. five bread rolls and two fish
___ O. enforcers of the law
___ P. denied the existence of angels
___ Q. guards of the tomb
___ R. a tax man
___ S. rye bread and cheese
___ T. from two to three years old

INFO BYTE
ASTUTE SOLDIERS

A centurion (an officer in charge of 100 Roman soldiers) and others who stood guard at the Cross were convinced by the natural phenomena that occurred when Jesus was crucified that Jesus was indeed the Son of God (Matthew 27:54).

(Answers: 1. R; 2. C; 3. O; 4. P; 5. A; 6. C; 7. Q; 8. D; 9. N; 10. H; 11. E; 12. J; 13. L; 14. K; 15. B)

Where the Action Is! (Mark)

SOME THINGS YOU'LL DISCOVER IN THIS CHAPTER

1. Jesus healed a paralyzed man who was lowered by a rope to get His attention.

2. Mark had close connections to leaders in the church, but he was not one of the original twelve apostles.

3. Jesus was able to do what He chose on the Sabbath because He is Lord of the Sabbath.

You may be a long-lost Roman if you are an action-oriented person. The Romans loved action of all kinds—from watching gladiators compete in the Colosseum to conquering the world—you name it. Perhaps their love of action explains why Mark wrote a Gospel of action. Wanting to present Jesus primarily to the first-century Romans, Mark chose to highlight Jesus' deeds and go light on recording Jesus' discourses and parables. As you read Mark's Gospel, you will notice that he wrote in the historic present tense instead of the past tense and often used the word *immediately* or one of its synonyms. He must have wanted his readers to feel that they were looking at instant replays of events in Jesus' life—kind of a you-are-there strategy. So hang on to your hat, we're off on an action adventure in the Gospel of Mark.

A Day in the Life of Jesus (Mark 1:1-39)

Mark begins his inspired record of Jesus' life and ministry by focusing on Jesus' baptism and temptation. Then he jumps right into a Day-Timer kind of account of a day in Jesus' ministry. Jesus

MARK WHO?

Mark was not one of Jesus' twelve disciples, but he seems to have been a close friend of Simon Peter, possibly even one of Peter's converts (1 Peter 5:13). His mother was Mary, a devout woman in Jerusalem (Acts 12:12). He was also a cousin to Barnabas, a highly regarded member of the early church. Mark accompanied Paul and Barnabas on their first missionary journey. Paul chose not to take Mark along on the next journey, but years later he and Paul were reconciled (Colossians 4:10; 2 Timothy 4:11; Philemon 24).

appeared in Galilee, preaching the gospel (literally, the "good news" about Jesus) and calling His first disciples—two pairs of fishing brothers: Simon (Peter) and Andrew, and James and John.

After calling these four men to be His disciples, Jesus entered the synagogue in the little fishing village of Capernaum at the northwest end of the Sea of Galilee. He taught in the synagogue with profound authority and validated His authority by healing a demon-possessed man.

Next stop: Simon Peter's home, where Jesus healed Simon's gravely ill mother-in-law. By evening, the news about this amazing Jesus had spread all over town. Everyone, including many diseased and demon-possessed people, rushed to Simon's house. Jesus healed those who needed His help.

Early the next morning, the disciples found Jesus praying in a secluded place. They informed Him that everybody was looking for Him. But it was time to move on and preach in nearby towns.

Ready to Go through the Roof
(Mark 1:40–9:50)

Mark reports that Jesus healed a leper, who then could not keep quiet about the healing (Mark 1:40-45). Later, in Capernaum again, Jesus gave strong legs to a paralyzed man whose friends had been unable to get past the crowd in the house where Jesus was staying. So they carried the paralyzed man onto the roof, tore an opening there, and lowered him to Jesus (2:1-12). Now that's perseverance!

Mark records Levi's (Matthew's) call to be a disciple and a confrontation Jesus faced with the Pharisees who objected to Jesus' eating with Levi's tax-collector friends and other known sinners (2:13-22). The Pharisees were soon accusing Jesus of violating the Sabbath by letting His disciples pick grain to eat as they passed through the grain fields. They said the disciples were guilty of working on the Sabbath. Jesus referred them to something similar that King David had done, and He identified Himself as the Lord of the Sabbath (2:23-28).

In chapters 3 and 4 of Mark, Jesus healed people, appointed and deputized His 12 disciples, debated the scribes, defined who His true family members were, taught a couple of parables, and quieted a violent storm that had unleashed its fury on the Sea of Galilee and the boat carrying Jesus and His disciples.

More acts of Jesus' miracles, confrontations, and teachings are recorded in Mark 5–9 with brief teaching episodes.

Jesus' Miracles, Confrontations, and Teachings Reported in Mark 5–9

The healing of a demon-possessed, crazed, and enormously strong man

The healing of a hemorrhaging woman

The restoring to life of the young daughter of a synagogue official

The commissioning of the disciples to preach and heal

The feeding of the 5,000

Jesus walking on water

Numerous healings in villages, cities, and the countryside

Confrontation with the Pharisees over what real cleanliness is

The healing of a Gentile woman's little daughter

The healing of a deaf mute

The feeding of the 4,000

More confrontation with the Pharisees

The healing of a blind man

Teaching about Jesus' impending crucifixion and resurrection

Jesus' transfiguration

The healing of a demon-possessed, mute boy

More teaching about Jesus' betrayal, crucifixion, and resurrection

Teaching about the value God places on every little child

Next Tour: Judea (Mark 10)

Jesus and His disciples entered Judea, where big crowds surrounded them and received Jesus' teaching. Once again, the Pharisees opposed Jesus and tried unsuccessfully to trip Him up in His teaching.

WHAT'S UP WITH THE GOOD BOOK?

"If a man is not familiar with the Bible, he has suffered a loss which he had better make all possible haste to correct."—*Theodore Roosevelt*

INFO BYTE
A LONELY OCCUPATION

Tax collectors led a lonely life in first-century Palestine. They were Jews who took money from their countrymen to feed Rome's coffers. They were also known to rip off the taxpayers by collecting more than was owed and pocketing the difference.

"Stay away from the love of money; be satisfied with what you have. For God has said, 'I will never fail you. I will never forsake you.'" (Hebrews 13:5)

At Jericho, Jesus healed a blind man in response to the man's remarkable faith.

When told by a crowd to be quiet, the blind man called out even more loudly for Jesus to show him mercy. When Jesus sent for him, the blind man threw aside his coat and rushed to Jesus. He must have believed strongly that Jesus would give him sight; otherwise he would not have thrown his coat aside. Imagine how hard it would have been for this blind man to recover his coat in a crowd if he'd remained blind!

Onward to Jerusalem and the Cross
(Mark 11–15)

These chapters cover the last week of Jesus' earthly life. They report His triumphant entrance into Jerusalem; the casting out of merchants from the temple; some teaching; confrontations with Pharisees, Herodians, Sadducees, and a scribe; teaching in the temple; commendation of a poor widow's offering; teaching about future events; the Passover; and Jesus' betrayal, arrest, trial, and crucifixion.

On His Way Back Home (Mark 16)

Mark reported Jesus' resurrection briefly, noting that the stone at the entrance to the tomb was enormous. He also recorded the meeting between the disciples and their risen Lord, when He commissioned them to preach the Good News about Himself throughout the world. He promised that supernatural signs would accompany their ministry. Mark's final action shots show Jesus ascending to heaven and taking a seat at God's right hand, and the disciples preaching with power from the Lord and with accompanying supernatural signs.

LET'S GET TESTY

Are the following items found in Mark's Gospel? Answer yes or no.

1. The shepherds' visit to Bethlehem___
2. The wise men's visit to Bethlehem___
3. The feeding of the 5,000___
4. Chasing the merchants from the temple___
5. Quieting a storm on the Sea of Galilee___
6. Healing Peter's father-in-law___
7. Jesus walking on water___
8. The betrayal of Jesus___
9. A comment about the size of the stone at the tomb___
10. The call of Levi (Matthew) to be a disciple___
11. Jesus' transfiguration___

(Answers: 1. no; 2. no; 3. yes; 4. yes; 5. yes; 6. no; 7. yes; 8. yes; 9. yes; 10. yes; 11. yes)

"TAKE YOUR MEDICATION THREE TIMES A DAY. ONE BEFORE *OPRAH*, ONE BEFORE *WHEEL OF FORTUNE*, AND ONE BEFORE *NIGHTLINE*."

Looking at the Doctor's Records (Luke)

"Doctor Luke" (Colossians 4:14) wrote this third synoptic Gospel (Matthew and Mark are the other two) to the Greeks. Because the ancient Greeks produced so many deep thinkers, philosophers, and orators and believed their culture could produce the perfect specimen of humanity, they needed the kind of Gospel Luke wrote—a Gospel containing many of Jesus' sermons and stories and stressing His perfect humanity. As you might expect from a man of science, Luke carefully researched eyewitness accounts of the life of Jesus and then organized his Gospel around the data he accumulated (Luke 1:1-3). He wanted to give the Greeks an accurate written record of Jesus' life and ministry so they would know the truth (1:4).

Because Luke's Gospel contains so many of Jesus' teachings, you shouldn't be surprised to learn that it is the longest Gospel. Also, Luke drew from an extensive Greek vocabulary as he compiled his Gospel. Mark, on the other hand, gave us the shortest Gospel account. Unlike Matthew's Gospel, the Gospel of Luke offers few examples of fulfilled prophecy. His Old Testament examples often show how God reached out to include Gentiles in the benefits of the covenants He made with the Jews.

SOME THINGS YOU'LL DISCOVER IN THIS CHAPTER

1. Luke was a medical doctor who had a detailed and precise approach to his Gospel presentation.

2. The disciples wanted to destroy a Samaritan village that didn't show them hospitality.

3. Jesus wept over the city of Jerusalem—the place where He came to share the Good News of salvation and become King.

INFO BYTES
KNOW YOUR DOCTOR

Luke accompanied the apostle Paul on missionary journeys (Acts 16:10-24; 2 Timothy 4:11; Colossians 4:14). Apparently, Luke was Greek, because he is listed in Colossians 4 with Gentile Christians. As such, he was the only Gentile writer among the New Testament writers. He wrote Acts as well as Luke.

THEOPHILUS WHO?

Luke addressed his Gospel to Theophilus (Luke 1:1). Some Bible scholars believe Theophilus was a government official. Others believe the name represents all who love God, since *theophilus* in Greek means "one who loves God." Luke's second book, Acts, is also addressed to Theophilus (Acts 1:1).

As you read Luke's Gospel, observe how he used details to reference the historical context in which Jesus lived and ministered. Also, notice his frequent references to the ministry of the Holy Spirit. Finally, watch how he emphasized Jesus' innocence under Roman law and zeroed in time and again on Jesus' ministry to the disenfranchised—Gentiles, women, the sick, and the poor.

"I'm Speechless. I'm Going to Have a Baby Boy!" (Luke 1:5-25)

A couple of devout "seniors" living in the time of Herod the Great got a big surprise; they were going to be first-time parents. The future dad was the first to hear about this amazing event. He was a priest by the name of Zechariah, and he was on the job when the angel Gabriel delivered the news to him. "Name the baby John," Gabriel told Zechariah. "He will be filled with the Holy Spirit even before birth, and he will prepare Israel for the Messiah."

Zechariah wasn't so sure about all of this. He didn't get all excited, leave work, and run down to the lumber store to get wood so he could start building a cradle. He reminded Gabriel that he and his wife were too old to start a family. His incredulity cost him. Gabriel told him he would be unable to speak until the baby arrived.

Soon, Zechariah's wife, Elizabeth, got pregnant, but if Zechariah felt like shouting "WOW," he couldn't. He had lost his voice!

An Even More Amazing Birth Predicted (Luke 1:26-56)

Elizabeth was six months along in her pregnancy when her cousin Mary, a virgin in Nazareth, received a visit from the angel Gabriel. *Déjà vu!* Gabriel told Mary that God had singled her out for a special honor. She would bear a son—God's Son, the Messiah—whom she should name Jesus. This supernaturally conceived Son would someday rule as the King of Israel forever. Then Gabriel told Mary that her elderly cousin Elizabeth was pregnant—a guarantee to Mary that nothing is impossible with God.

Mary hurried to the hillside home of Zechariah and Elizabeth, where she stayed for three months before returning to Nazareth. As soon as Mary arrived at the old couple's home, she received encouragement. Elizabeth's unborn child jumped for joy in her womb, and Elizabeth greeted Mary as blessed and spoke of Mary's unborn child as blessed. Elizabeth felt honored that the mother of her Lord should visit her.

That happy greeting caused Mary to sing praise to the Lord. Her song, often called the "Magnificat," extolled God for His compassion and mercy in remembering His promises to Israel.

IN CASE YOU'RE WONDERING
SON OF MAN

Luke applied the term "Son of Man" to Jesus 26 times in his Gospel. As such, Jesus was the perfect representative of the human race—someone who deserved the Greeks' close attention and admiration.

"I Can Talk. I Can Sing!" (Luke 1:57-80)

The birth of Zechariah and Elizabeth's little boy caused quite a stir in the neighborhood and among their relatives. They rejoiced with her (Zechariah couldn't express his joy audibly). Eight days later, when the baby was to be circumcised, everybody assumed his name would be Zechariah, after dear old Dad. But Elizabeth insisted he would be named John, in spite of not having even one relative by that name. Calling for writing material, Zechariah wrote down J-O-H-N. Immediately, he was able to talk again.

Old Zechariah chose his first words well; he burst into a song of praise to God. He linked the remarkable recent events with Old Testament promises of salvation. John would prepare the way for Israel to receive the Messiah.

As for John, he grew strong physically and spiritually. In adulthood, he lived in the desert and awaited the appointed moment to announce the arrival of Israel's Messiah. In the meantime, John preached that people needed to turn from their sins and get ready for the Messiah's arrival.

The Hills are Alive with the Sound of Angels
(Luke 2:1-20)

You have probably sung "Hark! The Herald Angels Sing." Now you can read the story upon which that Christmas carol is based. Luke 2 tells all about it.

WHAT'S UP WITH THE GOOD BOOK?

"The Holy Bible is an abyss. It is impossible to explain how profound it is, impossible to explain how simple it is."
—*Earnest Hello*

IN CASE YOU'RE WONDERING
WHY BETHLEHEM?

Wouldn't it have made more sense for the King of the Jews to be born in the historic and impressive city of Jerusalem? No! Bethlehem had been identified centuries before as the birthplace of Israel's long-awaited King (Micah 5:2).

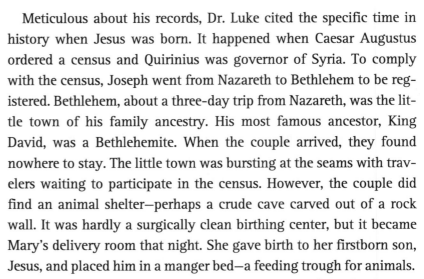

Meticulous about his records, Dr. Luke cited the specific time in history when Jesus was born. It happened when Caesar Augustus ordered a census and Quirinius was governor of Syria. To comply with the census, Joseph went from Nazareth to Bethlehem to be registered. Bethlehem, about a three-day trip from Nazareth, was the little town of his family ancestry. His most famous ancestor, King David, was a Bethlehemite. When the couple arrived, they found nowhere to stay. The little town was bursting at the seams with travelers waiting to participate in the census. However, the couple did find an animal shelter—perhaps a crude cave carved out of a rock wall. It was hardly a surgically clean birthing center, but it became Mary's delivery room that night. She gave birth to her firstborn son, Jesus, and placed him in a manger bed—a feeding trough for animals.

Nestled in the hills outside Bethlehem, a group of shepherds were alertly tending their sheep when they were jolted by the sudden presence of an angel of the Lord. He stood before them, and the Lord's glory lit up the night sky with stunning brilliance. The shepherds were petrified, but the angel calmed their fear. He assured them he carried terrific, joyful news. The Savior, Christ the Lord, had been born in Bethlehem, he told them, and they could find this baby wrapped in strips of cloth and lying in a manger.

Suddenly, a host of angels joined the angel of the Lord. Together, they sang praises to God and spoke of His intention to grant peace to those with whom He was pleased.

As soon as the angels departed, the shepherds decided to hurry to Bethlehem and find the baby. After finding Him, they told others what they had seen and heard on the hillside. Then, as they returned to their sheep, they praised God for what they had witnessed.

That's Our Boy! (Luke 2:21–52)

All parents think their child is special—the brightest or the best-looking. But Jesus, the child born to Mary, really was one of a kind—the best and the brightest. Joseph and Mary received affirmation of this fact when Jesus was only five weeks old. They brought

Jesus to the temple and were met by a devout old man named Simeon. The Lord had promised Simeon that he would not die until He had seen the Messiah. When Simeon saw little Jesus, he knew right away that this baby boy was the Messiah. It was enough to cause the old fellow to burst into praise. He praised God for allowing him to see the salvation Jesus would bring to Gentiles and Jews alike, and he blessed Mary and Joseph. However, he told Mary that she would experience sharp pain related to the Messiah's future.

Soon, an elderly and devout prophetess named Anna began thanking God and speaking about the Messiah to all who were eagerly looking for redemption.

Twelve years later Mary and Joseph went to the temple to celebrate the Feast of Passover. On their return trip home, they realized Jesus was not with them or their relatives. After backtracking, they found Him in the temple, surrounded by teachers and engaged in dialogue with them. Now 12 years old, Jesus held the teachers and all who heard him spellbound. His wisdom was amazing! Like any proud mother, Mary treasured this moment in her heart.

As Jesus grew older, His wisdom and physical stature increased, and He continued to gain the favor of both God and others.

Jesus' Baptismal Record and Family Tree
(Luke 3)

Dr. Luke sure kept good records. He pinpointed the time John began his public ministry. Tiberius Caesar was celebrating his 15th year of rule; Pontius Pilate was governor of Judea; Herod was tetrarch of Galilee; Herod's brother Philip was tetrarch of Iturea and Traconitis; Lysanius was tetrarch of Abilene; and Caiaphas and Annas were high priests. No *once upon a time* here—John and Jesus were historic figures who would profoundly influence Israel and even the whole world.

Quoting from the book of Isaiah, John summoned the nation to repent and receive the Messiah. Not given to soft words, John rebuked hypocrites who boasted of their religion while ripping off

IT'S A PROMISE!

"So be strong and take courage, all you who put your hope in the Lord!" (Psalm 31:24)

INFO BYTE
MARY'S PURIFICATION

After giving birth, a mother was considered unclean for 33 days beyond the day her baby boy was circumcised. (The circumcision was performed when the baby was eight days old.) She was obliged to give a burnt offering and a sin offering for her cleansing (Leviticus 12:4-6). Mary complied with this law.

their brothers. He assured them that the Messiah would not tolerate phony religion. Then John baptized the repentant and Jesus, who received affirmation from heaven. God the Father spoke His approval of Jesus as His Son, and the Holy Spirit descended like a dove upon Jesus.

Luke carefully noted that Jesus began His public ministry at about 30 years of age and that people assumed He was Joseph's son. Luke then presented Jesus' genealogy (probably through Mary) all the way back to Adam. In keeping with Luke's goal of featuring Jesus as the perfect man, his genealogical record showed that Jesus was the representative of the entire human race.

Slaying the Dragon (Luke 4:1-13)

Just before Jesus launched His public ministry, He faced the devil—the evil dragon (Revelation 12:9)—in a one-on-one confrontation. Jesus had not eaten for 40 days, so He was hungry when the devil tempted Him to turn stones into bread. Jesus struck a blow against the dragon by overthrowing the temptation. Next, the devil tempted Jesus by offering Him all the kingdoms of the world if Jesus would fall down and worship him. But Jesus declined, knowing that only God deserves to be worshiped. Finally, the devil tempted Jesus to show off by leaping from the top of the temple safely into the strong hands of protecting angels. Jesus successfully turned this temptation down, too. After all was said and done, Jesus had quoted appropriate Scripture in response to each temptation. He had chosen to obey God in every area of life.

There's a New Prophet in Galilee
(Luke 4:14-44)

Returning from the wilderness, where He was tempted, Jesus entered Galilee in the power of the Holy Spirit. News about Him spread like a grass fire on a hot, dry, windy July day. When He taught in the synagogues, people praised Him. One day in the synagogue of Nazareth,

his hometown, Jesus read publicly from the book of Isaiah. The passage He read predicted the coming of Israel's Messiah. After handing the book back to the synagogue attendant, He told the assembled worshipers that Isaiah's words had been fulfilled. However, the worshipers saw Him only as Joseph's son. Their unbelief brought such a stern rebuke from Jesus that they thrust Him out of Nazareth and tried to hurl Him off a cliff. Their wicked scheme failed. Jesus slipped out from among them and went on His way.

In Capernaum's synagogue, Jesus received a more cordial reception. When He taught on the Sabbath and healed a demon-possessed man, observers registered amazement and buzzed about Jesus' power. Later Jesus went to Simon Peter's home and healed Simon's mother-in-law of a high fever. The healing was so immediate and complete that the woman got out of bed and waited on Jesus and His companions. Before long, a crowd of the sick and demon-possessed had assembled at Simon Peter's home to receive healing.

The Catch of the Day (Luke 5:1-11)

Jesus saw two boats at the edge of the Sea of Galilee. He got into the one owned by Simon Peter and asked him to push out from the shore. Then, sitting in the boat, Jesus taught the crowds that had assembled on the shore. After the sermon, Jesus told Peter to position his boat farther from the shore and lower his nets. Peter whined that he and his partners had fished all night without catching even one fish, but he followed Jesus' instruction. Suddenly, the nets bulged with fish and nearly burst from the load. It took all four partners to drag the nets to shore. Then Jesus summoned the four fishermen to change careers—from catching fish to catching people. That day, the four turned their backs on a load of fish that might have made them rich.

Actions and Reactions (Luke 5:12-9:50)

Jesus' popularity with the people was exploding. After He healed a leper, news about Him spread and resulted in huge crowds gathering to hear Him and to be healed by Him (5:12-15). But Jesus did not fail to find some time for private prayer (5:16).

Of course, Jesus didn't win any popularity votes among the scribes and Pharisees. They quickly challenged His authority to forgive the sins of a paralyzed man whom He had healed. They bit their tongues, though, when Jesus asked them whether it was easier to forgive sins or to give a paralyzed man new legs. Only God could do both (5:17-26)!

Other Actions by Jesus during This Tour of Ministry in Galilee

Calling Levi (Matthew) the tax collector to be His disciple (5:27-29)

Healing a man with a shriveled right hand in the synagogue on the Sabbath (6:6-10)

Appointing 12 disciples (6:12-16)

Delivering a sermon about a bundle of blessings (6:17-49)

Healing a centurion's servant (7:1-10)

Raising a widow's son from death—during the young man's funeral procession (7:11-15)

Forgiving a sinful woman who washed and anointed Jesus' feet with a blend of tears and perfume (7:36-50)

Preaching about the kingdom of God (8:1)

Calming a wild storm on the Sea of Galilee (8:22-25)

Casting out demons (8:26-39)

Raising to life a synagogue official's daughter (8:41-56)

Curing a woman's 12-year hemorrhage (8:43-48)

Commissioning the disciples to preach and heal (9:1-6)

Feeding 5,000 people with only five bread rolls and two fish (9:10-17)

Radiating Jesus' glory on a mountain (9:28-36)

Healing a demon-possessed boy (9:37-43)

The Reactions to Jesus' Ministry during This Period

An accusation from the Pharisees and scribes that Jesus ate and drank with such lowlifes as tax collectors and sinners (5:30)

An accusation from the Pharisees that He and His disciples had
worked on the Sabbath by picking some grain and eating it
(6:2)

Rage on the part of the scribes and Pharisees at seeing Jesus heal
on the Sabbath (6:7-11)

Confidence on the part of witnesses to the raising of the widow's
son that Jesus was a great prophet (7:15-16)

Disgust on the part of a Pharisee who saw Jesus accept the
devotion of a sinful woman (7:37-39)

Fear and amazement on the part of the disciples upon seeing
Jesus quiet a raging storm (8:24-25)

Fear and rejection on the part of the people of the country of the
Gerasenes who had learned that Jesus had healed a demon-
possessed man (8:34-37)

The notion of some that Jesus was a resurrected John the Baptist,
by others that He was Elijah, and by others that He was a
resurrected Old Testament prophet (9:19)

The desire of Peter to stay on the mountain where Jesus had
revealed His glory (9:33)

Those Hawkish Disciples (Luke 9:51–10:24)

If you think Jesus' followers were a bunch of wimps attending a
perpetual Sunday school picnic, think again. The disciple Simon
Peter had a feisty disposition, occasionally argued with Jesus, and
even seemed ready to fight at the slightest provocation. James and
John were known as "the sons of thunder" before Jesus gave them
an attitude adjustment. As a matter of fact, James and John were so
enraged by the unwillingness of the residents of a Samaritan village
to let Jesus stay briefly in their village that they wanted to nuke the
place. Jesus didn't grant their request, of course. He explained that
He had come to save lives, not destroy them.

As the group journeyed further toward Jerusalem, Jesus explained the high standards involved in following Him. Discipleship
was a don't-hesitate, don't-quit proposition! Then He appointed 70

disciples and dispatched them two by two on a mission to cities and families throughout the region. They would learn firsthand what following Jesus involved.

Hey, Good Neighbor! (Luke 10:25-37)

You have heard the expression *good samaritan,* but did you know it is based on a parable Jesus told? Luke 10 reports that a scribe tested Jesus by asking how he could inherit eternal life. Jesus answered with a question of His own: "What does the law tell you?" The scribe's first answer was also his final answer. He quoted Deuteronomy 6:5 about loving the Lord with all your heart, soul, strength, and mind and Leviticus 19:18 about loving your neighbor as yourself. When Jesus affirmed his answer, the scribe asked, "Who is my neighbor?" Jesus responded by telling a parable about a traveler who was accosted by robbers and left for dead at the side of the road. Jesus said a priest saw the injured man but passed by on the other side of the road. Next, a Levite saw the victim but went on his way, choosing not to get involved. Finally, a Samaritan came along, compassionately administered first aid, and transported the victim to an inn, where he paid the innkeeper to take care of the victim. Also, he promised to return and pay any additional costs.

Jesus asked the scribe to identify the true neighbor in the story. When the scribe identified the Samaritan, Jesus told him to go and show mercy as the Samaritan had.

A Model Prayer and Mounting Opposition (Luke 11)

The disciples interrupted Jesus' prayer time by asking Him to teach them how to pray. He accepted the invitation, and taught them a model prayer, which most people call "the Lord's Prayer." He also encouraged them to pray persistently.

You would think everyone would have appreciated Jesus, but that was not the case. On one occasion some members of a crowd that had seen Jesus heal a mute man accused Him of doing miracles by the power of Satan. He promptly exposed that accusation as ridiculous. Why would Satan empower anybody to fight against Satan's own forces? On the other hand, Jesus indicated that if God had empowered Him to defeat Satan's forces, the kingdom of God must be at hand. Then Jesus scolded the unbelievers, stating that both the queen of the south and the men of Nineveh would testify against them at the judgment. The queen of the south (Sheba) had marveled at Solomon's wisdom, and the men of Nineveh had repented because of Jonah's preaching. Now one greater than both Solomon and Jonah was present, but the contemporary generation had rejected Him.

Surprisingly, a Pharisee invited Jesus home for lunch, but soon the Pharisee's hypocrisy was out on the table. He questioned why Jesus had not ceremonially washed before eating. Jesus replied that the Pharisees paid meticulous attention to outward religious practices but were unclean at heart. They did not love God, and they failed to practice justice. Jesus' accusations stirred up the Pharisees and scribes' animosity toward Him and sent them huddling to plan His downfall.

The Cost of Being the King's Kid
(Luke 12:1–19:27)

On His way to Jerusalem, Jesus spoke on a number of topics, giving all who heard Him timely tips for successful living. He warned His disciples to beware of hypocrisy (Luke 12:1-3). He urged them not to fear persecution because God, who cares what happens to sparrows, cares far more about the well-being of His children (12:4-12). Jesus also spoke against coveting possessions and urged His listeners to seek God's kingdom and serve God faithfully (12:13-48). He explained that those who followed Him could expect to be rejected by family members, and He chided those who could not discern the time in which they lived (12:49-59). Jesus used the opportunity of healing a woman with a severely bent back to underscore the importance of doing good on the Sabbath (13:10-17). He warned that many will be shut out from the kingdom of God, predicted His death, and lamented Jerusalem's rejection of Him

(13:18-35). Later, He healed a man with swollen limbs on the Sabbath and again stressed the legitimacy of performing deeds of mercy on the Sabbath (14:1-6). He taught, too, about humility, God's gracious invitation to participate in the kingdom, and the need to count the cost of becoming His disciple (14:7-35).

When the Pharisees and scribes protested that He welcomed tax collectors and sinners, Jesus told parables about a shepherd who left 99 sheep safe in their fold to retrieve a single lost sheep, a woman who lit a candle and swept her house thoroughly to recover a lost coin, and father who waited anxiously for the return of a wayward, runaway son (Luke 15). In each case, the recovery became an occasion of much joy. Each parable illustrated how heaven rejoices when a lost sinner returns to God.

The Lecture Series Continues

Turning to His disciples, Jesus spoke of the importance of faithful stewardship and the need to love God rather than possessions. The Pharisees, who overheard Jesus' remarks, ridiculed Him, but their mocking was met by a story Jesus told about a rich man who ended up in hell and a beggar who went to paradise (Luke 16). Death had turned the spotlight on the foolishness of building one's life only on riches.

Jesus also lectured briefly on forgiveness and humble service (17:1-10). After seeing only one of ten healed lepers return to thank Him, Jesus forgave the man's sins (17:11-19). Then Jesus described what things will be like just before His second coming, when he returns as Lord and King to bring history to a close (17:20-37).

Persistent and humble praying received a place in Jesus' lecture series (18:1-14). He also commended little children as model citizens of God's kingdom (18:15-17) and challenged a rich ruler to sell everything he owned, give the proceeds to the poor, and follow Him. Although the rich ruler was interested in eternal life, he did not want it badly enough to become a "sold-out" follower of Jesus (18:18-30).

As Jesus and His disciples approached Jericho, Jesus summoned a blind man to Him. This man had been crying loudly in a crowd for

Jesus to show him mercy. He got his wish; Jesus answered his request for sight, much to the amazement of the crowd (18:35-43).

A Bird's-Eye View

While passing through Jericho, Jesus caught sight of Zacchaeus, a tax collector. Because Zacchaeus was short, he had climbed into a tree for a look at Jesus. But Jesus called him to leave the tree and entertain Him at his house. The meeting was a life-changing event for Zacchaeus. He offered to pay back fourfold whatever he had swindled from his clients (Luke 19:1-10).

As He neared Jerusalem, Jesus told a parable about a nobleman who left on a journey after entrusting a sum of money to each of ten servants. When the nobleman returned, he asked for an accounting. He rewarded servants who had wisely invested the money, but he penalized the one servant who had simply kept his master's money in a safe place (19:11-27).

Ready or Not, Here I Come (Luke 19:28-48)

From a place near Bethany on the southeast side of the Mount of Olives, Jesus sent two disciples with explicit instructions to go to a nearby village, find an untamed colt, tell the owner that the Lord needed it, and bring it to Him. This colt served as Jesus' mount for His triumphal entry into Jerusalem. But as crowds outside the city welcomed Him joyfully because of His miracles, some miffed Pharisees told Jesus to quiet the crowds. Jesus refused to do so.

As He approached the city, Jesus wept over it and predicted its fall. Then He entered the temple and chased out the merchants who were profaning it. Instead of applauding Jesus for cleansing the temple, the religious leaders schemed to kill Him.

Clashing with the Clergy (Luke 20)

Luke reported a series of incidents in which the religious leaders questioned Jesus' authority. They tried to trip Him up by asking tough questions about John the Baptist, taxes, and domestic relationships in the afterlife. Because Jesus buried His critics with wise answers, they were afraid to continue the interrogation. Later, Jesus warned His disciples to beware of the religious leaders who loved only themselves while ripping off poor widows.

Signs Written across the Sky (Luke 21)

Have you ever read the daily newspaper and asked yourself, *What's this world coming to?* Jesus answered that question in part for some who were worshiping in the temple. He predicted the destruction of the temple, religious deception, international conflicts, natural disasters, signs from heaven, and persecution of believers. He also predicted that hostile enemies would surround Jerusalem, kill many Jews, disperse the population, and crush Jerusalem. When that happened, Jesus said, celestial disturbances would occur, and fear would immobilize people. But Jesus promised that when conditions were most dreadful, He would return with power and glory.

After-Supper Betrayal, Arrest, and Trial (Luke 22)

Doesn't it blow you away to hear about religious people vowing to kill others because their religious beliefs clash? As Luke 22 opens, we learn that the chief priests and scribes were plotting to kill Jesus when Passover—a highly sacred and solemn observance—was about to begin. And Satan was certainly on their side. He influenced Judas to meet with the plotters and offer his services. Judas agreed to betray Jesus for a sum of money (Luke 22:1-6).

After eating the Passover meal with His disciples, Jesus instituted the Lord's Supper, or Communion. The Communion bread represented His body, which would be nailed to the cross. The Communion cup represented His blood, which would be shed for the remission of sin. Jesus also announced that one of the disciples at the table would betray Him (22:7-23). Apparently, the solemnity of Jesus' words didn't sink into the disciples' understanding; they argued about which of them would be acclaimed as the greatest. Jesus assured them that greatness in His kingdom is equated with humble service, and He promised that His kingdom would include each of them at His table and a place of authority as well (22:24-30).

Nothing to Crow About

Jesus told Simon Peter that He would pray for him, because he must become a spiritual leader. But Jesus also told Simon Peter that he would deny Him three times before a rooster crowed (22:31-34). Then Jesus took all His disciples except Judas to the Mount of Olives, where He prayed intensely while the disciples slept. Abruptly, Judas appeared with a multitude to arrest Jesus, whom Judas identified by kissing Him (22:39-53).

Those who arrested Jesus took Him to the high priest's house. Outside, in the courtyard, Simon Peter denied knowing his Lord three times. That night, Jesus' guards beat and mocked Him. Early the next morning they dragged Him before the Sanhedrin, the highest Jewish court. He was interrogated and asked point-blank whether He was the Messiah. When He gave every indication that He was, they accused Him of blasphemy (22:54-71).

The Darkest Day in History (Luke 23)

Luke 23 records the treatment Jesus received at the hands of cowardly Governor Pilate and Herod, ruler of Galilee. Herod and his men made sport of Jesus, draped a kingly robe over Him, and sent Him back to Pilate. Although Pilate could not find any fault with Jesus, he released Him to an angry mob to be crucified. The crowd had gleefully called for the freedom of a known criminal, Barabbas, but the execution of Jesus. While hanging on the cross, flanked by two bandits on crosses, Jesus was mocked by the rulers and soldiers alike who watched Him die. But before dying, Jesus promised everlasting life to a repentant criminal on one of the crosses. Darkness covered the earth for three hours, and the heavy veil separating the temple's Holy Place from the Most Holy Place tore from top

INFO BYTE

IT'S FRIDAY...BUT SUNDAY'S COMIN'

Jesus died on a cross just outside Jerusalem, at a place called Calvary (Latin) or Golgotha (Hebrew). The Romans crucified each victim by driving nails through his wrists, fastening him to the crossbar. Then they raised the crossbar and secured it to the vertical beam that was already in place. Finally, they drove a nail through the victim's heels and into the vertical beam.

Crucified prisoners usually died of asphyxiation within a couple of days. However, Jesus died in about three hours. Unlike every other crucified person, Jesus chose the moment of death; He dismissed His own spirit after enduring not only excruciating pain but also the agony of bearing our sins and being separated from God.

to bottom. When Jesus dismissed His human spirit to His heavenly Father, a high-ranking officer at the foot of the cross glorified God because he was convinced that Jesus was righteous.

Joseph of Arimathea begged Pilate for permission to remove Jesus' body from the cross. After receiving permission, Joseph wrapped the body in linen and laid it in a tomb cut out of rock. Also, the devoted women who had followed Jesus to the cross and had remained there throughout His ordeal prepared spices and ointments for His body.

Sunday Is a Brand-New Day (Luke 24)

The culmination of the life and ministry of Jesus now took place. Jesus arose from the dead on the first day of the week. Two angels announced His resurrection to the women bringing spices and ointment to the empty tomb. They hurried to tell the good news to the disciples, and soon Peter was running to the tomb. When he entered he saw only the linen strips intact without a body.

Later, Jesus joined two of his followers on a walk to Emmaus. He shared with them from Scripture how the recent events had fulfilled prophecy, but they did not recognize Him until He ate with them that evening. When Jesus vanished from their sight after the meal, they rushed to Jerusalem and shared the Resurrection news with the eleven disciples and the other followers of Jesus. Suddenly, Jesus appeared among the group. They thought they were seeing a ghost until Jesus showed them His hands and feet.

After eating with His followers, Jesus shared Scripture with them and commissioned them to preach repentance and remission of sins. Then He led them to Bethany, at the Mount of Olives, blessed them, and ascended to heaven.

The joyful disciples returned to Jerusalem and entered the temple, where they worshiped God continually.

LET'S GET TESTY

CHECKING DR. LUKE'S RECORDS

Circle the number if the person or item is mentioned in Luke's Gospel:

1. The names of John the Baptist's parents
2. The parable of the Good Samaritan
3. The parable of the Lost Son
4. The parable of the Lost Coin
5. The parable of the Lost Sheep
6. Jesus' transfiguration
7. Zacchaeus
8. The fall of Jerusalem
9. The Son of Man coming with power and glory
10. An untamed colt
11. The call of Levi
12. Mary's purification offering
13. Caesar Augustus
14. Pilate
15. A repentant crucifixion victim
16. Mary's visit to Elizabeth
17. Simeon
18. Anna
19. A request to "nuke" a village
20. Story of a rich man and Lazarus

(Answers: All numbers should be circled.)

CHAPTER SIXTEEN

Pick a Miracle, Any Miracle! (John)

The apostle John was an old man when he wrote the Gospel of John around A.D. 85–90, but he had never lost the excitement that Jesus had brought into his life about 60 years earlier. Along with the other disciples, John had followed Jesus from village to village up and down Palestine and had seen Him perform many miracles. Those miracles served as incontrovertible proof that Jesus was the Son of God. After all, only God can perform miracles. John's passion was to construct a Gospel around eight of those miracles so his readers would see that Jesus is the Son of God and consequently believe in Him (see John 20:30-31).

Jesus' Eight Miracles in John's Gospel

1. Turning water into wine (2:1-11)
   At a wedding, Jesus changed water to wine when the supply of wine ran out.
2. Healing a government official's son (4:46-54)
   At Cana, Jesus told a government official that his dying son would live. On his way home to Capernaum the official learned

SOME THINGS YOU'LL DISCOVER IN THIS CHAPTER

1. John chose eight key miracles to demonstrate the character and nature of Jesus.

2. Raising Lazarus from the dead caused an angry reaction on the part of the Pharisees, who then plotted to kill Jesus.

3. Though Simon Peter boasted that he would never leave Jesus, he denied his Lord three times that very night.

that his son had recovered at the time Jesus had promised he would live.

3. Healing a paralyzed man (5:1-15)

A man paralyzed for 38 years received healing from Jesus at the pool of Bethesda in Jerusalem.

4. Feeding the 5,000 (6:1-14)

Using a boy's lunch of five barley loaves and two fish, Jesus fed at least 5,000 people. 12 baskets of leftovers remained after the meal.

5. Walking on water (6:16-21)

Jesus walked on the Sea of Galilee in a ferocious storm to reach His terrified disciples, who were crossing the sea by boat.

6. Healing a blind man (9:1-7)

A man born blind received his sight when Jesus mixed saliva and dirt, plastered it on the blind man's eyes, and commanded him to wash in the pool of Siloam.

7. Raising Lazarus from the dead (11:11-44)

Jesus merely spoke Lazarus's name and commanded him to come out of his tomb. Immediately, Lazarus came forth.

8. Jesus' own resurrection (20:1-10)

Jesus' crucified body was laid to rest in a tomb, but three days later He arose bodily as He had predicted.

Keys to Salvation

Of all the Gospels, John's is the most universal in appeal. He wanted his readers to know that God loves everybody (John 3:16). So he frequently used the word *everyone* (see, for example, John 3:15-16; 11:26) to show that Gentiles as well as Jews have access to salvation. Also, in keeping with his goals of sharing the Good News about Jesus, John frequently used the words *eternal life, life,* and *believe.*

Special Delivery (John 1:1-14)

John did not write the Christmas story into his Gospel, but he certainly gave us an astounding picture of what led up to the first

Christmas. He wrote that in *the* beginning, far before the beginning of Creation, Jesus, whom he called "the Word," existed with God and was God. He created everything and is the source of life and light. Then, one day, He came into the world that He had created, but He came as a real flesh and blood human being, as the virgin-born Jewish baby described by Matthew and Luke. Although Jesus' own nation—Israel—rejected Him, John and the other disciples saw His glory. Jesus exuded grace and truth. John also reported that whoever believes in Jesus becomes a child of God.

INFO BYTE
WHAT'S IN A NAME?

John called Jesus "the Word." The Greek word *logos* means "word" or "message." Jesus was God's word or message to humanity. Everything we need to know about God's character was communicated in Jesus' character and actions (see John 14:7-11).

A Lion of a Lamb (John 1:15-34)

John the Baptist prepared the way for the Jews to receive the Messiah. He called for repentance and told the people to make the way clear for the Messiah's arrival, and he baptized all who took his advice to heart. When Jesus came for baptism, John pointed Him out as the Lamb of God, a term Jews would immediately identify with the Passover Lamb.

Brother, Can You Spare the Time?
(John 1:35-51)

The following day, when John and two of his disciples saw Jesus, John told the two to look on Jesus as the Lamb of God. That was all the two needed to hear; they left John and followed Jesus. Andrew, one of the two, attracted his brother, Simon, to Jesus by telling him that Jesus was the Messiah. This meeting marked the beginning of a whole new life for Simon. Jesus even changed his name to Cephas (which is Peter in Greek), meaning "a stone."

Next, Jesus called Philip to be His disciple. Then Philip brought his brother, Nathaniel, to Jesus. At first Nathaniel was skeptical, but when he learned that Jesus knew all about him, he confessed that Jesus was the Son of God and Israel's King.

IN CASE YOU'RE WONDERING

WHAT EVER HAPPENED TO NICODEMUS?

Nicodemus may not have become a believer the night he met with Jesus, but it seems he became a believer eventually. John 19:38-40 reports that he joined Joseph of Arimathea in preparing Jesus' body for burial.

First, You Take Water. Then You Add a Little Miracle . . . (John 2:1-11)

Have you ever attended a wedding that ran out of punch? It can be more than a little embarrassing for the host and hostess. Jesus and His disciples attended a wedding in the village of Cana, Galilee, that ran out of wine. Mary, Jesus' mother, was present and perhaps with a dry voice told Jesus the wine had dripped its last drop. Jesus instructed the servers to fill six 20- to 30-gallon stone pots with water and take a sample to the master of ceremonies. The master of ceremonies tasted this wine made from water and asked the bridegroom why he had kept the best wine until then.

What This House Needs Is a Good Cleaning (John 2:13-25)

At Passover, Jesus went to Jerusalem, where He entered the temple. What He saw there made His righteous indignation boil. Merchants had turned the temple into a supermarket. He fashioned a whip from small cords and chased the merchants out. The temple, He said, was His Father's house, not a house of merchandise.

When Jesus' critics asked who had authorized Him to chase the merchants out of the temple, they got quite an answer. Jesus predicted that He would raise up His temple (body) three days after it was destroyed. The critics just didn't get it, but after Jesus' resurrection from the dead, a light went on in His disciples' heads. They understood then that Jesus was referring to His body as a temple.

Jesus performed many miracles at the Passover, and many believed in Him because of the miracles.

Don't Keep Me in the Dark (John 3:1-21)

Nicodemus, a Pharisee and high-ranking Jewish official, met Jesus at night. The lines of conversation between the two reveal that Nicodemus was convinced by Jesus' miracles that Jesus had come from God. Jesus replied by telling Nicodemus that no one can enter God's kingdom without experiencing a spiritual birth. He drew

Nicodemus's memory back to the time Moses lifted a bronze snake onto a pole. Snake-bitten Israelites were healed when they looked at the bronze snake. Even so, Jesus said, the Son of Man would be lifted up (on the cross), and whoever would believe in Him would escape punishment and receive eternal life. God had not sent His Son into the world to condemn the world but to save it. He demonstrated His love for the world by giving His Son. Whoever believes in the Son, Jesus told Nicodemus, will not perish but have everlasting life. Jesus explained further that He had come as a light, but those who practice evil reject the light.

IN CASE YOU'RE WONDERING
WHERE WERE THE DISCIPLES WHEN JESUS WAS AT THE WELL?

The disciples had gone into the city to buy food. They returned just as Jesus and the Samaritan woman were concluding their conversation.

Can Anything Good Come from Samaria?
(John 4:1-42)

Much to the shame of humanity, racial prejudice has existed for centuries. When Jesus lived on earth, the Jews and Samaritans disdained each other. It was typical for a Jew traveling north from Judea to Galilee to travel completely around Samaria, which lay between the two Jewish provinces. The traveler would bypass Samaria by crossing the Jordan River. Then he would journey north through Perea to the east of Samaria and finally cross the Jordan again to enter Galilee. But, unlike His fellow Jews, Jesus did not harbor prejudice toward the Samaritans or any other group of people. When He left Judea and journeyed to Galilee, He went right through Samaria and at one point stopped at a well, where He engaged a Samaritan woman in conversation.

The woman had come to the well at noon, an unusual time to draw water, because the sun would be scorching hot at that time of day. But perhaps she wanted to escape the stares and taunts of other women. After all, she had a bad reputation.

Jesus' request for a drink of water startled her. Why would a Jew ask anything of a Samaritan? However, as the conversation unfolded, she gradually understood that Jesus was different. She perceived Him to be a gentleman, a prophet—and when He revealed facts about her marital status, she believed He was the Messiah. A light had gone on at the well!

Quickly, the woman left her waterpot at the well, went into town, and announced that she had found the Messiah. Many believed and followed her as she retraced her steps to the well. Then the Samaritans entertained Jesus as their guest for two days.

Another Day, Another Miracle (John 4:46-54)

No sooner did Jesus arrive in Galilee than a government official invited Him to visit his sick son at Capernaum. Jesus told the official to return home; he would find his son restored to good health. The man believed, and that very hour his son recovered.

The Case of the Poolside Straggler (John 5)

Pools can be popular gathering spots, especially on hot summer days. You don't have to be at a pool long before you hear a kid shout, "Last one into the pool is a rotten egg!" At a pool near the Sheep Gate in Jerusalem, someone might have shouted in the time of Jesus, "First one into the pool gets healed!" That's because a great number of physically challenged people waited poolside for the water to stir, believing that healing powers accompanied the stirring.

One poolside person had been unable to walk for 38 years, but he hoped to reach the bubbling water someday and be healed. Unfortunately for him, he never reached the water in time. Others always got there before him. However, his fortunes changed when Jesus saw him lying poolside and asked him if he wanted to get well. When the physically challenged man answered by recounting his desperate attempts to reach the water, Jesus instructed him to get up, pick up his bed, and walk. Immediately, the man was healed.

It may seem odd, but the Jews who witnessed this miracle informed the healed man that the law (actually, their interpretation of the law) prohibited him from carrying his bed on the Sabbath. Instead of celebrating with the man, they criticized him. Later, when Jesus and this man met in the temple, Jesus challenged him to sin no more. Upon leaving the temple, the man told the critics that Jesus had healed him. This report led to a heated exchange between them and Jesus.

Jesus informed His critics that He was doing the will of His Father, who had authorized Him not only to perform works like the healing of the paralyzed man but even to judge and to raise the dead. Jesus rebuked His critics for failing to see that the Scriptures pointed to Him as the giver of life and for refusing to believe in Him.

There's More Where That Came From (John 6)

After confronting His critics, Jesus went across the Sea of Galilee. He sat on a mountainside with His disciples, where they had a commanding view of the huge crowd that had followed Him there. They were attracted to Jesus because of His miracles on behalf of the sick. Jesus asked His disciple Philip where they could purchase bread so the crowd could have lunch. This was only a test, not an actual alert; Jesus knew what He would do about lunch. Apparently Philip was a practical man. He answered that even 200-days' pay could not buy enough food for such a big crowd. That's when Andrew mentioned that a young boy had carried a sack lunch of five barley loaves and two fish.

That was enough for a young boy, but how could so many people share such a small amount of food? Jesus demonstrated His Creator ability by multiplying the five loaves and two fish over and over again. The 12 disciples performed the role of waiters and served the crowd—well over 5,000 in all—until everyone's hunger was fully satisfied. The tip? Twelve baskets of leftovers were gathered up—perhaps one for each disciple. Jesus had made a little go a long, long, long way! And the lunch guests were convinced that He was the Prophet whose coming the Old Testament Scriptures had predicted. As a matter of fact, they were ready to seize Jesus and make Him their king, but Jesus slipped away into the recesses of the mountain.

That evening, when the disciples were halfway across the Sea of Galilee, their boat floundered in the grip of a horrendous storm. But Jesus walked to them on the water, and as soon as He entered the boat, the storm subsided.

The next day Jesus addressed the multitude He had fed. He told them they were seeking Him because of His miracles and the food

INFO BYTE
FESTIVAL OF BOOTHS

The Festival of Booths was one of three Jewish festivals held after harvest. The Jews built temporary shelters from tree branches and lived in the shelters for seven days. The festival served as a reminder of Israel's journey from Egypt to the Promised Land, when the people lived in tents.

He had supplied. What they really needed to do, He said, was to believe in Him. He was the Bread of Life. Unlike the manna the Israelites had eaten in the wilderness, the Bread of Life supplied eternal life. Upon hearing these words, many who had followed Jesus turned away from Him. So Jesus asked His 12 disciples if they, too, would turn away. Simon Peter spoke for all. He replied that they would stay with Jesus because He had the words of eternal life, and they were convinced that He was the Holy One of God.

Jesus affirmed the 12 disciples but revealed that one of them was a devil. He was referring to Judas Iscariot, who would betray Him.

Something's Brewing at the Festival of Booths (John 7)

At the Festival of Booths in Jerusalem, Jesus stood up in the temple and taught with such knowledge and skill that the Jews questioned how He had become so learned without having received a formal education. Jesus replied that His teaching was from God, who had sent Him. Further, He accused the Jews of failing to obey the law of Moses and of plotting to kill Him. Again, Jesus declared that God had sent Him, and He asserted that the Jews did not know God.

Although many rank-and-file Jews believed in Jesus because of His miracles, the religious leaders were furious and sent officers to apprehend Him. Even some of the crowd that heard Jesus speak wanted to seize Him, while others believed He was either the Prophet or the Messiah. Later, the officers returned to the religious leaders empty-handed. They reported that no one had ever spoken the way Jesus spoke.

Lines in the Sand (John 8)

Early in this chapter John exploded the myth that a person has to be a goody-goody to be accepted by Jesus. The scribes and Pharisees brought a disgraced woman to Jesus. She had been caught in the act of adultery, a crime punishable by death by stoning under the law of Moses. What would Jesus say should be done with her?

First, Jesus wrote something on the ground—perhaps the sins of the religious stuffed shirts. Then He suggested that any accuser who had never sinned should throw the first stone. One by one the accusers left. Then Jesus forgave the woman but instructed her to go and sin no more.

The rest of the chapter reports that Jesus identified Himself as the Light of the World, the Son of Man who would be crucified, the One who sets people free, the One sent by the Father, the Speaker of truth, the Giver of life, and the One who existed before Abraham.

"I Am"

The Gospel of John records several identities of Jesus introduced by His words "I am."

I am the Bread of Life (6:35)
> Spoken after the feeding of the 5,000.

I am the Light of the World (8:12)
> Spoken after saving the life of a woman who had committed adultery. Jesus forgave her and commanded her not to sin again.

Before Abraham was, I am (8:58)
> Spoken to Jews who revered Abraham but wanted to kill Jesus.

I am the Good Shepherd (10:11)
> Spoken in a discourse about Jesus' relationship to believers, His sheep. He knows them, protects them, and lays down His life for them.

I am the resurrection and the life (11:25)
> Spoken to console Martha, whose brother Lazarus had died.

I am the Way, the Truth, and the Life (14:6)
> Spoken to Jesus' disciples in the upper room, where Jesus observed the Passover with them and taught them.

I am the true Vine (15:1)
> Spoken in the upper room to stress the importance of remaining in close fellowship with Jesus. A branch cannot bear fruit apart from the vine. Neither can a disciple be spiritually productive without drawing nourishment from Jesus.

Blind, but Now I See (John 9)

Seeing a beggar blind from birth prompted the disciples to ask Jesus whether the blind man or his parents had sinned. Jesus answered that the condition existed as an opportunity to display God's glory. Then Jesus spit on the ground, scooped up some spittle mud, and applied it to the blind man's eyes. He told the blind man to wash in the pool of Siloam. The blind man obeyed and returned with sight.

This miracle caused quite a buzz, especially among the Pharisees. Because Jesus had healed the blind beggar on the Sabbath, they accused Jesus of breaking the Sabbath. Others refused to believe the man had been blind in the first place, but the blind man's parents set them straight. When some critics asked how the blind man was healed, the parents advised them to ask their son. He was old enough to answer for himself, they insisted.

The inquirers told the former blind man that Jesus was a sinner. The blind man said he didn't know about that, but he did know that he used to be blind and now he could see. Then he stuck the proverbial knife into them by asking whether they, too, wanted to be Jesus' disciples.

Later, Jesus met the formerly blind man and identified Himself to the man as the Son of Man. The man promptly believed.

What Kind of Shepherd Do You Want? (John 10)

Jesus identified Himself as the Good Shepherd in contrast to others who were robbers, thieves, and mercenary hired men. Jesus indicated that His sheep recognize His voice and follow Him. He predicted that He would lay down His life for the sheep. These words caused a division among the Jews. Some slandered Jesus, saying He was demon possessed; others said He could not have healed the blind if He were demon possessed.

Later, at the Feast of Dedication (Hanukkah), when the Jews asked Jesus if He was the Messiah, Jesus pointed to His miracles as evidence and declared that He gives eternal life to His sheep. The

Jews reacted violently. They were ready to stone Him to death, believing He had committed blasphemy by claiming to be God. However, Jesus rebuked them and then escaped their grasp.

The Stench of Death and a Breath of Fresh Air (John 11)

This chapter tells a lot about Jesus' compassion and power. It begins with a message Jesus received from Mary and Martha that their brother, Lazarus, was sick. But Jesus waited two days before leaving for their home. By that time Jesus knew Lazarus had died, but He knew, too, that He would raise him to life.

When Jesus arrived, He found many Jews assembled there to comfort the grieving sisters. Martha told Jesus that Lazarus would not have died if Jesus had been there. Jesus answered that He is the resurrection and the life; therefore, anyone who believes in Him will live even if he dies. When He entered the house, Mary fell at His feet and repeated what Martha had said.

Jesus commanded them to open the tomb. Martha reminded Jesus that the stench would be awful because Lazarus had been dead for four days. Nevertheless, Jesus had the tomb opened and prayed. Then He called out Lazarus's name, commanding Lazarus to come forth. Immediately, Lazarus, bound tightly in graveclothes, came hobbling out of the tomb. Jesus commanded bystanders to unwrap him and let him go.

Lazarus was alive again and able to breathe fresh air!

Whereas many who witnessed this miracle believed, others rushed to tell the Pharisees what had happened. Like a pack of wolves, they huddled together to plan a way to kill Jesus.

Sweet Perfume and Stinky Pharisees (John 12)

Judas, the treasurer for Jesus and the disciples, showed his love of money when he objected to something Mary did for Jesus. She anointed Jesus' feet with expensive perfume. A little cash register went ding, ding, ding, in Judas's head and the total value of the

IT'S A PROMISE!

"Jesus told her, 'I am the resurrection and the life. Those who believe in me, even though they die like everyone else, will live again.'" (John 11:25)

perfume added up to 300 days' wages. Judas protested that the perfume could have been sold with the proceeds going to the poor. But we know what Judas really wanted to do with the money. Luke reported that Judas was a thief who had his hand in the cash purse. Jesus set the record straight; Mary had anointed Him in preparation for His burial.

The next day Jesus was welcomed to Jerusalem by a crowd spreading palm branches in front of Him as He rode a young donkey into the city. They proclaimed Him king!

Later Jesus predicted His death and performed many miracles. Even some of the Jewish leaders believed in Him but were afraid to admit it, because they feared the Pharisees would excommunicate them.

Table Talk in an Upper Room (John 13–17)

Observing the Passover Feast with His disciples in an upper room provided an opportunity for Jesus to teach a lesson on humility and give a series of discourses. Since none of the disciples jumped at the chance to wash Jesus' feet and the feet of the other disciples—something a household servant would have done—Jesus performed that service. During supper, He took off His robe, wrapped a towel around His waist, poured water into a basin, and began to wash the disciples' feet (John 13:1-5).

Simon Peter objected to having his feet washed by Jesus, but Jesus told Peter he would not belong to Him unless Peter submitted to the washing. Then, referring to Judas, Jesus explained that one of them was unclean. After putting on His robe and returning to the table, Jesus revealed that one of His men would betray Him. He would identify the betrayer by handing him bread dipped in sauce. The bread went to Judas, and Judas left the upper room after eating the bread (13:6-30).

Jesus commanded the disciples to love one another. This love would show the world that they belonged to Him. When Peter boasted that he would give his life for Jesus, Jesus announced that

Peter would deny Him three times that very night before a rooster crowed (13:31-38).

As the upper room conference continued, Jesus urged His disciples not to be afraid at the thought of His departure. He assured them that He was going away to prepare rooms for them in His Father's house. He would come again for them, He said, so they could always be together. He further spoke of Himself as the Way, the Truth, and the Life, and promised to send the disciples another Helper just like Himself (John 14).

Chapter 15 of John's Gospel records Jesus' description of Himself as the true Vine and His disciples as the branches. He told His disciples they would produce fruit if they maintained a vital relationship with Him. He also told them to anticipate persecution because they belonged to Him. After all, He explained, the world hated Him.

Again, Jesus announced that He would soon return to His Father, but He would send the Helper, the Spirit of Truth, to them. This Helper would guide them into all truth and glorify Jesus. Furthermore, the disciples would be able to ask anything in Jesus' name, and their request would be granted. Although they would face persecution in the world, they would have Jesus' joy in their hearts (John 16).

John 17 presents what is truly the Lord's Prayer. Jesus prayed, thanking His Father for the disciples and asking Him to protect them, unify them, and set them apart for His holy purposes.

There's a Bloomin' Betrayer in the Garden
(John 18)

After praying, Jesus left the upper room, crossed the Kidron Valley, and entered a garden. John tells us that Judas knew the place because Jesus and His disciples had often met there. So Judas escorted a battalion of Roman soldiers and temple guards to the spot. When Jesus identified Himself as the person they were looking for, they fell flat on their backs on the ground. Again He identified Himself, and told them to let His disciples go.

WHY TWO HIGH PRIESTS?

The Romans had deposed Annas from the high priesthood in A.D. 15, but many Jews still regarded him as their high priest. Caiaphas, Annas's son-in-law, was the official high priest when Jesus was put on trial.

Blustery Peter drew a sword but only sliced off the right ear of Malchus, the high priest's servant. Jesus then commanded Simon Peter to put the sword back into its sheath.

The arresting officers first took Jesus to Annas, the high priest's father-in-law, while Peter and the other disciples trailed behind. Standing around a fire with guards and household servants, Peter denied knowing Jesus. Inside, Jesus was fiercely interrogated. At one point a guard punched Him in the face because he thought Jesus had answered the high priest rudely. After the interrogation, Annas tied Jesus and sent Him to Caiaphas the other high priest.

While Jesus was being dragged off to face Caiaphas, Simon Peter denied his Lord again. After the third denial, a rooster crowed.

After appearing before Caiaphas, Jesus was led to Governor Pilate, who asked Him whether He was the King of the Jews. Jesus explained that His kingdom wasn't of this world. When pressed again for an answer, Jesus offered that He had indeed been born for that purpose and had come to bring truth.

Pilate asked, "What is truth?" then appealed to the assembled crowd for a decision about Jesus' fate. When Pilate asked whether he should set Jesus free, the crowd shouted "No." The angry mob told Pilate to set Barabbas, a known criminal, free.

Dead and Buried (John 19)

Probably in an effort to appease the crowd without ordering Jesus' execution, Pilate scourged Jesus. His soldiers shoved a crown of thorns on Jesus' head and draped a purple robe over Him. They pretended Jesus was a king and mocked Him. They also punched Jesus in the face. Then Pilate led Jesus outside, told the mob he found Jesus not guilty, and asked the mob what Jesus' fate should be. The mob screamed for Jesus to be crucified.

Again, Pilate tried to release Jesus, but when he presented Jesus to the crowd a final time as their king, they insisted that Caesar was their only king and that Jesus should be crucified.

Jesus was crucified between two criminals, with a superscription above His head, which Pilate had prepared and refused to remove. It read JESUS THE NAZARENE, THE KING OF THE JEWS. Soldiers stripped Jesus of His outer garments, ripped them into four parts, and distributed the parts among themselves. Jesus' seamless robe became a gambling prize.

Before He died, Jesus saw His mother, Mary, and John standing nearby. He charged John with Mary's care and then cried out that He was thirsty. Soldiers raised a sponge dipped in sour wine to Jesus' lips and, after tasting it, He cried out, "It is finished," and dismissed His spirit.

Because the Jews did not want the three victims of crucifixion to remain on their crosses on the Sabbath, they asked Pilate to have their legs broken. The shock and torture would hasten their deaths. However, after the soldiers broke the two criminals' legs, they discovered that Jesus had already died, so they did not break His legs. Unknowingly, they had fulfilled Old Testament prophecy that none of the Messiah's bones would be broken.

With Pilate's permission, Joseph of Arimathea and Nicodemus took Jesus' body, anointed it heavily, wrapped it in linen, and placed it in a garden tomb.

INFO BYTE
PILATE

Pilate was governor of Judea, A.D. 26–36. He struggled between fear of the Jews and his opinion that Jesus was innocent. He followed the law of convenience by turning Jesus over to the crowd for crucifixion.

Alive and Well (John 20–21)

But death could not keep Jesus in its grip; He arose a few days later and appeared first to Mary Magdalene and then to ten disciples, who were huddled behind locked doors because they feared reprisal by the Jews. The disciple Thomas was absent at the time, but about a week later he was present with the ten when Jesus appeared in their midst. Thomas would not believe until Jesus invited him to touch His hands and side (John 20).

One day, Simon Peter led the other disciples on a fishing expedition. Did Peter think the experience of following Jesus was over and that it was time to go back to his fishing trade? *Déjà vu!* They caught nothing until a stranger showed up and directed them to a huge catch of fish. Peter recognized at once that the stranger was

Jesus. He jumped overboard and swam to Jesus. The other disciples dragged the net full of fish—153 to be exact—to shore. There, the disciples enjoyed a breakfast prepared in advance by Jesus.

After breakfast, Jesus challenged Simon Peter's love for Him and instructed him to feed and care for Jesus' little lambs and sheep. He also predicted that Peter would be crucified as an old man.

John concluded his Gospel by affirming that he had chosen to record only a few of Jesus' many deeds. To record them all, John insisted, would require more books than the world had room for.

LET'S GET TESTY

Name That Miracle!

Fill in the blanks
to identify the miracles recorded in John's Gospel.

1. At a wedding, Jesus turned _____ into _____.
2. Jesus healed a government official's _____.
3. Jesus healed a paralyzed man at a _____.
4. Jesus fed over 5,000 people with just ____ loaves and _____ fish.
5. Jesus _____ on water.
6. A man born blind received his sight when Jesus put spittle mud on his _____ and told him to _____ in the _____ of Siloam.
7. Jesus raised _____ from the dead after he had been dead _____ days.
8. Jesus Himself _____ from the grave.

(Answers: 1. water, wine; 2. son; 3. pool; 4. five, two; 5. walked; 6. eyes, wash, pool; 7. Lazarus, four; 8. arose)

CHAPTER SEVENTEEN

The Church Is on Fire!
(Acts)

Faulty wiring caused a small-town church to burst into flames in the dead of night. But in the little town, where residents were unaccustomed to hearing sirens, many awoke, threw on some clothes, and rushed to the fire. Standing next to each other and watching the flames and smoke billow from the church spire, a deacon and an atheist exchanged casual hellos. Then the deacon directed a cutting remark to the atheist, "I never expected to see you at church."

"Well," replied the atheist, "this is the first time I've seen the church on fire!"

Bad joke? Maybe. But it could be a wake-up call for any church that would rather exhort mild-mannered people to be more mild-mannered than reach out to its community with a life-changing message about the risen Savior.

The book of Acts, written by Luke as his second historical document (the Gospel of Luke was his first), covers 30 years of the early church's progress, from its beginning at Jerusalem to its establishment in Europe. Acts is indeed the story of the church on fire.

SOME THINGS YOU'LL DISCOVER IN THIS CHAPTER

1. Peter added 3,000 members to the church of Jesus Christ on his first try at preaching the Good News.

2. Paul terrified the leaders of Philippi, who had beaten and jailed him, with the news that he was a Roman citizen and that they could be in deep trouble.

3. It took nearly 500 military men to prevent the fulfillment of an oath on the part of a number of Jews to kill Paul at any cost.

171

Mission Impossible? (Acts 1)

Knowing what you know about the disciples, would you have trusted them with a significant assignment? Peter didn't have enough courage to tell a little servant girl that he was a follower of Jesus. Thomas had been a first-rate skeptic. James and John were hotheads. All of the disciples had deserted Jesus during His arrest and trial. Later, they had locked themselves in a room because they feared the Jews. Not exactly a highly talented job pool, were they? But their risen Lord and Savior would empower His disciples to turn the world upside down.

For 40 days after His resurrection, Jesus appeared to His disciples and taught them about the kingdom of God. Then, as the group assembled on the Mount of Olives, they received a command from Jesus to stay in Jerusalem until they were baptized with the Holy Spirit. Their assignment would be to serve as Jesus' witnesses in Jerusalem, throughout Judea and Samaria, and to the ends of the earth.

After giving His men the task of evangelizing the world, Jesus ascended into heaven. However, two men in white clothing assured the disciples that He would return someday.

Upon returning to Jerusalem, the disciples gathered in the upper room of the house they were staying in with other believers. About 120 were present for prayer when Peter led them in electing a successor to Judas Iscariot. Matthias got the nod.

INFO BYTE

PENTECOST

The word *pentecost,* a Greek word meaning "50," identifies the Jews' fourth annual feast. It was celebrated 50 days after the firstfruits of the wheat harvest were waved before the Lord (Exodus 23:16; Leviticus 23:15-21).

Hey, This Church Is Growing Fast (Acts 2)

Ten days after Jesus' ascension, Jews from all around the Mediterranean world gathered in Jerusalem to celebrate Pentecost. That's when the Holy Spirit filled the believers and enabled them to speak in other languages. As a result, Jews from foreign lands heard the believers speak about God's mighty deeds in their native languages, and they were amazed. However, the apostle Peter explained that the phenomenon had been predicted by the prophet Joel. Then Peter preached about Jesus' miracle-loaded life, His crucifixion, resurrection, and ascension, and declared that Jesus, whom they had crucified, had been honored by God as Lord and Messiah. He urged his audience to repent and be baptized in Jesus' name.

Three thousand listeners responded to Peter's message by believ-ing and being baptized. All 3,000 united together and devoted themselves to the apostles' teaching and other spiritual pursuits. Daily, the Lord added others to this remarkable body of believers known as the church.

IN CASE YOU'RE WONDERING

IS THE CHURCH A BUILDING OR A PEOPLE?

The word *church* translates from the Greek word *ekklesia*, meaning "called out." The Lord has called out believers from the world to be members of the church, also identified in the New Testa-ment as the body of Christ.

Hot Times in the Old Town (Acts 3–7)

Before His crucifixion, Jesus had told His disciples they would be persecuted. His prediction came true. Peter and John were the first targets. They were arrested and tossed into jail after healing a lame beggar at the Beautiful Gate of the temple and preaching about Christ to the assembled onlookers (Acts 3:1–4:3). Nevertheless, many believed, and Peter and John didn't let a little jail time discourage them. When they were brought before the same council that had con-demned Jesus, they didn't back down in the least. Peter told the coun-cil that the lame beggar had been healed by the name of Jesus, whom the council members had crucified. But God had raised Jesus from the dead and was offering salvation through Jesus alone (4:4-12).

After conferring privately, the council decided to command Peter and John to stop speaking and teaching in the name of Jesus and then release them. But Peter and John told the council they could not obey the order (4:13-22).

When Peter and John reported to their fellow believers what had happened, the believers were filled with the Holy Spirit and spoke the Word of God boldly. Furthermore, the believers banded together as a caring and sharing community, meeting one another's needs regard-less of the personal cost. Barnabas, one of the disciples, sold some property and donated the proceeds to needy believers (4:23-37).

A (Too) Hot Piece of Property

Hypocrites in the church are nothing new; the early church had a few of its own to deal with—specifically, Ananias and his wife, Sapphira. They wanted the whole church to think they were super-spiritual, so they sold a piece of property, kept some of the money from the sale, and gave what was left to the church,

IT'S A PROMISE!

"For I will give you the right words and such wisdom that none of your opponents will be able to reply!" (Luke 21:15)

pretending that it was the total amount of the real estate transaction. Their scheme backfired, though. Peter confronted Ananias and reminded him that he hadn't been required to give anything, but he had lied to the Holy Spirit. Immediately, Ananias dropped dead. Three hours after the church's young "ushers" buried Ananias, Sapphira showed up. When Peter asked her if the donation represented the total amount of the sale, she answered, "Yes." Then Peter broke the news to her about her husband, and she dropped dead. The ushers buried her next to her husband (5:1-11).

The early church had received a powerful lesson about how much God detests hypocrisy.

As the church grew, so did persecution by the religious authorities. They threw the apostles into jail, but an angel of the Lord opened the prison doors so they could get out and preach again. Upon learning that the apostles were preaching again, the religious authorities arrested and reprimanded them. Then they beat the apostles, commanded them to stop speaking in Jesus' name, and released them. The apostles were joyful that they had suffered for Jesus, and they went right back to teaching and preaching about Jesus, the Messiah (5:12-42).

Eventually, a people problem arose in the church. Greek members thought their widows were being neglected. They accused the apostles of taking better care of the widows of the Hebrew members. To solve the problem, the apostles directed the church to elect seven men, qualified and highly regarded, to distribute meals to all the needy widows. One of the elected men was Stephen, who became a powerful witness for Christ, much to the dismay of the religious authorities, who dragged him before them for trial (Acts 6).

You're Gonna See Jesus

The religious authorities received quite a sermon from Stephen when they asked him to give an account of himself. Stephen rehearsed Israel's long history from Abraham to the present, underscoring God's goodness and Israel's disobedience. When Stephen concluded by charging the religious leaders with the sin of rejecting God's message and the Messiah, he felt the full blast of their fury.

The religious authorities gnashed their teeth at Stephen, but he looked up to Jesus in heaven and announced that he saw the Son of Man standing at God's right hand. That was the last straw. The religious authorities forced him to a place outside the city, where they laid their robes at the feet of a young man named Saul and stoned Stephen. As Stephen was dying, he knelt, committed his spirit to Jesus, and prayed for forgiveness for his assailants (Acts 7).

The Heat Gets Hotter (Acts 8–12)

Stephen's martyrdom sparked a raging fire of persecution against the church in Jerusalem. Many believers were scattered throughout the regions of Judea and Samaria. However, all the apostles stayed in Jerusalem (Acts 8:1).

Leading the reign of terror against believers was Saul, the young man who had tended the robes of those who stoned Stephen. He conducted a house-to-house search for believers. When he found believers, whether male or female, he carted them off to jail (8:3).

The persecution didn't stop the believers from spreading the gospel. Wherever they went, they spoke about Jesus, the Messiah. Philip, who had been elected by the church at Jerusalem to care for the widows, went to the city of Samaria, preached there, and healed many people (8:4-8).

When the apostles got wind of what was happening in Samaria, they sent Peter and John to check it out. Could Samaritans enjoy salvation by faith just as the Jews had? Sure enough, everything checked out A-OK, and Peter and John even took time to preach in Samaritan villages before returning to Jerusalem (8:14-25).

Philip could have questioned the Lord when He told him to hit the road—a desert road. But he didn't, he simply obeyed and headed off into the desert. Soon, he saw an Ethiopian official returning from Jerusalem by caravan. The Spirit told Philip to chase down the Ethiopian's chariot. Philip did so, heard the Ethiopian reading from Isaiah, and asked whether the Ethiopian understood what he was reading. The question led to an invitation for Philip to hop aboard the chariot and explain Isaiah's message. Philip began with the passage being read and proclaimed Jesus to the Ethiopian. When the caravan reached an oasis, the Ethiopian asked to be baptized. After the baptism, Philip was snatched away by the Holy Spirit, and the new believer—the Ethiopian—continued down the road rejoicing. As for Philip, he kept preaching throughout Samaria (8:26-40).

Meanwhile, back in Jerusalem, young Saul's hatred had reached the boiling point. He threatened to destroy believers, and he gained permission from the high priest to arrest believers in Damascus and drag them back to Jerusalem in chains (9:1-2). Little did he know that he would be arrested by the risen Christ (the Greek word for "Messiah") before reaching Damascus.

The Original "Damascus Road Experience"

Just outside Damascus, Saul was startled by a dazzling light from heaven. Blinded by it, he fell to the ground. In the moments that followed, Saul learned that Jesus was truly alive and in command of the situation. Jesus told Saul to enter Damascus and await further instructions there. Led by the hand, sightless Saul entered Damascus. Three days later, the Lord sent a believer named Ananias to visit Saul. At first Ananias hesitated, knowing what kind of villain Saul was, but the Lord prevailed. He assured Ananias that He had big plans for Saul; He would send Saul as His chosen messenger to the Gentiles, to kings, and to the Jews. When Ananias met Saul, he rehearsed what the Lord had told him. Immediately, Saul received his sight, was baptized, ate food for the first time in three days, and stayed for several days with the believers in Damascus (9:3-19).

Saul started to preach Christ in the synagogues, much to the amazement of the Jews who knew his reputation. Now he became the target of the Jews' hatred and had to escape from Damascus by being put into a basket and lowered by a rope down the city's wall. When he reached Jerusalem, Barnabas befriended him, but Greek Jews tried to kill him. It seemed best to the believers to send Saul to Tarsus, his hometown. Because Saul was no longer persecuting the church, the believers in Judea enjoyed some peace, and the church kept growing (9:20-31).

The apostle Peter hadn't gone underground during all the perse-

cution in Jerusalem. He kept preaching and healing. While visiting Joppa, on the Mediterranean coast, he raised a woman to life who had performed many charitable deeds for believers there. This miracle persuaded many residents of Joppa to become believers (9:32-43).

Not-So-Favorite Food

Chapters 10 and 11 report how the Lord broke down Peter's racial prejudice and persuaded him to preach to Gentiles in the home of a Roman military officer, a seeker of truth. The story reads like science fiction, but it's all true. It involves a UFO—a sheet lowered from heaven—full of creeping, crawling things, a new diet for Peter, and a visit by three strangers. Chapter 11 also reports how persecution served as the impetus for carrying the gospel to the Gentiles in Antioch of Syria. Many Antiochians believed that Barnabas was dispatched there from Jerusalem to teach them. But Barnabas didn't go alone. He stopped in Tarsus, found Saul, and took him along. The two partners taught in Antioch for a full year.

A Justified Jailbreak

As we read chapter 12, we bump up against another Herod. Like his grandfather, Herod the Great, who tried to kill Baby Jesus, this Herod was politically motivated and diabolical. He ordered the beheading of James, the brother of John. Because this execution pleased the Jews, he arrested Peter and incarcerated him under heavy guard in the bowels of his prison. No doubt he intended to behead Peter, too. But the church prayed for Peter, and the Lord sent an angel to spring Peter from jail. The angel found Peter sleeping and chained to guards. He woke him and told him to get up. Peter's chains fell off, and he put a coat on and followed the angel past several guards, out of the prison, and into the street. When the angel left, Peter went to the home of John Mark's mother, where believers were praying for him.

True to form, Herod executed the guards who had not been able to secure their prisoner, but what goes around comes around. One day, when Herod strutted his royal stuff and allowed people to call him a god, he was touched by an angel—actually struck down by an angel. Then worms ate him alive until he died.

INFO BYTE
JOPPA

This ancient city lay on the Mediterranean coast about 30 miles northwest of Jerusalem. King Hiram of Lebanon had floated timber to Joppa for use in constructing Solomon's temple, and later, Jonah had boarded a ship at Joppa intending to sail to Tarshish.

IN CASE YOU'RE WONDERING
PETER'S SLUMBER PARTY

How could Peter sleep in such perilous circumstances? He must have known he was slated for execution. Perhaps he remembered Jesus' promise that Peter would die as an old man (John 21:18). He was only 40-something when he was in prison. Or he may have cashed in on the promise of Isaiah 26:3.

INFO BYTE
WHAT'S IN A NAME?

At Antioch believers were called "Christians" for the first time (Acts 11:26). The name, meaning "followers of Christ," is used only two other times in the New Testament—in Acts 26:28 and 1 Peter 4:16.

The heat of persecution reached an all-time high under Herod, because the government teamed up with the religious authorities to crush believers. But the church kept on growing stronger.

Taking the Show on the Road (Acts 13–14)

The church at Antioch, begun by missionaries, became strong enough to send out its own missionaries, Barnabas and Saul, with John Mark as their assistant. In Acts 13, Saul's name changes to Paul. Because he would be preaching in Gentile countries, his Greek name, Paul, would be more appropriate than his Jewish name, Saul.

Leaving from Seleucia, the missionary team sailed first to Cyprus, then to the mainland. At this point, John Mark left and went home to Jerusalem. Paul and Barnabas continued on to Antioch in the province of Pisidia (not to be confused with the Antioch in Syria). As was their *modus operandi,* they entered the synagogue at Antioch. When they were invited to speak, Paul took the floor and shared the Good News that the crucified, risen Jesus was Israel's Messiah and was offering forgiveness to everyone who believes in Him. The sermon enjoyed a favorable response: Paul and Barnabas were invited back for the following Sabbath, and many of the Jews became believers. A big crowd showed up the next Sabbath, but jealous Jews bad-mouthed Paul and Barnabas so severely that the two decided to move on and begin preaching to the Gentiles. Nevertheless, a beachhead for the gospel had been established, and the Good News soon spread throughout the region.

Chapter 14 reports that Paul and Barnabas preached next in Iconium, where many believed but many did not. Those who opposed Paul and Barnabas schemed to kill them, but this plot was discovered, and Paul and Barnabas moved on to Lystra. Paul healed a disabled man there, but the response was not what he and Barnabas wanted. The Lycaonians thought the two were gods. They called Barnabas "Zeus" and Paul "Hermes," and only Paul's impassioned insistence that there is only one living God restrained the crowd. Surprisingly, the crowd's mood did a 180-degree turn when Jews from Antioch arrived and turned the crowd against the missionaries. The frenzied crowd dragged Paul outside the city, stoned him, and left him for dead. However, those who believed stayed with Paul until he revived. The next day, he and Barnabas left for Derbe, where many believed. Then they backtracked and appointed elders in the young churches they had founded.

After sailing home to Antioch, the two missionaries reported to the church there, highlighting how God had brought the Gentiles to faith.

The Fewer Rules the Better (Acts 15:1-35)

Things were going great at Antioch until some guys from Judea showed up and told the Gentile believers they could not be saved unless they were circumcised (which was what the Old Testament commanded all Jewish males to do). The issue was so contentious that the church sent Paul and Barnabas to take the matter up with the apostles and elders in Jerusalem. When they reached Jerusalem, they told the church, the apostles, and the elders what God had done through their ministry to the Gentiles. But strict Jewish Christians insisted the Gentiles must submit to circumcision. After much discussion and Peter's support for the Gentiles, the apostle James recommended that the Gentiles be accepted without circumcision. He suggested writing a letter to them urging them to stay away from idolatry, keep themselves sexually pure, and abstain from eating blood and the meat of strangled animals. His recommendation carried, and Paul and Barnabas returned to Antioch to report the good news and deliver the letter.

Hitting the Road Again (Acts 15:36-21:36)

Two good men had one big argument. Paul wanted to travel to the cities where he and Barnabas had preached on their first missionary journey, but Barnabas wanted to take John Mark with them. Paul objected, reminding Barnabas that John Mark had split during the first journey. The disagreement grew so intense that Barnabas took John Mark and went one way, while Paul chose Silas and headed off in a different direction (Acts 15:36-41).

At Derbe and Lystra, Paul added another team member, Timothy.

INFO BYTE

ANOTHER PASSENGER AND TEAM MEMBER

Luke, the writer of Acts, joined missionaries Paul, Timothy, and Silas at Troas. Notice the switch of pronoun from "they" to "us" (Acts 16:8, 10).

His mother was Jewish and his father was a Gentile. As they visited Gentile churches, they shared the letter from the church leaders in Jerusalem. When the team tried to enter Asia, the Holy Spirit would not let them do so. Then, at Troas on the coast, Paul had a vision in which he heard a man pleading with him to go to the Greek province of Macedonia. Believing that God had given him this vision, Paul led his team to a ship heading for Europe (16:1-12).

A Whole Lot of Shaking Going On

The missionaries docked at Samothrace and continued by foot to Philippi, an important Macedonian city. A businesswoman named Lydia was converted there and opened her home to the missionaries as a preaching center. One day, Paul freed a slave girl of a demon, but her owners were anything but happy about it. The demon had empowered her to foretell the future, a power that had brought her owners big money. Now their business had gone belly-up. Enraged, they managed to have Paul and Silas flogged and thrown into prison. Apparently, some anti-Semitism was involved, because Timothy and Luke did not meet the same fate (16:13-24). Nevertheless, Paul and Silas were anything but despondent. They held a midnight praise concert for the prisoners. Suddenly, an earthquake shook the jail. Cell doors flew open and the prisoners' chains snapped. The jailer woke up, supposed that his prisoners had escaped, and therefore prepared to commit suicide. But Paul assured him everyone was present and accounted for. Then Paul led the jailer and his family to become Christians (16:25-39).

The following day, the jailer told Paul that the city rulers had consented to release him and Silas. But Paul said they had better come in person, because they had beaten and jailed two Roman citizens. This news frightened the rulers so much that they came in person to beg Paul and Silas to leave their city. The missionaries did leave, but only after meeting the believers at Lydia's house and encouraging them (16:40).

It's Tuesday.... Is This Athens or Corinth?

From Philippi, Paul's group traveled south to Thessalonica, where Paul went to the synagogue and declared that Jesus had died and risen again. Some Jews believed, as did many Gentile men and a number of prominent women. But persecution erupted, forcing the missionaries to leave. At Berea they were well-received, but Jews from Thessalonica dogged their steps, stirred up trouble, and caused Paul to leave Berea. However, Silas and Timothy stayed behind.

Next stop, Athens, the seat of Greek government, philosophy, and idolatry. Paul spoke to the Athenians about the true God, unknown to them, and challenged them to repent so they would not experience judgment at the hands of Jesus, whom God raised from the dead. Some jeered Paul; others said they would like to hear from him again; and some believed (17:15-34).

Corinth was Paul's next stop. There he found a Jewish husband and wife team of tent makers, Aquila and Priscilla. Since Paul, too, was a tent maker by trade, he stayed at their home. Silas and Timothy caught up with Paul at Corinth. Paul's preaching in the Corinthian synagogue stirred up a hornet's nest, so Paul moved to a house next to the synagogue and preached from there. The synagogue's leader and his family believed, and so did many other Corinthians. But the angry Jews trumped up a phony charge against Paul and wanted the city magistrate to punish him. However, the magistrate threw the case out of court. Paul's stay at Corinth had lasted a year and a half (18:1-17). On his way home to Antioch, Paul dropped off Aquila and Priscilla at Ephesus (18:18-22).

For two years Paul preached, taught, and performed miracles in Ephesus. Even handkerchiefs and cloths carried from Paul to the sick brought healing. If imitation is the highest form of flattery, Paul might have felt flattered when seven sons of Sceva, a Jewish priest, tried to cast out demons as Paul had done. However, a demon told them it recognized the names of Jesus and Paul but didn't know Sceva's sons. Then the man possessed by that demon pounced on the impostors, overpowered them, and sent them away "streaking" and wounded (Acts 19:1-16).

Wild about Diana

When Paul's ministry put a severe damper on the silversmiths' business of crafting and selling silver shrines to honor Ephesus's chief goddess Artemis (Diana), the silversmiths gained the support of other tradespeople and stirred up a public riot against Paul and his traveling companions. Fortunately, the town clerk informed the mob that their assembling was illegal and they should let the courts handle their complaint (19:17-41).

After leaving Ephesus, Paul traveled to Troas, where he gathered the believers together for a lengthy report. When his talk reached the midnight hour, a young man named Eutychus dozed off in the worst seat in the house—a third-story window ledge. He fell out of the open window and died on impact. Paul restored him to life and went right back to talking until dawn (Acts 20:1-12).

At Miletus, a seaport, Paul called for the church leaders in Ephesus. When they arrived, he summarized his faithful ministry at Ephesus and told the leaders he was heading for Jerusalem. He knew he would be arrested there, but he was prepared for that eventuality. Then he charged the leaders with the task of teaching and protecting the believers at Ephesus (20:13-38).

Customized Lying

Along the way to Jerusalem, Paul visited believers. A prophet at Caesarea warned Paul not to go to Jerusalem, but Paul would not be talked out of doing what he thought was the will of God (21:1-14). When he reached Jerusalem, he shared preacher stories with the apostles. Trouble struck quickly. A lie circulated throughout the city that Paul had been teaching Jews to stop practicing Jewish customs. So Paul and some other men tried to overturn the lie by undergoing a Jewish purification ceremony. This action didn't help; the Jews still considered Paul a traitor to Judaism and dragged him out of the temple. They would have killed him, but a Roman military commander and his men rescued Paul, arrested him, and took him into their custody (21:15-36).

Paul's Third Missionary Journey
(Acts 21:37–28:31)

In a letter Paul had written to the Romans, he expressed a desire to visit Rome (Romans 1:10), but he could not have imagined how he

would get there. Acts 21:37–28:31 describes the circumstances that took Paul to Rome.

First, Paul assured the Roman commander that he was not the Egyptian who had instigated a revolt and had led 4,000 members of the Assassins into the desert. He identified himself as a Jew and a citizen of Tarsus and asked permission to address the Jews. Permission granted, Paul spoke in Hebrew to the assembled Jews (21:37-40). His personal conversion story and account of his commission to preach to the Gentiles stirred the Jews' anger. The commander ordered that Paul be scourged, but just as the soldiers were about to scourge him, Paul announced that he was a Roman citizen. Because it was unlawful to scourge a Roman citizen, the commander released him (Acts 22). The next day, though, Paul was brought before the Jewish council. When he claimed that his conscience was clear, Paul found himself on the receiving end of a punch ordered by the high priest. Things went downhill from there. So the commander took Paul back to the soldiers' barracks. Upon learning that a number of Jews had taken a solemn oath to kill Paul, the commander mustered 200 soldiers, 70 horsemen, and 200 spearmen and whisked him away in the dead of night to Caesarea (Acts 23).

On the High Seas

Following a number of appearances before political notables and a request to bring his case before the emperor, Caesar, Paul was put on a ship captained by a Macedonian Greek. Luke accompanied Paul, as did other prisoners, a military officer, and his soldiers (Acts 24:1–27:1). At an Asia Minor seaport, Paul and the other passengers were transferred to another ship bound for Italy. It was anything but smooth sailing. A cyclone churned the Mediterranean waters and threatened to tear the ship apart. But Paul had conveyed God's promise to all on board that everyone would survive. The ship ran aground off the island of Malta, but all on board made their way safely to shore (27:2-44).

The First Snakehandler

Getting shipwrecked is enough to make most grown men cry, but getting bitten by a poisonous snake after surviving a shipwreck might carry most grown men right to their grave. Paul experienced both disasters and kept his cool. The snakebite incident occurred after the islanders had built a fire for the shipwrecked crew and passengers. Paul was putting some sticks on the fire when a viper crept out of the wood and onto his hand. At first, the islanders took this as a sign that Paul was a murderer, but when he didn't fall down dead, they changed their minds, raising him all the way from the status of murderer to that of a god. Before leaving for Rome on another ship that had docked at Malta for the winter, Paul healed the father of the island's chief ruler and many other afflicted islanders. Finally, Paul set foot on Italian soil and was met by Christians. At Rome, he was allowed to rent a house for two years and share the message of Christ with all who visited him. Although he was under house arrest the whole time, the gospel could not be held in check (Acts 28).

LET'S GET TESTY

Acts in Acts

Put the following historic events in order by number:

1. Jesus appears to Saul near Damascus.
2. Jesus ascends to heaven.
3. Stephen is martyred.
4. Paul's ship is shipwrecked.
5. John Mark leaves Paul and Barnabas.
6. Barnabas and Paul split up.
7. Paul and Silas sing in jail at midnight.
8. Paul receives his sight at Damascus.
9. At Pentecost 3,000 Jews believe in Christ.
10. Paul preaches at Athens.

(The correct order is 2, 9, 3, 1, 8, 5, 6, 7, 10, 4.)

ite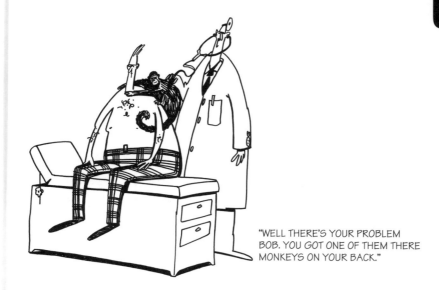

"WELL THERE'S YOUR PROBLEM BOB. YOU GOT ONE OF THEM THERE MONKEYS ON YOUR BACK."

CHAPTER EIGHTEEN

To Rome with Love (Romans)

Rome is known as "the eternal city." It isn't eternal, of course, but it *is* ancient. Paul's letter to the Romans addressed residents in Rome who had received eternal life through faith in Jesus Christ (Romans 6:23b). We don't know how these Romans became believers. Paul never preached at Rome, but Acts 2:10 may hold the answer. Jews from Rome had attended Pentecost and become believers. Perhaps, after returning home, they started a church. Paul wanted to visit Rome and strengthen the faith of the believers there and asked the recipients of his letter to pray that this would happen (Romans 15:30-32). The letter to the Romans combines deep theological truth and practical assistance for Christian living.

In His Majesty's Service (Romans 1:1-17)

Paul began his letter by identifying himself as a servant and an apostle of Jesus Christ. He wrote that Jesus was a descendant of David and had risen from the dead. After greeting his readers warmly, Paul mentioned that he was praying for them and wanted

SOME THINGS YOU'LL DISCOVER IN THIS CHAPTER

1. Great biblical characters were in good standing with God not because of what they did that was good, but because of their belief in Him.

2. Though all of nature demonstrates that God exists, humans still deviate into all kinds of idolatry and rebellion.

3. Believers can trust that God will work out everything for good in the lives of His children, including our trials.

185

WHAT'S UP WITH THE GOOD BOOK?

"The Bible is a stream wherein the elephant may swim and the lamb may wade."—*Gregory the Great*

to visit them and preach the gospel at Rome. He believed he owed Jews and Gentiles alike an opportunity to hear the gospel, for the gospel could save both Jews and Gentiles if they would believe.

Back to Nature (Romans 1:18-32)

What's your favorite scenic view? An impressive mountain? A sweeping river valley? A high waterfall? A starry sky? A flaming sunset? A stand of tall birch trees in a green meadow? According to Paul, nature clues human beings in to the fact that God exists. However, the heathen chose to reject nature's message about the true God and worship idols. They degenerated further by engaging in sexually deviant behavior, other forms of immorality, and blasphemy. God's wrath, therefore, was directed at all those who had rejected Him.

Good People Don't Go to Heaven?
(Romans 2:1–3:23)

In chapters 2 and 3, Paul wrote something that blows away the popular belief that good people go to heaven. First, he explained that Gentiles who try to lead a respectable, moral life should not look down their noses at the pagan. They are no better off than the pagan, because they think their so-called righteousness earns them a ticket to heaven. In reality, Paul pointed out, God knows how sinful self-righteous people are. He sees their hearts. Instead of repenting, these hypocrites proudly trust in their good deeds to get them to heaven (2:1-16).

The Jews are no better off if they rely on their religious credentials for salvation instead of believing in Christ. Being custodians of the law of Moses doesn't win any points with God. Again, Paul stressed that God examines the heart, not religious performance or pedigrees (2:17-29). Religious do-gooders and pagans fall into the same category—they are sinners under God's judgment. But God has made it possible for sinners of all kinds to be saved. Jesus died to deliver all who believe in His name. Sin pays terrible wages—death—but God freely gives eternal life to all who believe in Jesus (3:1-31).

Here's What Really Counts with God
(Romans 4–5)

The Jews held Abraham and David in high esteem. Abraham, of course, was the father of the Hebrew race; David was Israel's most beloved king. However, neither Abraham nor David came into a favorable standing (justification) with God by doing anything meritorious. God brought them into His favor because they believed Him. Abraham's faith made him acceptable to God long before the law of Moses existed, and David's faith made him acceptable to God after the law of Moses had been given. The law contributed nothing to either man's salvation. God's terms have not changed, Paul told the Romans. God still brings into His favor anyone who simply believes. Jesus' resurrection proved that God had accepted Jesus' sacrifice on the cross as sufficient to save all who trust in Him (Romans 4)

But Paul also taught the benefits of being justified by faith. Believers have peace with God, access to God, and joy. Even life's roughest trials can't pin believers to the canvas, because they have hope. They know a better day is coming. Trials just make believers more patient. Believers also possess the love of God, which the Holy Spirit has placed in their hearts. And they won't experience God's wrath, because Jesus has saved them from God's wrath. Adam introduced sin and judgment to the human race, but Jesus Christ brought the gifts of righteousness and eternal life (Romans 5).

Me and My Evil Twin (Romans 6–8)

Paul's message in Romans 1–5 shouted, "Stop trying to save yourself; trust Jesus Christ to save you." His message in chapters 6–8 builds on that message and points out how those who trust in Christ can lead successful Christian lives. Chapter 6 explains that every Christian is identified with Christ and has been set free from the power of sin. But being set free doesn't give anyone *carte*

IT'S A PROMISE!

"Since God did not spare even his own Son but gave him up for us all, won't God, who gave us Christ, also give us everything else?" (Romans 8:32)

blanche to live just any old way. Christians are free to honor and serve God (Romans 6).

If you think the apostle Paul walked around with a halo over his head and sang, "Hey, Look Me Over," you need to read Romans 7. He confessed that he fought a continual battle with sinful desire. On the one hand he wanted to do right, but on the other hand he felt a strong urge to do wrong. He concluded that only Christ could deliver him from sin's tyranny.

Chapter 8 reads like a victory speech. He informed his readers that the Holy Spirit produces righteousness in believers' lives (8:1-4). The Spirit, who gives life and peace, lives in believers (8:9), leads them (8:14), assures them that God is their Father (8:15-17), plants within them a firm hope (8:18-25), and prays for them (8:26-27). Believers can be confident that everything that happens in their lives—even hard trials—are designed by their heavenly Father to build Christlike qualities into their lives (8:28-30). Not even the harshest trials or death itself can separate believers from God's love revealed in Christ (8:31-39).

Time Out for Israel! (Romans 9-11)

The Jews really had a lot going for them. As a people they had received God's law and covenantal promises, but they spurned their privileges and rejected the Messiah. Therefore, God turned His attention to the Gentiles (Romans 9).

Of course, Paul was a Jew with a deep love for his fellow Jews. He longed to see them believe in Jesus, who had fulfilled the law. However, on the whole, the Jews had failed to trust in Jesus, preferring to establish their own righteousness by keeping the law—an impossible task! By turning to the Gentiles, God threw the gospel invitation wide open to both Jews and Gentiles. On an individual basis, salvation comes to whoever believes in Jesus. But, as Paul mentioned, no one can believe without hearing the Good News, and no one can proclaim the Good News without being sent to do so (Romans 10).

It's not like God has forgotten or abandoned Israel. Paul told the Romans that God has set the nation aside for a while, but a believing remnant of Jews exists, and someday God will fulfill all His promises concerning Israel. Someday, the Messiah will deliver the nation from her sins and reconcile her to God (Romans 11).

You Gotta Walk the Walk (Romans 12–16)

Paul made it clear to the Christians in Rome that faith and daily relationships are closely linked. In chapter 12 Paul urged them to yield their bodies and minds to God. This act of dedication would enable them to know and do God's will. Every Christian, Paul taught, has received at least one spiritual gift to be employed in ministry on behalf of others. Christians ought to love others, be kind to one another, and put others' interests ahead of their own. They should be efficient, zealous servants of the Lord who exude joy, hope, and patience. They should be prayerful, charitable, cordial to their enemies, empathetic, compassionate, and humble. Instead of retaliating when mistreated, Christians ought to repay evil with kindness and leave matters in the Lord's hands.

Chapter 13 instructs Christians to be good citizens and to lead lives that are above reproach. In chapters 14 and 15, Paul appealed to the Christians in Rome to accept one another without judging on the basis of religious observances or dietary restrictions. He emphasized that the kingdom of God doesn't major on food or drink but on righteousness, peace, and joy. Then he shared some personal travel plans with his readers and invited their prayers for him. He asked them to pray specifically that he would be delivered from his enemies, that his ministry in Jerusalem would be well received, that he would arrive in Rome with joy, and that he and his readers would be mutually refreshed.

Paul closed his letter to the Romans first by commending Phoebe, a sister in Christ and a valued servant in the church at Corinth. Then he sent warm greetings to individuals in the church at Rome and wished everyone the Lord's grace before signing off with praise to the only wise God (Romans 16).

LET'S GET TESTY

Reviewing Romans

Answer T for true and F for false.

1. Paul was an apostle and servant of Jesus Christ. ___
2. The book of Romans mentions Noah. ___
3. The book of Romans mentions Abraham. ___
4. The book of Romans mentions David. ___
5. If a person performs enough religious deeds, he or she will gain salvation. ___
6. Christians are exempt from being good citizens. ___
7. Phoebe was a Christian woman. ___
8. The Holy Spirit prays for believers. ___
9. It isn't important what believers do with their bodies. ___
10. Paul wanted to visit Rome. ___

(*Answers: 1. T; 2. F; 3. T; 4. T; 5. F; 6. F; 7. T; 8. T; 9. F; 10. T*)

CHAPTER NINETEEN

Setting Things Straight (1 and 2 Corinthians)

The members of the church at Corinth thought they were God's gift to the Christian community. They had lots of self-esteem, but much of it was unfounded. Sure, many of them were knowledgeable and some were outstanding orators, but in matters of morality and spirituality the Corinthians were still in preschool. The apostle Paul had learned that the Corinthian church was being torn apart by arguments (1 Corinthians 1:11). Later, he learned that the Corinthians had begun to doubt his authority, thinking he wasn't really an apostle. So within a year he wrote two letters to the Corinthians to set them straight about such issues as unity, morality, doctrine, church organization, and his apostleship. First Corinthians addresses most of these issues, whereas 2 Corinthians takes up the issue of Paul's apostleship.

Stop Playing King of the Hill
(1 Corinthians 1–4)

Playing king of the hill isn't strictly a kids' pastime; adults play the game too. At work, in government—even at church, some

SOME THINGS YOU'LL DISCOVER IN THIS CHAPTER

1. The Corinthians sometimes focused more on the strengths of their individual leaders than on Christ.

2. They also sometimes confused their freedom in Christ with the liberty to do what they wanted and then be forgiven if they were wrong.

3. This church had delayed in giving an offering to poorer churches, and Paul sought their generosity.

191

PROSPEROUS BUT DECADENT

Corinth was situated strategically below the isthmus connecting Greece and the Peloponnese. It was a commercial giant, but also a center of idolatry and immorality. Its temple of Aphrodite housed 1,000 prostitutes. Being a Corinthian was closely associated with being a drunk. The Romans had burned Corinth in 146 B.C. but had it rebuilt and given Roman colony status in A.D. 44.

adults invest time and energy into their efforts to become king of the hill. The Corinthian church had its share of candidates for king of the hill, although the candidates themselves had no such aspirations. Their followers were the culprits. Some thought the orator Apollos was the greatest; others thought Paul deserved the top spot; others gave Peter the nod; and the rest believed the honor should go to Christ. Although Paul greeted the Corinthians cordially and complimented them on their communication skills and knowledge, he pointed out the inappropriateness of building fan clubs in the church. Only Christ deserves every believer's adoration and devotion (1 Corinthians 1).

In chapter 2 Paul reviewed his stay at Corinth. He had neither enticed nor entranced the Corinthians with persuasive language and human wisdom. Instead, he had presented Jesus Christ clearly in the power of the Spirit. Human wisdom, he wrote, cannot make any sense of spiritual truth; only the Holy Spirit can enlighten the mind to understand it.

Not one to beat around the bush, Paul told the Corinthians to grow up; they were acting like a bunch of babies. Worse still, they were acting like they had never become Christians. They needed to understand that God's servants all have a part to play in building the church. If each fulfills his divinely assigned role, his work will endure and he will be rewarded. However, if anyone builds for show or for his own glory, his work will come to nothing and he will lose his reward. The Corinthians, Paul wrote, were God's building, and he, Apollos, and Peter were just subcontractors (1 Corinthians 3).

In chapter 4 Paul stressed how important it is for God's servants to be faithful. God had entrusted Paul with the gospel, and he had faithfully proclaimed it. He and the other apostles had suffered ridicule and persecution as God's servants, but they endured every attack. Paul had introduced the Corinthians to Christ and longed to see them progress spiritually. He had sent Timothy to them to instruct them, but he promised to go to Corinth in person. He did not want to have to discipline the Corinthians during his visit. He much preferred to be loving and meek.

Get a Grip! (1 Corinthians 5–6)

Some things had gotten out of control in the Corinthian church—big time! One member was having an affair with his stepmother, and the church wasn't the least bit concerned. Paul told the church to take charge of this situation by excommunicating the offending member. The non-Christian world has plenty of immoral people, Paul wrote, but the church should never condone immoral conduct in the church (1 Corinthians 5).

The Corinthians were fighting over more things than just who should be king of the hill. Instead of resolving personal disputes peaceably within the church, they were hauling one another to court. Also, some of the Corinthians must have been leading trashy lives, because Paul pointed out that they had been set free from immorality but were not free to continue in it. They needed to understand that God had redeemed them for Himself and that the Holy Spirit lived in their bodies. So instead of defiling the temple of the Holy Spirit—the body—they should glorify God in their body and spirit (1 Corinthians 6).

To Tie the Knot or Not (1 Corinthians 7)

Sexual impurity is a huge no-no, Paul wrote, but sexual relations within marriage are encouraged (7:1-9), and married couples ought to stay married. Running back to mother or chasing a wife back to mother is frowned upon (7:10-16). Singles are free to marry, but a Christian should marry only another Christian (7:25-40).

Give Me Liberty (1 Corinthians 8–10)

Christians don't always see eye to eye on issues not mentioned specifically in the Bible. In Corinth, some Christians thought it was OK to buy meat of an animal that been sacrificed to an idol. Those baby back ribs tasted just fine to them. But others could not eat such meat without upsetting their conscience and perhaps their stomach. Paul advised that the meat eaters had liberty to eat the meat, but if doing so would offend their Christian brothers and sisters whose

WHAT'S UP WITH THE GOOD BOOK?

"The Bible is a window in this prison world, through which we may look into eternity."—*Timothy Dwight*

consciences were sensitive, the meat eaters should pass on their liberty (1 Corinthians 8).

Nothing in the Bible says preachers ought to be destitute. Paul explained that he had liberty to accept a salary or to decline. Because God had called him to preach, he would preach with or without pay. Whatever it took to reach Jews and Gentiles, that's what he was willing to do. His greatest reward would be the victor's crown that he looked forward to receiving at the end of the Christian race (1 Corinthians 9).

Liberty isn't spelled l-i-c-e-n-s-e, according to Paul. Christians do not have license to do whatever feels good. When the Israelites committed sexual sins and worshiped idols in the desert, they fell under God's judgment. Paul believed Christians should learn from what happened to Israel. Resisting temptation and running from idolatry are appropriate actions (1 Corinthians 10:1-14). Christians should determine their response to questionable issues by considering what effect it might have on another Christian, by safeguarding their conscience, and by endeavoring to honor God (10:15-33).

Setting Things Straight in Church
(1 Corinthians 11–14)

In this section Paul appealed to the Corinthians to do things in an orderly fashion, from the way they observed the Lord's Supper to the way they used their spiritual gifts. He pointed out that love is the greatest quality and serves as the centerpiece for all spiritual gifts. Without love, Paul insisted, preaching is just noise, faith is invalid, and charity is worthless.

An Open Grave and an Open Checkbook
(1 Corinthians 15–16)

What difference does it make that Christ arose? Paul answered this question in chapter 15. Christ arose as predicted by Scripture. Without His resurrection, preaching would be meaningless, and faith

would be groundless. Because Christ arose, Christians can anticipate their own resurrection. Life extends beyond the grave!

In chapter 16 Paul taught that Christians ought to open their checkbooks and support the Lord's work regularly. Then he concluded his first letter to the Corinthians by promising to visit Corinth to pick up a collection for needy Christians in Jerusalem, by commending a few believers, and by sending warm greetings.

By the Time I Get to Corinth
(2 Corinthians 1–2)

Some of Paul's detractors at Corinth had accused him of being insincere. Paul had promised to visit Corinth, but hadn't shown up there, so was he insincere? He explained that he was sincere but had delayed his visit so that the Corinthians would have more time to set matters straight. He did not want to have to exercise apostolic discipline when he arrived (1:1-24). In the interim he wanted the Corinthians to discipline and then forgive the adulterer mentioned in 1 Corinthians 5:1-5 (2:1-11). Paul then described his ministry of proclaiming the Word of God (2:14-17).

Check Out My Résumé (2 Corinthians 3–7)

In this section of 2 Corinthians, Paul's writing is mainly autobiographical. Usually, he didn't say much about himself in his New Testament letters, but his opponents at Corinth had been accusing him of fraud. If they could convince enough people that Paul was not a genuine apostle, they could convince them that his message, too, was unreliable. So Paul defended his apostolic ministry in order to substantiate the message God had given him to preach. He testified that God had empowered his ministry and made it productive. People's lives had been changed, and those same people were being transformed gradually into the image of the Lord (3:1-18). Also, Paul insisted he had not engaged in deception but had clearly preached Christ, not himself (4:1-7). Although Paul had suffered much persecution for the sake of the gospel, he was willing to endure it for the good of those to whom he ministered (4:8-15). Through all his trials, he kept on ministering and focusing on the eternal prize (4:16-18). His ministry was positively affected by the recognition that he was accountable to Christ and would one day be reviewed by Him (5:1-14). Further, Paul's ministry was characterized by love and an intense desire to see God and sinners reconciled (5:15-21). He had always willingly sacrificed his own interests for the sake of the ministry (6:1-10) and had preached faithfully against wickedness (6:11–7:1). Paul had wronged no one and truly cared about the Corinthians. When he heard from Titus that they had disciplined an offending church member, he rejoiced (7:2-16).

What Happened to the Offering Plates?
(2 Corinthians 8–9)

Because Paul was a selfless minister of the gospel, he cared about poor Christians in Jerusalem and was collecting an offering for them from Gentile churches. The Macedonian churches had given joyfully in spite of their poverty and trials (8:1-5). After starting to contribute, the Corinthians had stalled for a year or so; therefore, Paul had sent Titus and another believer to Corinth to revive the project (8:6, 16-23). Paul urged them to practice generosity, knowing that Jesus had given His all for them (8:9). Their participation in this project would prove their love (8:7-8, 24). God rewards cheerful givers, Paul assured the Corinthians (9:1-10), and demonstrated His own generosity by giving the gift of His Son (9:15).

Back to the Main Subject
(2 Corinthians 10–12)

In this closing section of 2 Corinthians, Paul returned to his main subject—the defense of his apostleship. He wrote that the Lord commended him (10:18). Furthermore, Paul asserted that he was jealous for the Corinthians, not wanting to see anyone beguile them, and he had never charged for his ministry to the Corinthians (11:7-9). Then

Paul indicated that the Lord had given him revelations (12:1-10) and had performed miracles through him (12:11-12). In closing, Paul delivered some exhortations and greetings to the Corinthians.

LET'S GET TESTY

Who Were the Corinthians?

Underline the correct words in the parentheses below.

The city of (Colosse/Corinth) was home to the Corinthians as well as 1,000 (prostitutes/Jewish priests) who served (Apollos/Aphrodite). The Corinthian Christians had chosen sides behind Christian leaders, including Paul, Peter, and (Apollos/Aphrodite). Paul taught that Christians were God's (building/poetry). He urged the Corinthians to discipline a member who was having (an affair/a tantrum). Paul told them they had liberty but were not free to (sin/vote). He affirmed the (Resurrection/registration) and encouraged his readers to give (regularly/when they felt like it). In 2 Corinthians Paul defended his (territory/apostleship/mother-in-law). He also urged the Corinthians to complete (an offering/a building).

(Answers: Corinth; prostitutes; Aphrodite; Apollos; building; an affair; sin; Resurrection; regularly; apostleship; an offering)

"SHE'S NOT BUYING IT, JOHN. IT'S FAITH PLUS WORKS AROUND THE HOUSE."

CHAPTER TWENTY

Take Those Chains from Your Hearts (Galatians)

Picture it. A chain gang has been set free, but after a brief time of freedom the former chain gang members clamp on ankle bracelets and link themselves together by chains wrapped around their waists. It just doesn't make any sense, does it? But something like that happened in the first century in Galatia, a province in Asia Minor. The churches in Galatia had experienced the liberating power of the gospel when the apostle Paul preached in the area during his first missionary journey, but after Paul left, some smooth-talking false teachers persuaded them to chain themselves to ceremonies and rules required by Old Testament law. Paul's letter to the Galatians was written to tell the Galatian churches to take those chains from their hearts, because the Old Testament law was never intended to save anyone. It's purpose was to show people their sin so they would depend on Jesus to save them.

Fickle Faith (Galatians 1)

The false teachers used the old *ad hominem* (meaning the person is the problem) argument against the message Paul had preached to the

SOME THINGS YOU'LL DISCOVER IN THIS CHAPTER

1. The Galatians were trying to be acceptable to God by religious observances rather than recognizing the fact that they were already accepted by faith in Christ.

2. Paul and Peter had a dispute over whether the Gentiles had to conform to certain Jewish laws.

3. Paul told the Galatians that faith and love matter most, under the guidance of the Holy Spirit.

199

AMAZING GRACE

Grace means "unmerited favor." The Galatians were trying to merit God's favor by observing religious laws, but Paul insisted that only God's unmerited favor brings people into a right relationship with Him. Paul used the word *grace* at the beginning of his letter (1:3) and at the end as well (6:18).

Galatians. They attacked the man, believing the message would lose credibility if the audience considered the messenger a phony. So Paul countered the *ad hominem* argument right from the start by identifying himself as a divinely-appointed apostle (1:1). A number of Christians joined him in sending greetings to the Galatian churches (1:2). Obviously, they considered him an apostle and embraced the message he preached! Then he reiterated the essential point of his message: Jesus voluntarily died for our sins so we could be delivered from sin. In verse 1 Paul had identified Jesus as risen from the dead.

In the rest of the first chapter, Paul expressed amazement that the Galatians had abandoned the true gospel and embraced the false teachers' "gospel." He warned that God will destroy every teacher of a counterfeit gospel, and he rehearsed how God had revealed the true gospel to him and how that gospel had changed his life dramatically for the good.

And in This Corner . . . The Champion of the Gospel (Galatians 2)

Paul, a real champion of the gospel, had to defend its message of grace on two separate occasions. Once, he took Barnabas, a Jew, and Titus, a Gentile, to a meeting in Jerusalem convened by church leaders to determine whether male Gentile Christians needed to be circumcised and observe Jewish practices. Certain false teachers of the let's-make-the-Gentiles-become-Jews persuasion crashed the meeting and opposed Paul. But Paul emerged as the winner. The church leaders agreed not to make the Gentile Christians conform to Jewish ways, and they recognized that God had called Paul to be an apostle to the Gentiles just as He had chosen Peter to be an apostle to the Jews.

Later, in Antioch, Paul was back in the ring defending God's grace. This time he contended against the apostle Peter, who had eaten with Gentile Christians until certain Jewish Christians showed up. Then he abruptly changed tables, choosing to eat with the Jewish Christians and giving the impression that Gentile Christians were second-class citizens. Even Barnabas, who had ministered alongside Paul, switched tables. However, Paul didn't let this snubbing go uncorrected. He rebuked Peter publicly.

The Law Served Its Purpose (Galatians 3)

Paul charged that the Galatians must have fallen under a spell cast by false teachers. They seemed to have forgotten what God had done for them on the basis of faith, not works. So Paul gave them a history lesson, showing that Abraham had received a right relationship with God long before the law was given to Israel at Mount Sinai. He insisted that God gave the law to reveal the sinfulness of the human heart so that sinners would realize they needed to accept by faith what Jesus did for them on the cross. According to Paul, the law served as a guide to bring people to Christ. All who believe in Christ experience true unity and become Abraham's spiritual descendants and heirs.

IN CASE YOU'RE WONDERING

WHO WERE THE FALSE TEACHERS?

The false teachers, often called "Judaizers," were Jews who insisted that Gentiles must become Jews and keep the law of Moses in order to gain a right relationship with God.

Grow Up! (Galatians 4)

Engaging in allegory, Paul compared the plight of those who tried to find favor with God by observing the law to a child under the supervision and discipline of caregivers. Such a child would not receive his independence or a share of his father's wealth until he reached maturity. Paul argued that people under the law are like that immature child. However, God sent His Son to deliver people from the law so they could be God's mature children and receive all the benefits of that relationship. God's children, Paul wrote, have God's Spirit in their hearts and can address God affectionately as their Father.

Paul further assured the Galatians that he longed to see them grow up spiritually, and he reminded them that as Abraham had to cast Hagar and Ishmael out of his house for the sake of peace, so they needed to cast the false teachers out of their midst.

WHAT'S UP WITH THE GOOD BOOK?

"Of the whole of Scripture there are two parts: the law and the Gospel. The law indicates the sickness, the Gospel the remedy."—*Philip Melanchthon*

Secret Power from Within (Galatians 5)

Those who boasted that they were strict Jews needed to understand that God is not impressed with outward religion; He cares about the

"So don't get tired of doing what is good. Don't get discouraged and give up, for we will reap a harvest of blessing at the appropriate time." (Galatians 6:9)

condition of the heart. Faith and love matter to Him. Paul told his readers to submit their lives to the Holy Spirit's guidance. Trying to live by a set of rules without depending upon the Spirit would result in immorality and wickedness, but a life controlled by the Spirit would result in Christlike character.

Don't Shoot Your Own Wounded (Galatians 6)

Perfect people don't exist. So when a Christian falls into sin, other Christians should not jump all over his or her case. Jumping on somebody who is down is hardly the way to help him or her get back up. Paul told the Galatians to try to restore a fallen brother or sister. Also, he told them to help one another bear their burdens. And those who were well-versed in the Scriptures should help others learn the Scriptures. He further encouraged the Galatians to keep on doing the right thing, knowing that God will ultimately crown every worthwhile effort with success. Finally, Paul reminded his readers about the persecution he endured for the sake of Christ, and then he wished for them the grace of the Lord Jesus Christ.

LET'S GET TESTY

Did Paul Say That?

Underline each incorrect statement.

1. The letter to the Galatians was written by Paul
2. to a church in Galatia,
3. a province in Italy.
4. The Galatians had departed from the gospel Paul preached
5. and had embraced a phony gospel
6. that taught that Gentile believers must become Jews.
7. Even Paul's apostleship was being doubted in Galatia,
8. but Paul defended his apostleship.

9. At one time Paul went to Antioch for a meeting of church leaders

10. assembled to address the issue of whether Gentile converts must become Jews.

11. Paul took Barnabas and Timothy to this meeting.

12. The church leaders agreed with Paul's perspective that Gentile converts did not have to become Jews.

13. Later, at Antioch, Paul rebuked Peter

14. because Peter snubbed the Gentiles when Jews arrived.

15. Paul cited Noah as someone who had a right relationship with God before the law was given to Israel.

16. The law was given to reveal sin.

17. Christlike character is produced by the Holy Spirit, not by the law.

18. Paul challenged the Galatians to expel the false teachers just as Abraham had expelled Hagar and Ishmael from his home.

19. He also challenged them to help carry one another's burdens,

20. and he closed his letter by wishing them the grace of the Lord Jesus Christ.

(Answers: The incorrect answers are 3, 9, 11, and 15.)

CHAPTER TWENTY-ONE

Some Jail Mail (Ephesians, Philippians, and Colossians)

SOME THINGS YOU'LL DISCOVER IN THIS CHAPTER

1. Paul warned the Ephesians that they would need all of God's armor to overcome the traps of the devil.

2. Both Paul and Silas had been beaten and jailed in Philippi, but their response was to sing hymns in jail.

3. To the Colossians Paul stated clearly just who Jesus is—an exact representation of God.

Letters from inmates vary considerably, but many follow a similar pattern: an outpouring of regret for crimes committed, a resolve to start a new life, and an appeal for help. The apostle Paul also wrote letters from jail. He was under house arrest in Rome at the time. But none of his letters expressed regret, a desire for a different kind of life, or an appeal for help. Quite the opposite! Joy spilled from his letters. He exulted in the life Jesus had given him and resolved to follow Jesus faithfully forever. Also, he wrote of his love and concern for those who received his letters. In this chapter we will peek over the shoulders of three groups of first-century Christians and scan their letters from Paul.

Equal Opportunity Ephesians (Ephesians 1–6)

As you know from previous sections in this guide, often Jewish Christians and Gentiles didn't waltz together down a church aisle. It seems a wall of prejudice separated them. Paul's letter to the Ephesians was intended to break down that wall. Paul insisted that all

IT'S A PROMISE!

"God saved you by his special favor when you believed. And you can't take credit for this; it is a gift from God."
(Ephesians 2:8)

INFO BYTE
EPHESUS

The city of Ephesus on the coast of Asia Minor boasted a good economy, strong politics, and its famous temple of Diana. Paul had stopped at Ephesus briefly on his second missionary journey. On his third missionary journey, Paul stayed in Ephesus for more than two years.

206

believers were "holy people" (1:1), God's adopted children (1:5), redeemed and forgiven (1:7), marked for an eternal inheritance, and members of the church with the risen Christ as their head (1:22-23). Obviously, then, God doesn't play favorites.

In chapter 2 we learn that in spite of the Ephesians' ungodly past, they were saved by God's grace through faith in Jesus Christ (2:1-9). Furthermore, God works in the lives of believers so they will do good works (2:10). Although Gentiles historically were separated from Israel and her covenants of promise, now believing Gentiles enjoy all the privileges enjoyed by believing Jews. Together, both are united in Christ and have equal access to the Father (2:11-22).

The truth that both Jewish believers and Gentile believers are members of Christ's body, the church, had been revealed to Paul (3:1-13). He was praying that the Ephesians would gain a richer understanding of Christ's presence in their lives, His love, and His power (3:14-20). As Paul reflected on this wonderful truth, he offered praise to the Lord (3:21).

Privilege brings responsibility, of course, so Paul urged the Ephesians to work at getting along with one another (4:1-6), to use their spiritual gifts for the good of the church (4:7-16), and to lead a disciplined and compassionate life (4:17-32). Even their speech should be free of dirty and coarse language (5:4). Children of light should reflect the light in all they do and say (5:8-12). Instead of living under the influence of wine, children of the light should live under the influence of the Holy Spirit (5:18). Doing so would have a profoundly positive impact upon relationships with fellow believers (5:19-21), marriage (5:22-33), parenting skills (6:1-4), and employee-employer relationships (6:5-9).

Paul's final words put the Ephesians on alert that Christians struggle against the devil and his forces, so we need to wear God's armor and pray at all times (6:10-18). Paul requested prayer that, while he was in prison, he would be able to share boldly the message of Christ (6:19-20). He had sent Tychicus to bring the Ephesians up to date on his personal circumstances and to encourage them (6:21-22).

Jailhouse Joy (Philippians 1)

Jailhouse blues just weren't in Paul's song repertoire. He was totally joyful under house arrest in Rome and undergoing a court trial. He gives some reasons for his joy in his letter to the Philippians. After greeting his friends at Philippi and expressing confidence that God would keep up His good work in their lives, he reported that because of his imprisonment many Christians were taking a bolder stand for Christ (1:12-14). Also, Paul knew that his life was in God's hands. If the Roman court set him free, he would keep on serving Christ. If the court ordered his execution, he would enter Christ's presence (1:20-23). Either way, he couldn't lose!

WHAT'S UP WITH THE GOOD BOOK?

"Take all this book upon reason that you can, and the balance on faith, and you will live and die a happier and better man."—*Abraham Lincoln*

Purple Stocks Are Hot (Philippians 2)

Philippi was the first city in Europe evangelized by Paul (Acts 16). As a Roman colony, it was an influential center of Roman culture. Citizens of Philippi were also Roman citizens, and many of them tried to pattern their dress and lifestyle after their counterparts in Rome. Lydia, a seller of purple cloth in Philippi, seemed to operate a successful business. Likely the Philippians' desire to dress like the purple-attired Roman aristocrats sent Lydia's sales soaring. Paul and Silas had been beaten and jailed in Philippi, but they sang hymns at midnight and God turned the jail into a "rescue mission."

In chapter 2 Paul appealed to his friends at Philippi to increase his joy by caring for one another and being united in mind and purpose, following Christ's model of humility and caring (2:1-10). Their cooperation and exemplary lives would further enhance his joy (2:12-18). Paul had dispatched two selfless representatives, Timothy and Epaphroditus, to Philippi to inquire about the Philippians and report back to him (2:19-30).

IN CASE YOU'RE WONDERING

BELIEVERS IN CAESAR'S PALACE?

Some of the believers in Caesar's palace may have been imperial guards assigned to guard Paul. Conceivably, Paul may have introduced them to faith in Christ, and they in turn introduced their fellow guards. As Paul indicated in Philippians 1:12-13, his imprisonment had advanced the gospel, and even the praetorian guard knew he was in prison for the sake of Christ.

Let's See the Résumé Again (Philippians 3–4)

Religious credentials and an outstanding pedigree might have some individuals walking around with their noses puncturing the clouds,

INFO BYTE
COLOSSE

This beautiful city was situated about 100 miles east of Ephesus near the cities of Laodicea and Hierapolis. It sat in the rich, fertile Lycus Valley by the Lycus River and was famous for its black wool. The church at Colosse may have been founded by Epaphras (Colossians 1:7).

but not Paul. His credentials and pedigree were strictly triple-A, but he recognized that he could not *earn* salvation. He testified that Christ alone gives salvation and true righteousness (3:1-14). Paul anticipated the day when Christ will come and transform every believer's body into one like His (3:15-21).

In chapter 4 Paul urged two feuding Christians at Philippi to bury the hatchet and channel their combined energies into ministry (4:1-3). Rejoicing in the Lord is what Paul hoped the Philippians would do (4:4). After all, there was good reason to rejoice. The Lord was close at hand, and God's remarkable peace was available (4:5-9). Then Paul wrote a thank-you note. He rejoiced that the Philippians had always supported his missionary work. They had just recently sent a care package to him, which he said pleased God as well as him (4:10-18). He assured the Philippians that God would meet their needs and signed off with greetings from believers at Rome, some of whom were members of Caesar's palace (4:20-23)

You Can't Improve on Perfection (Colossians)

Some athletes seem to perform almost flawlessly. They appear to be perfect at what they do, but sports records are made to be broken. Eventually, a rising superstar will break what seems to be an unreachable golf course record or home run record or the record for the highest number of points scored in a basketball game. But even that feat will be performed by an imperfect human being. Paul's letter to the Colossians presents Jesus Christ as God's perfect Son and our perfect Savior. No one will ever knock Him from the top spot!

Just Who Is This Jesus? (Colossians 1)

In the first century a group of religious philosophers known as the Gnostics insisted that all matter was evil and only spirit was good. So they had a big problem with Jesus. How could He be truly God, when He lived in a material, evil body, they asked. Paul set the record straight for the Colossians, who were probably being hounded by the Gnostics. He wrote that Jesus is God's beloved Son

and our Redeemer (1:13-14). He is also the exact image of God, not just a reflection of God, and the Creator of everything (1:15-16). He holds all things together, and He arose from the dead (1:17-18). It seems Paul was reminding the Colossians that Jesus Christ is absolutely perfect.

Looking for Smarts in All the Wrong Places (Colossians 2–4)

True wisdom, Paul wrote, is found in Jesus Christ (2:3). So the Colossians didn't need to waste their time looking for secret knowledge in the religion of the Gnostics (2:7-9). Nor did they need to try to be made perfect by adhering to religious rules and observances. They were complete in Christ (2:10-23).

The rest of Paul's letter encouraged the Colossians to get on with the business of leading a spiritually productive life. As Christians, they should rid their lives of hostile emotions and abusive speech. They should be kind, humble, patient, gentle, compassionate, and forgiving, and live as Christ's representatives in the church, in the home, in the workplace—everywhere (3:1–4:6). In closing, Paul told the Colossians he was sending Tychicus and Onesimus to encourage and inform them, and he sent a number of personal greetings to them.

INFO BYTE

WHAT'S IN A NAME?

The name *Gnostics* comes from the Greek word *gnosis*, meaning "knowledge." The Gnostics taught that they had superior knowledge—secret knowledge—found nowhere else.

LET'S GET TESTY

Letter Perfect

See if you can get a perfect score by selecting the correct answer for each of the following statements.

____ 1. This letter mentions joy or rejoicing several times.

    A. Philippians

    B. Ephesians

    C. Colossians

___ 2. In the Colossian letter, Paul refuted

    A. narcissism

    B. Gnosticism

    C. neorealism

___3. The temple of Diana was located in this city.

    A. Colosse

    B. Philippi

    C. Ephesus

___ 4. Paul told these people that all wisdom is found in Christ.

    A. The Ephesians

    B. The Colossians

    C. The Philippians

___ 5. The letter to the Ephesians teaches that believing Jews and believing Gentiles are

    A. cousins

    B. ten lost tribes of Israel

    C. one in Christ

___ 6. Lydia, a businesswoman in Philippi sold

    A. stocks and bonds

    B. purple cloth

    C. souvenirs

___ 7. Paul told these Christians to put on the whole armor of God.

    A. The Philippians

    B. The Colossians

    C. The Ephesians

___ 8. The Philippian letter indicates that the gospel had spread to Caesar's

    A. navy

    B. palace

    C. sports arena

___ 9. This church sent a care package to Paul in prison.

    A. The Ephesian church

    B. The Philippian church

    C. The Colossian church

___10. Paul instructed the Ephesians to live under the
 influence of
 A. the Holy Spirit
 B. religion
 C. the law of Moses

(Answers: 1. A; 2. B; 3. C; 4. B; 5. C; 6. B; 7. C; 8. B; 9. B; 10. A)

CHAPTER TWENTY-TWO

"C'MON RANDY, WE DON'T KNOW WHEN THEY'RE COMING BACK, BUT WE JUST CAN'T WAIT AROUND AND DO NOTHING. WE'VE GOT THINGS TO DO LIKE DIGGIN' UP GARDENS AND RUNNIN' DOWN CATS."

Heads Up! Eyes Open! (1 and 2 Thessalonians)

During the Y2K scare, some people were trying to convince the rest of us that the world was on the brink of disaster and about to experience the second coming of Christ. Of course, no one can predict Jesus' return to earth to take his people home to be with him in heaven, and the Bible raises a red flag warning about setting a date for Jesus' coming. Somehow the Thessalonian Christians feared they had missed Jesus' return, so they needed clarification about the Second Coming. So Paul wrote 1 and 2 Thessalonians to assure them that Jesus' coming again was still in the future and to encourage them to stay alert and maintain an active faith while waiting for that unscheduled event. First Thessalonians was one of Paul's earliest New Testament letters.

You're Doing Fine, Thessalonica!
(1 Thessalonians 1)

Paul had been in Thessalonica only three weeks before persecution drove him away from the city. Later, he sent Timothy back to Thessalonica to learn how the new Christians were getting along.

SOME THINGS YOU'LL DISCOVER IN THIS CHAPTER

1. Some Thessalonians thought that since they were expecting the Lord to return soon, they could remain idle and simply wait.

2. Before Christ returns, a lawless, evil person will rule and set up a kingdom against God.

3. The Thessalonians had become model believers for those around them, exhibiting the most important virtues: faith, hope, and love.

213

INFO BYTE
THE LORD'S RETURN

At the end of every chapter in
1 Thessalonians you will find a reference
to the Lord's return. (See 1:10; 2:19;
3:13; 4:16-17; 5:23.) His return will
fulfill the promise He made to His disciples in the upper room (see John 14:3).

IT'S A PROMISE!

"Keep on praying. No matter what
happens, always be thankful, for this is
God's will for you who belong to Christ
Jesus." (1 Thessalonians 5:17-18)

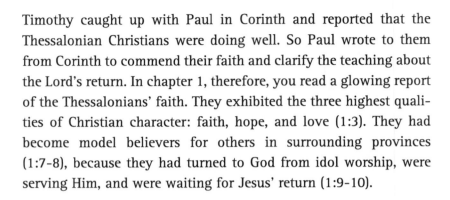

Timothy caught up with Paul in Corinth and reported that the
Thessalonian Christians were doing well. So Paul wrote to them
from Corinth to commend their faith and clarify the teaching about
the Lord's return. In chapter 1, therefore, you read a glowing report
of the Thessalonians' faith. They exhibited the three highest qualities of Christian character: faith, hope, and love (1:3). They had
become model believers for others in surrounding provinces
(1:7-8), because they had turned to God from idol worship, were
serving Him, and were waiting for Jesus' return (1:9-10).

If I Could See You Now (1 Thessalonians 2–3)

Paul cherished the brief time he had with the Thessalonians,
preaching the gospel and nurturing those who believed (2:1-12).
Upon hearing of their outstanding spiritual progress, he thanked
God continually for them (2:13-14). Paul longed to see them again,
but when he planned a trip to Thessalonica, he was hindered by
Satan. However, he knew he would see them eventually—at the
coming of Christ—and they would be his glory and joy (2:17-20). In
chapter 3, Paul rehearsed how he had sent Timothy to them and
how Timothy had returned with a glowing report. Knowing that the
Thessalonians were getting along well in the faith gave Paul great
comfort in the midst of his trials. He assured them that he was praying for an opportunity to visit them, and he was also praying for
their further spiritual development.

All's Well That Ends Well (1 Thessalonians 4–5)

Christians should not sit around idly twiddling their thumbs as they
anticipate Christ's return. According to Paul, Christians ought to be
wide awake and looking for opportunities to represent Christ well
(4:1-12). Furthermore, when they bury their Christian loved ones,
they don't have to grieve as though they have no hope. Paul
encouraged the Thessalonian Christians to look forward to the
Lord's return, when living Christians and departed Christians will

be united together with Christ (4:13-18). Unbelievers face a hopeless end, but believers have an endless hope (5:1-11). But Paul exhorted the Thessalonian Christians to live a heavenly life on the earth while waiting for the fulfillment of their hope. He urged the Thessalonians to respect and support their spiritual leaders; to try to get along with others; to lead a prayerful, thankful, and joyful life; to cooperate with the Holy Spirit; and to exercise caution regarding religious teaching (5:12-22).

The Bullies Are Going to Meet Their Match
(2 Thessalonians 1)

Because the Thessalonians were being persecuted, they thought they had missed the Lord's return for the church and had slipped into the Day of the Lord. But Paul assured them the Lord hadn't returned yet. He wrote that when He does return, He will take vengeance on those who bullied believers and rejected the gospel, and He will be glorified among His people. Paul told his readers that he was praying always for them.

The Counterfeit Christ
(2 Thessalonians 2:1-12)

Every schoolkid knows there is always one bully who is worse than all the other bullies. You know his *modus operandi:* he hangs around after school, waiting to beat up on his pick of the day. Paul admitted that times were really already vile and lawless in the first century, but he predicted they would be much worse after the appearance of the biggest bully of them all. He identified the bully as the man of sin, aka the man of lawlessness and an evil man (2:3, 8-9). The man of lawlessness will be so brazen as to oppose even God. His sinfulness will push him where no man has ever gone before. He will sit in the temple and declare that he is God (2:4). His power, which will come from Satan, will enable him to gain a big following by performing counterfeit miracles, signs, and wonders

INFO BYTE
THESSALONICA

Strategically located as a Greek seaport, Thessalonica enjoyed a booming economy and became a free city under Augustus. As the capital of Macedonia, it enjoyed a good view of Mount Olympus. When Paul preached in Thessalonica, the city's population was about 200,000. To review Paul's visit to Thessalonica, read Acts 17:1-10.

WHAT'S UP WITH THE
GOOD BOOK?

"The Spirit is needed for the understanding of all Scriptures and every part of Scripture."—*Martin Luther*

IN CASE YOU'RE WONDERING
PAUL'S SIGNATURE

By signing his letter, Paul attested to its genuineness. False teachers were not above writing letters and claiming Paul had written them.

(2:9). But God will silence this bully and end his reign of blasphemy and tyranny. When the Lord returns, He will zap him with His brightness. The big bully will be out of business—permanently! And all his followers will be punished too (2:8-12).

An Exhortation to End Well
(2 Thessalonians 2:13–3:18)

Knowing that the Thessalonian Christians were on the winning team and destined for glory, not judgment (2:13-14), Paul prayed for them and exhorted them to remain loyal to the truth (2:15). He prayed that they would have encouragement, hope, and success in every good thing they said and did (2:16-17).

Paul ended his second letter by asking his readers to pray for him so his preaching would produce positive results (3:1-2). He expressed further confidence in them and warned them about false teachers and troublemakers (3:3-10). Addressing a few idle busybodies, he underscored the principle of "will work for food" and told them to mind their own business (3:11-12). Then he offered a prayer on behalf of the Thessalonians, and signed the letter in his own handwriting (3:16-18).

LET'S GET TESTY

Returning Once Again to the Lord's Return

Answer yes or no to each of the following statements.

1. Paul told the Thessalonians they had missed the Lord's return. _____

2. Almost every chapter of 1 Thessalonians concludes with a reference to the Lord's return. _____

3. Paul wrote 1 and 2 Thessalonians because the church at Thessalonica needed some clarification about the Lord's return. _____

4. The promise of the Lord's return ought to give believers hope. ____

5. Big trouble lies ahead for those who do not prepare for the Lord's return. ____

6. The bodies of dead Christians will be resurrected at the Rapture. ____

7. In light of the Lord's return, Christians should resign their jobs. ____

8. When the Lord returns, He will be glorified in believers. ____

9. When the Lord returns to judge His enemies, He will destroy the man of sin. ____

10. When the Lord returns, He will pardon all who followed the man of sin. ____

(Answers: 1. no; 2. yes; 3. yes; 4. yes; 5. yes; 6. yes; 7. no; 8. yes; 9. yes; 10. no)

CHAPTER TWENTY-THREE

Two Sons in the Ministry (1 and 2 Timothy and Titus)

SOME THINGS YOU'LL DISCOVER IN THIS CHAPTER

1. Timothy and Titus were Paul's sons in the faith and learned the responsibilities of leading a church.

2. Money is not evil, but the love of it produces all kinds of evil behavior and thinking.

3. Titus had to minister on the island of Crete, appointing leaders in a land of liars and lazy louts.

Most of Paul's New Testament letters were addressed to churches, but he also wrote letters to individuals. Titus received one such letter, and Timothy received two. Both Timothy and Titus were young pastors, whom Paul regarded highly. He referred to each of them as his son in the faith (1 Timothy 1:2; Titus 1:4).

Timothy had joined Paul's missionary team on Paul's second missionary trip (Acts 16:1-3). His mother was Jewish, but his dad was a Gentile (Acts 16:1). Apparently, when Paul was released from house arrest in Rome, he advised Timothy to stay at Ephesus and serve as the church's pastor (1 Timothy 1:3). Titus, too, had traveled with Paul and had remained at Crete to be the pastor of the church there (Titus 1:5). It seems Paul was released from house arrest, went on another missionary trip, was arrested again, and thrown into a Roman prison to await execution. That's when he wrote 2 Timothy.

Being a Pastor Is Not for Wimps
(1 Timothy 1–2)

Anyone who thinks a pastor just sits around all day sipping tea with the garden club needs to read Paul's warnings and instructions to

Timothy. He charged his young son in the faith with the responsibility to teach God's Word and reject myths and endless speculations about family histories (1:3-6). The gospel, which was to be Timothy's message, had introduced Paul to the grace that had transformed his life and established him in the apostolic ministry (1:12-16). Paul admitted that Timothy was involved in spiritual warfare, but good things had been prophesied about Timothy that should encourage him to fight the good fight (1:18). Timothy was instructed to lead his congregation in praying for all classes of people, including government officials (2:1-3). He wanted Timothy to know that God wants all people to acknowledge the truth and come to Him through Jesus Christ, who is the way to God (2:4-8). Paul further instructed Timothy about the role of women in his congregation (2:9-15).

WHAT'S UP WITH THE GOOD BOOK?

"We believe that God never contradicts in one part of the Scriptures what He teaches in another, and never contradicts in revelation what He teaches in His works and providence."
—*William Ellery Channing*

The Lord Is Looking for a Few Good Men
(1 Timothy 3)

Paul set the standards high for church leaders. He said an elder must be above reproach, faithful to his wife, self-controlled, wise in his behavior, reputable, hospitable, and able to teach. He must not drink heavily or be violent. He must be gentle, peaceable, and free of greed. Also, his family life should be excellent, demonstrated by children who respect and obey him (3:1-7). Deacons, too, must meet the highest qualifications (3:8-13).

Here's Your Job Description, Timothy
(1 Timothy 4–6)

The second part of Paul's first letter to Timothy cites the following responsibilities in Timothy's pastoral job description:

Job Description for a Pastor

Point out the error of those who insist you must deny your appetites and not get married (4:1-6).

Lead a self-controlled, godly life, and instruct others to do the same (4:7-11).

Model the Christian life in speech, conduct, love, faith, and purity (4:12).

Heed the Scriptures and teach them publicly (4:13-16).

Be respectful of older men and women, and consider the younger women as your sisters (5:1-2).

Make sure needy widows are taken care of (5:3-10).

Encourage young widows to stay busy and remarry (5:11-16).

See that church workers are supported financially (5:17-18).

Don't listen to accusations without checking them out. Then deal with sin promptly and firmly (5:19-20).

Don't rush to ordain (5:22).

Instruct slaves to respect their masters and work hard (6:1-2).

Flee covetousness, but pursue spiritual goals (6:6-11).

Fight the good fight of faith (6:12).

Warn the rich not to be conceited and certain of the future because they have lots of money. Instruct them to put their confidence in God, not money (6:17-19).

Keep the faith (6:20).

Avoid godless, meaningless discussions (6:20).

It seems the huge responsibilities resting on young Timothy's shoulders had given him some stomach distress. So Paul advised him to use a little wine for medicinal purposes (5:23). But Timothy did not have to go it alone at Ephesus; God's grace would be with him (6:21).

IN CASE YOU'RE WONDERING
DID PAUL ENDORSE DRINKING?

In his first letter to Timothy, Paul instructs him to stop drinking only water and to drink a little wine for his stomach's sake. In the ancient world, wine was often used as an antiseptic and was added in small amounts to drinking water. Rather than endorsing the sin of drunkenness, Paul was just encouraging Timothy to be mindful of his health.

IN CASE YOU'RE WONDERING
WHAT'S WRONG WITH BEING RICH?

Paul did not teach that being rich is inherently evil. He taught that the love of money, not money itself, is a root of all kinds of evil (1 Timothy 6:10).

Mixed Memories (2 Timothy 1)

It has been said that the older a person becomes, the more often he or she strolls down memory lane. Paul, a seasoned servant of Christ, took a stroll down memory lane when he wrote 2 Timothy, his last New Testament letter. In the first chapter, he remembered Timothy and longed to see him again (1:1-4). He recalled Timothy's sincere trust in the Lord, a trust that his

mother and grandmother had both exhibited (1:5), and he urged Timothy to rekindle the gift God had given him for ministry (1:6-7). His memories of Timothy were good.

Paul also remembered that God had saved him and Timothy by grace and had called Paul to be a preacher, an apostle, and a teacher (1:5-11). He also remembered that God would safeguard what he had entrusted to Him (1:12). These, too, were good memories.

Another good memory Paul enjoyed was that of Onesiphorus, who had visited Paul in prison and ministered to him. Onesiphorus had also ministered effectively in Ephesus (1:16-18). It was good to remember Onesiphorus!

But some of Paul's memories were not so good. He remembered that some men had deserted him in Asia. He named Phygelus and Hermogenes as two of the offenders (1:15). Memories of the deserters, and especially the memory of Phygelus and Hermogenes, were anything but good.

You're in the Army Now (2 Timothy 2:1–4:5)

An army of wimps can't win battles. Like a battle-savvy sergeant, Paul told Timothy to be a strong, disciplined, single-minded soldier (2:1-19). As a soldier of the Lord, Timothy was advised by Paul to rid his life of bad habits and pursue qualities suited to a dedicated follower of Christ (2:20-26). Paul instructed Timothy on how to recognize a growing enemy and how to stand against this enemy by continuing in Scriptural teaching (2 Timothy 3). Then, as a commanding officer delivers a charge to his troops, Paul gave a stirring charge to Timothy to preach the Word in spite of popular demand for a message that reinforces what the audience wants to hear (4:1-5).

Old Soldiers Never Die (2 Timothy 4:6–22)

The executioner's sword was poised to flash down on Paul's neck and end his life, but Paul was ready for that event. He had no regrets. He had fought the good fight. He had completed the course.

He had guarded the faith. He anticipated that the executioner's sword would transport him into the presence of Christ, where he would receive a crown of righteousness. Also, he believed every faithful believer will receive a similar crown. The end of 2 Timothy lists those who abandoned Paul as well as his true friends and enumerates some requests Paul made of Timothy.

Good Leaders Who Can Deal with Louts
(Titus 1–2)

Titus might have had a hard time appointing qualified leaders for the church in Crete, because Cretans were infamous liars, louts, and scoundrels (1:10-16). Nevertheless, Titus was responsible to appoint leaders whose character was beyond reproach and honoring to God (1:6-9). But his responsibility went beyond appointing leaders; he was also to teach wholesome doctrine (2:1) and instruct older men, older women, and young men to conduct themselves in noble ways (2:2-6). Titus himself was charged by Paul with the task of being a sterling example to others (2:7-8). Even slaves were to be taught by Titus to conduct themselves in a manner pleasing to God (2:9-10). Paul assured Titus that God's grace revealed in Christ is intended to transform sinners into godly servants of Christ (2:11-15).

Ideal Citizens (Titus 3)

In the closing chapter of Titus, we read a number of exhortations calling the Cretan Christians to be ideal citizens and to avoid strife. His final words conveyed his personal plans, requests, and greetings.

LET'S GET TESTY

Reviewing Letters to Two Sons

Answer T for true, F for false.

1. Second Timothy was written from a prison in Rome. ___
2. Timothy served as pastor at Crete. ___
3. Titus's mother was Eunice. ___
4. Timothy and Titus received lists of leaders' qualifications. ___
5. Paul told Titus to be a strong soldier. ___
6. Cretans had a good reputation. ___
7. Money is the root of all evil. ___
8. Onesiphorus encouraged Paul. ___
9. Paul anticipated a crown of righteousness. ___
10. Timothy had never set foot inside Ephesus. ___

(*Answers:* 1. T; 2. F; 3. F; 4. T; 5. F; 6. F; 7. F; 8. T; 9. T; 10. F)

CHAPTER TWENTY-FOUR

Guess Who I Ran into in Jail? (Philemon)

Paul's letter to Philemon, a Christian in Colosse, unfolds a fascinating drama and highlights Paul's compassion and diplomatic skills. The letter was written as a plea to Philemon when Paul was incarcerated at Rome. Philemon's slave, Onesimus, had run away and gone to Rome. For some unmentioned reason, Onesimus landed in prison and met the apostle Paul there. More importantly, Onesimus met Jesus Christ there. Paul mentioned this runaway slave as his son, whom he had introduced to Christ in prison (1:10). Apparently, at the end of his prison term, Onesimus was returning to Philemon at Paul's advice (1:12). The letter from Paul was intended to smooth the way for Onesimus to be received by Philemon (1:12).

Paul began his letter by identifying himself and Timothy, who must have been visiting at the time (1:1). He greeted Philemon, Apphia (probably Philemon's wife), Archippus (perhaps the pastor of the church at Colosse), and the believers who worshiped in Philemon's house (1:2). After wishing them all grace and peace (1:3), Paul commended Philemon for his love and faith and mentioned how joyful he was because Philemon refreshed the hearts of other believers (1:4-7).

SOME THINGS YOU'LL DISCOVER IN THIS CHAPTER

1. Onesimus, a runaway slave who became a believer in Christ, was willing to return to his master, Philemon, who was also a believer.

2. Paul was willing to handle all debts on the part of Onesimus.

225

WHY DIDN'T PAUL DENOUNCE SLAVERY?

Paul was an apostle, not a social reformer although changes in society certainly took place as a result of his teaching. His main emphasis was on emancipation from sin's slavery through faith in Christ. Although he did not openly denounce slavery, he sowed seeds that brought emancipation to fruition. He taught that free citizens and slaves alike were one in Christ. (Galatians 3:28)

WHAT'S IN A NAME?

Paul was using a play on words when he referred to Onesimus as previously unprofitable but profitable now (1:11). The name Onesimus means "profitable."

Paul asked Philemon to welcome Onesimus back, indicating that Onesimus had been an unprofitable slave before running away but was now profitable (1:8-11). He hoped that Philemon would receive Onesimus as warmly as he would receive Paul (1:12). After becoming a Christian, Onesimus had become such an encouragement to Paul that Paul would have gladly kept him around, but he knew sending him to Philemon was the right thing to do (1:13-14). He commented that Onesimus had run away for a brief time, but was now a believer—a brother forever (1:15-16).

Onesimus may have stolen from Philemon before hitting the pavement headed for Rome. So Paul told Philemon to charge to his (Paul's) account whatever Onesimus owed him. He promised to repay the debt. However, Paul reminded Philemon that Philemon owed him his very soul (1:17-19).

Closing his letter of appeal, Paul asked Philemon prepare a guest room for him. He believed Philemon's prayers for him would result in his release from prison (1:22). After sending greetings from a few fellow Christians, Paul wished for Philemon the grace of the Lord Jesus Christ (1:23-25).

LET'S GET TESTY

A Letter from Jail
Match the following:

_____ 1. She was likely Philemon's wife   A. Onesimus

_____ 2. Philemon's home   B. Timothy

_____ 3. He was visiting Paul   C. Archippus

_____ 4. A runaway slave   D. Paul

_____ 5. He referred to his personal charge account.   E. Apphia

_____ 6. Likely the pastor at Colosse   F. Colosse

(Answers: 1. E; 2. F; 3. B; 4. A.; 5. D; 6. C)

CHAPTER TWENTY-FIVE

J. OWENS
EXECUTIVE RECRUITING, INC.

"EVEN THOUGH YOUR JOB AS HIGH PRIEST WAS ELIMINATED, THERE'S NOTHING TO BE ASHAMED OF. YOU'RE OVERQUALIFIED FOR MOST JOBS, BUT STILL VERY MARKETABLE."

Things Are Much Better Now (Hebrews)

You could summarize the letter to the Hebrews in one succinct statement: It doesn't get any better than this. The Hebrews who embraced Christianity had left behind a religion steeped in Old Testament ceremonies, rituals, laws, and symbolism. Through the gospel they had learned that Jesus Christ had fulfilled everything the Old Testament religion hinted at. The former religious observances were simply a shadow of the reality to be found in Jesus Christ. Therefore, what Jesus provides for those who trust in Him is much better than anything believers in Old Testament times understood and experienced.

The Angels Aren't in First Place (Hebrews 1–2)

The writer to the Hebrews began his letter by showing that Jesus Christ is superior to the angels. Unlike the created angels, Jesus is God's Son, and He created everything (1:2). He is also the exact representation of God the Father, and He sat down at the Father's right hand after dying to cleanse us from our sins (1:3). God had never

SOME THINGS YOU'LL DISCOVER IN THIS CHAPTER

1. We are not really sure who wrote the book of Hebrews, but Paul tops the list.

2. Jesus is higher than the greatest of angels as well as Moses.

3. Melchizedek is a mysterious figure who typifies Jesus Christ in His role as our high priest.

IN CASE YOU'RE WONDERING
WHO WROTE HEBREWS?

No one can say for sure. Names in the hopper include Paul, Barnabas, James, Luke, Philip, Apollos, and Priscilla. Paul's name seems to be at the top of the list, but it's anyone's guess. Whoever wrote Hebrews was certainly familiar with Old Testament history and practices.

IT'S A PROMISE!

"Since he himself has gone through suffering and temptation, he is able to help us when we are being tempted." (Hebrews 2:18)

called any of the angels His Son, nor did He exalt any of the angels to the place of authority Jesus occupies (1:4-14). By His birth as a human being, Jesus humbled Himself temporarily to a rank lower than the angels, but God raised Him from the dead and crowned Him with glory and honor (2:5-9).

A Better House Builder (Hebrews 3:1–4:13)

Moses, the lawgiver, built the tabernacle according to God's instructions, but Jesus built a better house for God—a house of believers (3:1-6). Moses led the Israelites through the desert, but he could not lead them into the Promised Land. However, Jesus leads believers into God's rest (3:7–4:13).

The Best One-Time Offer Ever (Hebrews 4:14–10:31)

In this section of Hebrews, the writer shows that Jesus is the great High Priest for all believers. As High Priest, Jesus outranks Aaron, Israel's first high priest. Now in heaven, Jesus understands our weaknesses and trials, sympathizes with us, and is available to provide the help and grace we need to meet our daily challenges (4:14-16). Aaron was appointed by God to minister on Israel's behalf, but Jesus is an eternal high priest after the order of Melchizedek (5:1–7:22). He did not come from the priestly tribe of Levi, as did Aaron, but He predated Aaron and serves as an eternal High Priest (7:24). Jesus is also superior to all other priests. The other priests had to offer sacrifices for their own sins as well as for the people's sins, but Jesus did not have to offer any sacrifice for Himself because He is sinless. He offered Himself as the perfect sacrifice for the sins of all. His was a one-time, never-to-be-repeated sacrifice (7:26-27).

A Direct Line to God

Because Jesus, the believers' High Priest, offered a perfect sacrifice for sin, God seated Him at His own right hand (8:1) and introduced a covenant that is much better than the former one He made with the Israelites at Sinai (8:6-13). In chapter 9 this theme is expanded. Under the old covenant, the high priest had to make atonement once a year, every year, for his own sins and for Israel's sins. At that time, he passed through the curtain separating the Holy Place from the Most Holy Place (9:1-6). Then, in the Most Holy Place, he sprinkled blood on the ark of the covenant (9:7). But Jesus entered the presence of God after offering His blood once and for all for our sins (9:11-14, 24-26). As a result, New Testament believers have direct access to God (9:27) and are urged to enter God's presence (10:22), hold tightly to their hope (10:23), encourage one another (10:24), and not neglect their meeting together (10:25).

This section of Hebrews ends with a solemn warning about God's judgment. Because only Jesus' sacrifice for sin is acceptable to God, all who reject it will suffer God's judgment (10:26-39).

INFO BYTE
MEL WHO?

Melchizedek! As Hebrews 7:1-4 explains, his name means "king of righteousness," but he was also "king of peace." Melchizedek brought bread and wine to Abraham and his men after they rescued Lot and the other hostages from their captors. Abraham reciprocated by paying a tithe, or ten percent of all he had, to Melchizedek (Genesis 14:18-20).

Faith Is the Key to God's Hall of Fame
(Hebrews 11)

In both Old Testament and New Testament times, there has been only one way to know and serve God—by faith (11:6). As you read the list of heroes of the faith in Hebrews 11, you will probably recognize them from your reading of part 2 of this guide. The list includes men and women from Abel to unnamed heroes of a much later era. Some of the experiences described in 11:35-38 fit those endured by believers living in the period between the close of the Old Testament and the beginning of the New Testament. All of these heroes of the faith died anticipating what believers today enjoy through faith in Christ (11:39-40).

WHAT'S UP WITH THE GOOD BOOK?

"The Bible is a vein of pure gold, unalloyed by quartz or any earthly substance. This is a star without a speck; a sun without a blot; a light without darkness; a moon without its paleness; a glory without a dimness."
—Charles H. Spurgeon

With Privilege Comes Responsibility
(Hebrews 12–13)

In view of things being much better now, believers ought to run the Christian race patiently, looking to Jesus (12:1-2) without getting discouraged (12:3-13). It is important, too, to try to live in peace

DON'T FORGET THE INMATES!

The reference to prisoners (13:3) adds to the reasons some cite for believing Paul wrote Hebrews. He certainly was well acquainted with prisoners from personal experience.

with everyone (12:14). Bitterness has no place in a believer's heart (12:15); nor does immorality belong there (12:16).

Further exhortations close the letter to the Hebrews:

Important Signs of a Christian

Loves fellow believers (13:1)

Shows hospitality to strangers (13:2)

Remembers those in prison (13:3)

Esteems marriage highly (13:4)

Shuns the love of money (13:5)

Honors spiritual leaders (13:7)

Follows the spiritual leaders' example (13:7)

Avoids false teachings (13:9)

Is willing to suffer for Jesus' sake (13:12-13)

Praises God continually (13:15)

Does good and gives properly (13:16)

Obeys and cooperates with spiritual leaders (13:17)

Prays (13:18)

LET'S GET TESTY

What's Better in Hebrews?

Select the correct answer for each statement.

___ 1. Hebrews 1 and 2 describes Jesus as superior to

    A. carpenters

    B. Pharisees

    C. angels

    D. none of the above

___ 2. Hebrews 3 describes Jesus as superior to

    A. Abraham

    B. Moses

    C. David

    D. Mephibosheth

___ **3. Moses built the tabernacle, but Jesus built**

    A. a house of believers

    B. a house of prophets

    C. a house of memories

    D. a house of stories

___ **4. Unlike the priests, Jesus passed through**

    A. Egypt

    B. Jerusalem

    C. the temple

    D. the heavens

___ **5. Unlike the sacrifices the priests offered for sin, Jesus' sacrifice was**

    A. temporary but perfect

    B. partial payment for sin

    C. final and perfect

    D. involuntary

(Answers: 1. C; 2. B; 3. A; 4. D; 5. C)

CHAPTER TWENTY-SIX

Show-Me Faith (James)

Anyone from Missouri, the Show-Me state, should be able to identify with the book of James. It definitely insists, "Show me your faith!" You can't read far in James without recognizing this brief book's practical approach to life. It examines faith in the laboratory of everyday life and judges it to be genuine if it passes a series of tests.

Pumped Up about Trials (James 1)

James wrote to Jewish Christians who had been scattered by persecution to foreign lands. Ironically, James told those displaced persons to be joyful when trials struck them. Trials, he explained, build endurance, which rounds out character. Trials also bring opportunities to seek God's wisdom and to prove that one's faith is genuine. Furthermore, God awards the crown of life to those who faithfully endure trials.

Temptation, too, tests one's faith. God doesn't tempt anyone, James assured his readers. God gives only good things to His

SOME THINGS YOU'LL DISCOVER IN THIS CHAPTER

1. Trials and temptations in life are really God's opportunity to build our character.

2. Real faith is not just head knowledge or belief but the meeting of needs of those around us.

3. Many of our problems come from our many desires that are selfish and not spiritual.

233

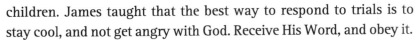

IN CASE YOU'RE WONDERING
WHO WROTE JAMES?
Likely, James, Jesus' brother (a son of Mary and Joseph), who became a leader in the Jerusalem church (Acts 12:17; 15:13; 21:18).

IT'S A PROMISE!

"But if you keep looking steadily into God's perfect law—the law that sets you free—and if you do what it says and don't forget what you heard, then God will bless you for doing it." (James 1:25)

children. James taught that the best way to respond to trials is to stay cool, and not get angry with God. Receive His Word, and obey it.

James compared the Word of God, the Bible, to a mirror and contrasted two kinds of Bible readers. One reader looks into the mirror of Scripture, sees himself as Scripture shows him to be, but does nothing to change his life. The other reader looks at himself in the mirror of Scripture, sees himself as he is, but makes appropriate changes in his life. The second person, James said, will be blessed.

Faith and Snobbery Are Mutually Exclusive (James 2)

James taught that genuine faith and snobbish attitudes and actions lie poles apart. He denounced the practice of favoring the rich over the poor and reminded his readers that they were suffering harsh treatment at the hands of the rich. As far as God is concerned, James pointed out, showing favoritism is a sin. Real faith, he taught, swings into action on behalf of anyone in need. Genuine faith provides food and clothing. On the other hand, dead faith wishes a destitute person well but offers no assistance. James cited the examples of Abraham and Rahab to drive home the truth that genuine faith proves itself by taking positive action.

A Wagging Tongue Stirs Up a World of Trouble (James 3)

According to James, believers ought to control their tongues. If they don't, they can cause a lot of damage, just as a small fire can do a lot of damage to a forest. James taught that praising God and cursing fellow human beings aren't compatible; believers should speak only wholesome words.

Humble Pie Is Sweet (James 4)

Selfishness and greed cause quarreling and aggression, James told his readers. But God wants His people to humble themselves and submit to His will. Part of the process of humbling oneself involves sorrow for sin and a desire for God's cleansing and nearness. Because life is brief, James advised that believers give God control of their day planners and depend upon Him to write in the appointments He wants them to keep.

Be Patient, Praise, and Pray (James 5)

Sometimes life just doesn't seem fair. James appealed to his first-century readers to wait patiently for the coming of the Lord. He pointed out that the Lord will punish abusive and stingy bosses someday. He hears the cries of those whose bosses rip them off, and He will reward those who patiently endure. But James also appealed to his readers to sing praises when they suffered and to pray. He assured them that much is accomplished through the prayers of righteous people, and he cited the example of Elijah. When Elijah prayed for a drought, not a single raindrop fell for three and a half years. When he prayed again, rain fell in sheets and ended the drought.

James concluded his letter by encouraging believers to win back anyone who strays from the truth.

WHAT'S UP WITH THE GOOD BOOK?

"The Bible is meant to be bread for our daily use, not just cake for special occasions."—*Anonymous*

INFO BYTE
DON'T SOW WILD OATHS

James warned against swearing an oath. His warning doesn't rule out court oaths, but oaths that are senseless, casual, profane, or blasphemous—wild oaths as opposed to solemn oaths.

LET'S GET TESTY

About Faith!

Answer T for true, F for false.

___ 1. James taught that faith is enough to please God.

___ 2. Trials are opportunities to show that one's faith is genuine.

___ 3. Showing favoritism is a violation of faith.

___ 4. When trials strike, a believer should ask God for wisdom.

___ 5. God tempts us to see if we are strong.

___ 6. Whoever endures trials successfully will receive the crown of life.

___ 7. Real faith provides help for the destitute.

___ 8. Showing favoritism is a sin.

___ 9. Greed leads to strife.

___10. Unwholesome words can cause a lot of trouble.

(Answers: 1 and 5 are false.)

CHAPTER TWENTY-SEVEN

Simon Says
(1 and 2 Peter)

How many times did you play "Simon says" when you were a kid? Unless you were exceptionally good at the game, you probably bombed out when the leader rapidly barked a command without first saying "Simon says." Don't feel bad. We've all been there.

The letters called 1 and 2 Peter were written by Simon Peter, the bombastic disciple whose life Jesus changed impressively forever. Jesus molded Simon Peter's character from crumbling clay into a rock-solid work of art. Simon, the fisherman, became Peter, the apostle to the Jews. As you read Peter's letters, watch for indications of Peter's rock-solid character, and be alert to his instructions on how to lead a successful Christian life.

Life Is Tough and Then We Hit the Jackpot
(1 Peter 1)

The recipients of Peter's letters were dispersed Jewish believers. Persecution had driven them from their homes and thrown them into unstable and unfavorable circumstances. However, Peter wished them God's grace and peace, and he reminded them that the

SOME THINGS YOU'LL DISCOVER IN THIS CHAPTER

1. All Christians are members of a royal family, which includes being a kingdom of priests, stones in God's temple, and a holy nation.

2. We need to watch out for false teachers who might lead us astray and will themselves reap severe judgment.

3. God's schedule and ours are not the same in terms of Jesus' return, and we shouldn't become complacent in our lives if we see no sign of it.

INFO BYTE

ANGELS' INTEREST IN SALVATION

The ark of the covenant, upon which Israel's high priest sprinkled the blood of a bull and goat, featured two golden angels on its top—one on each end—peering down at the mercy seat, the ark's covering (Exodus 25:17-22). Peter's allusion to angels' interest in salvation may have drawn his Jewish believers to this Old Testament imagery.

risen Christ had given them a living hope and an eternal inheritance. In spite of losing their earthly home and possessions, they would never lose their eternal inheritance because God was safeguarding it for them. Peter commented that his readers were joyful about this inheritance and that present trials would only prove their faith. He applauded their love for Christ and their indescribable joy.

Peter also spoke of the Old Testament prophets' predictions about the gospel, which his readers had received. He mentioned that angels show an intense interest in the salvation believers have received, and he called upon his readers to think clearly, be self-controlled, stay hopeful, be holy, fear God, and love one another with all their hearts. He pointed out that God had redeemed them by the blood of Jesus Christ and given them a new birth. Like a seed, the Word of God had produced new life in them, Peter said, and although physical life is only temporary, God's Word is eternal.

Live Like Royalty (1 Peter 2)

Members of a royal family are taught to conduct themselves with royal bearing. Similarly, Peter taught his readers to live like members of God's royal family. He underscored the need to discard evil behavior and evil intentions as well as the need to crave pure spiritual milk.

Members of God's Royal Family	Responsibilities of Members of God's Royal Family
Living stones in God's temple (2:5)	Be careful how you live (2:12).
God's holy priests (2:5)	Submit to authority (2:13).
A chosen people (2:9)	Live as God's servants (2:16).
God's holy nation (2:9)	Respect everyone (2:17).
God's possession (2:9)	Love fellow believers (2:17).
The people of God (2:10)	Fear God (2:17).
	Respect the king (2:17).
	Obey your masters [employers] (2:18).
	Patiently endure undeserved suffering (2:20).
	Follow in Jesus' steps (2:21).

Peter portrayed Jesus, who led a sinless life and died on the cross for sinners, as the perfect model of behavior (2:21-24). Peter emphasized that Jesus is also the Shepherd and Guardian of believers' souls (2:25).

A Fisherman's Tips on How to Fish for Souls (1 Peter 3–4)

Jesus had called Simon Peter to fish for souls. In turn, Peter called on believers to fish for souls. He gave some wise advice to wives of unbelieving husbands in 3:1-7, telling them how to win over their husbands by their good behavior. In the rest of the chapter, Peter advised all believers to suffer ill-treatment without retaliating, and when asked about their hope, believers should be ready to provide an explanation. Peter reminded his readers that Jesus suffered for sinners in order to bring them to God. In chapter 4, Peter instructed his readers to be willing to suffer for Christ, knowing that new life in Christ is far better than the old life in sin. Peter also taught that believers should invest the rest of their lives in God's service, employing their spiritual gifts wisely and counting it a privilege to be called Christians.

Look after One Another; Watch Out for the Devil (1 Peter 5)

The final chapter of 1 Peter implores spiritual leaders to care for God's people willingly. Younger believers received an exhortation from Peter to submit to the authority of their spiritual leaders. All of the believers, Peter wrote, should serve each other humbly and also humble themselves before God.

Peter knew well how treacherous the devil is. So he put his readers on the alert and told them to stand against the devil by being strong in the faith. In closing, Peter wrote about God's support for His suffering family members and sent greetings and the blessing of peace.

WHAT'S UP WITH THE GOOD BOOK?

"The Bible redirects my will, cleanses my emotions, enlightens my mind, and quickens my total being."
—E. Stanley Jones

IT'S A PROMISE!

"Give all your worries and cares to God, for he cares about what happens to you."
(1 Peter 5:7)

INFO BYTE
HIS MAJESTY

Peter, James, and John had seen the majesty of Jesus Christ on the Mount of Transfiguration (see Matthew 17:1-8). The experience left a lasting impression on Peter's understanding of who Jesus is.

The Goal Is Excellence (2 Peter 1–2)

Peter's second letter warned believers about false teachers. Apparently, Peter believed that the best defense is a good offense. He wanted God's grace and peace to actively propel believers into a better knowledge of Christ so they would experience God's power and become more like Him (1:1-4). Peter taught that a morally excellent life is a process that begins with faith and builds the following qualities one upon the other: goodness, knowledge, self-control, perseverance, godliness, brotherly kindness, and love (1:5-7).

Peter told the believers that he and the other apostles had not engaged in fiction, but in fact. They had seen Jesus Christ's majesty and were proclaiming what the Scriptures taught about Him (1:16-21). Then Peter gave a history lesson to show how God deals with false teachers. They will not escape His judgment, just as rebellious angels, Noah's wicked contemporaries, and Sodom and Gomorrah did not escape His judgment (2:1-8). Nevertheless, the Lord protects His people in the midst of wicked people (2:9). The rest of chapter 2 paints an accurate but dismal picture of false teachers (2:10-22).

Same Old, Same Old? (2 Peter 3)

If you've heard the expression, "slow as the second coming of Christ," you have rubbed shoulders with people like those censured in 2 Peter 3. Peter identified them as scoffers who believe the world just keeps moving along in the same-old, same-old way. As Peter pointed out, scoffers in Noah's time followed that philosophy until the Flood destroyed them and the earth. He explained that God's schedule and ours aren't the same. Someday, Jesus will return and destroy the present heavens and earth. Then He will introduce new heavens and a new earth. Being aware of this future event, Peter advised believers to be careful how they live, to guard themselves against false teachers, and to get to know Christ better.

LET'S GET TESTY

Simon Says

Write yes next to each instruction Simon Peter gave in his letters. Don't make a move if Simon didn't give the instruction.

1. Simon says, "Think clearly." _____
2. Simon says, "Be self-controlled." _____
3. Simon says, "Be holy." _____
4. Simon says, "Fear God." _____
5. Simon says, "Love one another with all your hearts." _____
6. Simon says, "Get rid of deceit." _____
7. Simon says, "Crave pure spiritual milk." _____
8. Simon says, "Respect everyone." _____
9. Simon says, "Be careful how you live." _____
10. Simon says, "Follow in Jesus' steps." _____
11. Simon says, "Live on a mountain." _____
12. Simon says, "Repay evil with evil.." _____
13. Simon says, "Withhold taxes." _____
14. Simon says, "Don't trust anyone over 30." _____
15. Simon says, "Get to know Christ better." _____

(Answers: The Yes instructions are 1, 2, 3, 4 5, 6, 7, 8, 9, 10, and 15.)

CHAPTER TWENTY-EIGHT

All in the Family
(1, 2, and 3 John)

Most Bible teachers believe the apostle John, who wrote the Gospel of John, also wrote 1, 2, and 3 John. Tradition suggests he wrote these brief letters around A.D. 90 from Ephesus. This means, of course, that John was old when he wrote these letters. He may have been as old as 90 and perhaps even older. So reading John's letters is like listening to a great-grandfather—maybe even a great-great grandfather—dispense loving counsel to all his family members. Don't be surprised to find John addressing his readers as his "dear children."

Walk the Walk (1 John 1)

John was an eyewitness to Jesus' ministry and life on earth, and he enjoyed fellowship with the Father and His Son, Jesus Christ. He identified the Father as the God of absolute light (1:5) and insisted that all who claim to have fellowship with God but walk in darkness are liars (1:6). According to John, those who fellowship with God walk in the light and enjoy fellowship with one another and are

SOME THINGS YOU'LL DISCOVER IN THIS CHAPTER

1. John warned his "dear children" about those who do not love in truth, and he taught the supreme importance of love in our lives.

2. One of the key tests of true teaching is to check if the teacher confesses that Jesus Christ came as the Son of God in the flesh.

3. John commended believers for serving others but says no to controlling others.

243

cleansed from all sin by Jesus' blood (1:7). John made it clear that those who talk the talk without walking the walk are simply deceiving themselves (1:8). However, those who confess their sins find forgiveness and cleansing (1:9-10).

Lessons for Little Children (1 John 2–4)

With great parental concern, John counseled his "dear children" not to sin, but he assured them that Jesus Christ is alongside the Father in the role of defense attorney for any believer who sins (2:1-2). But John quickly pointed out that those who know Jesus Christ also obey Him (2:3-6). True believers also love one another (2:7-11). John appealed to his "dear children" to separate themselves from the lusts and boastful pride that characterize ungodly society (2:15-16). He advised that doing the will of God is what really matters now and eternally (2:17).

John also warned his "children" about antichrists—false teachers who try to deceive believers by teaching that Jesus is not the Christ (2:18-23). However, John was confident that the Holy Spirit would safeguard their faith (2:24-27).

Love, John wrote, is a powerful divider of those who are God's children from those who are not. He explained that God's children love one another; whereas those whose lifestyle is marked by sin, not love, do not know God (3:7-15).

John passed along a simple test his "dear children" could use to determine whether a prophet was legitimate or false. A prophet was legitimate if he affirmed Jesus Christ's incarnation; false if he denied the incarnation (4:1-6). Again, like a paternal caregiver, John exhorted his "dear children" to love one another (4:7-21). He stated that believers love because God first loved them (4:19).

Make Sure You're Sure (1 John 5)

Closing his first letter, John wrote to give his readers full assurance of salvation through Jesus Christ. First, he cited obedience to God's commandments as evidence of belonging to His family (5:1-5).

Next, he identified three witnesses—the water of baptism, the blood of Christ, and the Holy Spirit—that testify to the fact that Jesus is God's Son (5:6-9) and affirmed that whoever believes in God's Son has eternal life (5:10). Then John made a clear distinction between those who have eternal life and those who do not. He explained that those who have the Son of God have life, whereas those who do not have the Son of God do not have life (5:11-12). John's purpose in writing his first letter was to enable believers to know for sure that they possess eternal life (5:13). His final word of advice to his "dear children" was concise: stay clear of idol worship (5:21).

Dear Lady (2 John)

Scholars offer two possible identifications for the lady addressed in John's second letter. Some believe she was an actual person who, with her children, was living according to God's truth. Others suggest the term "lady" represents a church. John expressed his love for this lady and her children and greeted them cordially (1:1-3). He had met some of this lady's children and was delighted to learn of their devotion to the truth (1:4). Then he reminded the lady about the importance of obeying the commandment to love one another (1:5-6) and the need to watch out for antichrists, whom he described as deceivers and deniers of Christ's incarnation (1:7-8). John instructed the lady not to welcome any of these false teachers into her house (1:10-11). John had many other things to share with this lady, but he hoped to be able to do so in person (1:12). He closed his letter with greetings from the children of the lady's chosen sister, perhaps her nephews and nieces or another church (1:13).

Gaius—What a Guy! (3 John)

A highly personal letter, 3 John gives high marks to a man named Gaius, whom John loved in the truth. Gaius enjoyed outstanding spiritual health, but it seems his physical health was not faring as well. John wished him better health (1:2). Upon receiving a good report from some believers about Gaius's obedience to the truth,

INFO BYTE
THE INCARNATION

John's teaching that the Son of God came into the world as a real human being (often called the Incarnation) was diametrically opposed to the teaching of false teachers known as Gnostics. The Gnostics taught that spirit is good but matter is evil. Therefore they rejected the concept of God taking upon Himself a human body.

IN CASE YOU'RE WONDERING
HOUSEGUESTS NOT WELCOME!

We can't say dogmatically that the lady's "house" was a residence. It may have been a house church. In New Testament times, believers met in individual homes for fellowship, instruction, and worship. John may have been telling a church to bar false teachers from its meetings, or he may have been telling an actual lady not to entertain false teachers in her home.

John was very happy (1:4). He commended Gaius for opening his home to itinerant ministers of the gospel (1:5-8).

Another member of the church where Gaius was a member was quite different from Gaius. His name was Diotrephes, and his game was king of the hill. He loved to be in charge and was a first-century "control freak," slamming John and chasing good people out of the church (1:9-10). As far as John was concerned, Diotrephes wasn't a true believer (1:11).

John mentioned a third person, Demetrius, and commended him. Everyone spoke highly of Demetrius (1:12).

Not wishing to write down everything he wished to impart to Gaius, John expressed the hope that he would see him soon and speak with him in person. He ended his letter with a brief benediction and greeting (1:14).

LET'S GET TESTY

Family Matters

Underline the most appropriate word(s) in each of the following sentences.

1. Most likely, 1, 2, and 3 John were written by the apostle John from Corinth/Jerusalem/Ephesus.

2. The apostle John was likely about 60/75/90 years old when he wrote these letters.

3. John identifies deniers of Christ's incarnation as errant brothers/antichrists/misinformed theology students.

4. Reference is made in 3 John to Gaius, Diotrephes, and Danarius/Diocletian/Demetrius.

5. John commended Gaius for his hospitality/intelligence/counsel.

6. Some believe that "lady" in 2 John represents a ship/a duchess/a church/a sorority.

7. John cited obedience to God's commands/church membership/recitation of the Lord's Prayer as evidence of belonging to God's family.

8. According to John, believers like/love/tolerate/attend church with/strike business deals with one another.

9. John wrote that whoever has a baptismal certificate/the Son/a kind heart/a clean record has life.

10. John had information about Jesus' life and ministry because he was an eyewitness/a student of history/an avid reader.

(Answers: 1. Ephesus; 2. 90; 3. antichrists; 4. Demetrius; 5. hospitality; 6. a church; 7. obedience to God's commands; 8. love; 9. the Son; 10. eyewitness)

CHAPTER TWENTY-NINE

"LIKE THE SIX OF US WOULDN'T KNOW A WOLF IF WE SAW ONE. C'MON!"

Stand Your Ground! (Jude)

SOME THINGS YOU'LL DISCOVER IN THIS CHAPTER

1. Jude was a half brother of Jesus who warned against those who departed from the purity of the faith.

2. Jude portrayed the true nature of these renegades as despicable in every way.

Although it has only 25 verses, Jude's letter covers a big chunk of time, all the way from at least the dawn of human history to the first century. It hands down a scathing indictment of false teaching and marshals God's people to stand their ground in the defense of truth. Jude identified himself at the beginning of his letter as a servant of Jesus Christ and a brother of James (1:1).

Although he had intended to write to believers about salvation, Jude changed his mind. Apostasy—false teaching—posed such a threat to believers that he saw a critical need to warn them about it and rally them to contend for the truth that had been given to them (1:3). He explained that some ungodly teachers, who had turned against Christ, had wormed their way into the churches and were teaching that it's OK to live like the devil (1:4). Like a lawyer arguing a case in court, Jude presented evidence to show that God punishes those who turn against Him.

JUDE'S ID

Although Jude didn't state the fact, he was one of Jesus' half brothers. Like James, Jude was the son of Mary and Joseph. Jesus, of course, was born of the virgin Mary. Joseph was not Jesus' biological father, because Jesus was the Son of God. We can infer from verse 1 that Jude was humble.

IN CASE YOU'RE WONDERING
CLIPPED WINGS!

The angels referred to in verse 6 probably followed Lucifer (Satan) in his rebellion against God before the dawn of human history. These incarcerated angels may have cohabited with women (Genesis 6). Other fallen angels, like Satan, are not chained. They actively advance the cause of evil and oppose God. Someday all rebellious angels will be consigned to hell (Matthew 25:41).

Evidence That God Punishes Those Who Turn against Him

Israelites delivered from Egypt, only to turn against God, fell dead in the desert (1:5).

Angels who rebelled against God are incarcerated and awaiting final judgment (1:6).

The region of Sodom and Gomorrah burned to a crisp under God's judgment (1:7).

Apostates: What More Can We Say?

The picture Jude painted of apostates is not pretty, but it is accurate. He portrayed them as immoral, disrespectful, scoffers, disobedient, brutish, faithless, self-willed, aggressive, mercenary, arrogant, profane, self-indulgent, worthless, unfruitful, disgraceful, morally polluted, aimless, and marked for judgment (1:8-15). Jude also depicted them as malcontents, complainers, braggarts, and self-seeking flatterers (1:16). However, Jude reminded believers that these apostates had been predicted and were now present (1:18-19). Jude said flat out that they did not have the Spirit (1:19b).

In verses 20-23, Jude presented a strategy for dealing with apostates. Believers should build their lives on the truth, pray in the Holy Spirit, remain in the circle of God's love, wait patiently for the full realization of eternal life, and try to rescue those who stray from the truth.

Jude's last words overflow with encouragement. He ascribed glory to God for who He is and for the salvation He provides, and he assured believers that God is able to safeguard them and escort them someday into His glorious presence (1:24-25).

LET'S GET TESTY

Do You Know Jude?

Answer T for true, F for false.

____ 1. Jude was Jesus' cousin.

____ 2. He had intended to write about angels.

____ 3. He was deeply concerned about apostasy.

____ 4. He reminded his readers about what happened in the days of Elijah.

____ 5. He mentioned judgment experienced by Sidon and Gomorrah.

____ 6. Certain fallen angels are incarcerated and awaiting final judgment.

____ 7. Apostates are meek.

____ 8. Apostates are unfruitful.

____ 9. Believers ought to build their lives on the truth.

____10. God is able to safeguard His people.

(Answers: 1. F; 2. F; 3. T; 4. F; 5. F; 6. T; 7. F; 8. T; 9. T; 10. T)

IT'S A PROMISE!

"Your word is a lamp for my feet and a light for my path." (Psalm 119:105)

WHAT'S UP WITH THE GOOD BOOK?

"There's no better book with which to defend the Bible than the Bible itself." —D. L. Moody

CHAPTER THIRTY

"OH, I ALREADY KNOW WHO WINS, I JUST CAME FOR THE SPECIAL EFFECTS."

What's This World Coming To? (Revelation)

Wow, you made it to the last book of the Bible. Way to go! As you may already know, of the 66 books of the Bible, Revelation is probably the hardest one to understand. But it is also the only one that offers a blessing to those who read it (Revelation 1:3). That offer alone kind of pulls you into Revelation, doesn't it?

Various Bible scholars offer different views on this captivating book of the Bible. Some take the preterist view. They see the prophecies in Revelation as fulfilled in the church's early history. The historical view regards the book of Revelation as an unfolding of church history from the first century until the end of time. The futurist view sees all the events portrayed in chapters 4–22 as still future. Those who take the idealist view see the book as a presentation of principles in the ongoing conflict of good and evil.

If you're ready and set, let's go!

Reunited on an Island (Revelation 1)

The writer of Revelation identifies himself in verse 4 as John. Most Bible scholars believe this was the apostle John, who also wrote the

SOME THINGS YOU'LL DISCOVER IN THIS CHAPTER

1. The book of Revelation is based on visions given to the apostle John near the end of his life on the island of Patmos.

2. This book is based on letters to seven churches in what is now Turkey, challenging them to hold fast in the midst of persecution and give their best to God.

3. In the end, God wins the last tremendous conflict, and His Son Jesus Christ reigns forever and ever.

INFO BYTE
REVELATION

The Greek word translated *revelation* means "disclosure" or "unveiling." As Revelation 1:1 states, this book is a disclosure or unveiling of Jesus Christ. The title could be interpreted to mean a disclosure *about* Jesus Christ or *belonging to* Jesus Christ.

Gospel of John and 1, 2, and 3 John. John was on the island of Patmos when he received this revelation of Jesus Christ (Revelation 1:1, 9). Although it is likely that he had been banished to Patmos by the Roman emperor Domitian, John was not despondent, because he had a deep sense of Jesus' love and a strong hope in His return (1:5-7).

The Total Jesus Revealed

While John was in deep communion with God on Sunday, the Lord's Day, he received a visit from Jesus Christ, whom he hadn't seen since His resurrection. Jesus spoke with a loud voice that sounded like a trumpet and commanded John to write what he saw to seven churches in Asia Minor (1:9-11). John's glimpse of Jesus was awesome. Jesus stood in the midst of seven gold lamp stands. He wore a robe and a golden sash. His hair was woolly white like snow, and His eyes were like blazing fire. Jesus' feet resembled bright bronze. His voice sounded like roaring water. He was holding seven stars in His right hand. A sharp double-bladed sword protruded from His mouth, and His face shone like the noonday sun (1:12-16). This vision of Jesus sent John reeling to the ground, but Jesus lifted him up, calmed his fear, identified Himself as the eternal keeper of the keys to death and hell, and instructed John to write what he had seen in these visions and what would take place in the future (1:17-20).

The Ultimate Church Growth Assessment
(Revelation 2–3)

Jesus dictated letters to seven churches in Asia Minor. Each letter contained a customized message for a church that included a description of Jesus, a commendation, a criticism, a challenge, and a promise. The churches were located at Ephesus, Smyrna, Pergamum, Thyatira, Sardis, Philadelphia, and Laodicea.

The church at Ephesus guarded the faith and worked hard, but it had lost the love it once had for the Lord. Jesus called upon this church to remember its former condition, repent, and become again what it once was (2:1-7).

Suffering and poverty characterized the church at Smyrna, but

the church was spiritually rich. Jesus predicted a future wave of persecution and appealed to the church at Smyrna to remain faithful unto death. He promised the crown of life to those who heeded His counsel (2:8-11).

Jesus commended the faithfulness of the church at Pergamum. His faithful witness, Antipas, had been martyred at Pergamum, but the church stayed its course. Nevertheless, false teachers were beginning to gain an audience, so Jesus called upon the church at Pergamum to repent (2:12-17).

The church at Thyatira had made good progress in Christian character and conduct, but its armor was beginning to crack. Immorality and idolatry were invading the church, due to the influence of Jezebel (likely a woman in the church). In effect Jesus told the church, "Either you correct this problem, or I will" (2:18-29).

The church at Sardis was hypocritical. Looking at it from the outside, people thought everything was just fine. But Jesus knew better and told the church to come alive and return Him and to the teachings it used to value (3:1-6).

A great opportunity for evangelism awaited the church at Philadelphia, but Jewish adversaries threatened the church. Jesus commended the church's obedience and called for perseverance. He promised to come quickly and counseled the church to safeguard its crown (3:7-13).

The seventh church to receive a letter from Jesus did not receive a commendation from Him. This was the church at Laodicea, which considered itself rich and lacking nothing. However, Jesus pronounced it lukewarm, wretched, miserable, poor, and blind. He challenged it to turn to Him so its spiritual needs would be met, and He said He was knocking at the church door. He promised to enter the life of anyone who opened the door to receive Him (3:20-21).

Beamed Up to Heaven (Revelation 4–5)

After writing the letters to the seven churches, John saw an open door in heaven and heard a voice like a trumpet calling him up to

IN CASE YOU'RE WONDERING
WHERE WAS PATMOS?

Patmos was an island in the Aegean Sea, southwest of Ephesus, a city on the coast of Asia Minor (now Turkey). Patmos covered about 30 square miles.

INFO BYTE
THE POOR RICH CHURCH

The church of Laodicea could readily identify with Jesus' mention of gold, white garments, and eye ointment. The city's leading industries were banking, production of wool cloth, and the manufacturing of eye salve.

INFO BYTE
KEY IDENTIFICATIONS

It seems obvious from the terminology in Revelation 4–5 that the Person on the throne is God and the Lamb who took the scroll is Jesus Christ.

heaven so he could see future events (4:1). John saw in heaven a glorious Person on a throne. The Person's appearance resembled dazzling jewels. Circled around the Person's throne were 24 other thrones, upon which 24 elders were seated. The elders wore white robes and had gold crowns on their heads. Lightning flashed and thunder roared from the main throne, and seven blazing lampstands and a sea of crystal-like glass appeared before it.

John also saw four living beings around the throne. They all served as attendants to the Person on the throne, and they sang day and night of the holiness of the eternal and almighty Lord God. Each living being had six wings but a distinctly prominent physical characteristic:

- The first being resembled a lion.
- The second being resembled an ox.
- The third being had a human face.
- The fourth being resembled an eagle.

When these four living beings gave glory, honor, and thanks to the Person on the throne, the 24 elders fell down and worshiped Him. They laid their crowns at His feet and lauded His character and creative power.

Next, John saw a scroll in the hand of the Person on the throne (5:1). It was sealed with seven seals, which no one was found worthy to break in order to unroll the scroll. John wept because no one was found, but one of the elders told him to stop weeping because the Lion of the Tribe of David was worthy to break the seals and open the scroll.

John saw a slain Lamb step up to the throne and take the scroll from the right hand of the Person on the throne. This action caused heaven to erupt in a concert of music and praise in honor of the Lamb. Millions of angels joined the 24 elders in ascribing praise to the Lamb. The four living beings responded with "Amen," and the 24 elders fell down and worshiped God and the Lamb.

Hoofbeats and Horrific Pounding
(Revelation 6–7)

John watched the Lamb open the seven seals one by one (Revelation 6:1). Here's what he observed:

Seal Judgments

First seal: Thundering hoofbeats. A rider on a white horse went forth to fight and win battles. He carried a bow and wore a crown (6:2).

Second seal: A rider on a red horse went forth to take peace from the earth. He carried a mighty sword and had the power to rob the earth of peace. War and mass carnage resulted (6:3-4).

Third seal: A rider on a black horse carried a pair of scales. What John heard suggests that inflation and famine strike the earth when the hoofbeats of the black horse pound the planet (6:5-6).

Fourth seal: A rider named Death rode out on a pale horse, and the Grave followed him. Death and the Grave received authority over one-fourth of the world's population. Together, they killed, spread famine and disease, and unleashed wild animals upon humanity (6:7-8).

Fifth seal: Martyrs under the altar cried to God for vengeance on their killers. Each received a white robe and the promise that vengeance would come in a little while (6:9-11).

Sixth seal: A great earthquake occurred. The sun eclipsed. The moon turned blood-red. Stars fell. The sky rolled. Mountains and islands disappeared. Earth's terrified movers and shakers fled to caves and called on mountain rocks to fall on them and hide them from the Lamb's wrath (6:12-17).

A brief intermission occurred in heaven between the opening of the sixth and seventh seals. During the intermission, an angel placed a seal of protection on each member of a select group of people—144,000 servants of God from the 12 tribes of Israel (Revelation 7).

Seventh seal: When the Lamb opened this seal, heaven experienced half an hour of silence (8:1).

IT'S A PROMISE!

"All who are victorious will be clothed in white. I will never erase their names from the Book of Life, but I will announce before my Father and his angels that they are mine." (Revelation 3:5)

IN CASE YOU'RE WONDERING
THE LOCUST STRIKE FORCE

The locust invasion was predicted by the prophet Joel (see Joel 2). Although John described awfully weird locusts, some Bible scholars believe the locusts could easily be understood today to mean a highly advanced military force.

The Angels' Brass Ensemble
(Revelation 8:2–9:21)

Seven trumpet judgments followed the breaking of the seventh seal. But first, John observed an angel mixing an incense burner with the prayers of believers. The angel offered this mixture on a gold altar before the throne. Then John saw the smoke from this offering ascend to God. Next, he saw the angel fill the incense burner with fire from the altar and throw it down to the earth. Thunder, lightning, and an earthquake resulted. Seven angels took this occurrence as a signal to blow their trumpets (8:2-6).

Here's what John saw happen when the first six trumpets blasted:

Trumpet Judgments

First trumpet: Hail and fire mixed with blood fell onto the earth, burning up one-third of the earth, one-third of the trees, and one-third of the grass (8:7).

Second trumpet: A blazing mountain was hurled into the sea. One-third of the water turned to blood. One-third of marine life died. One-third of the ships at sea were destroyed (8:8-9).

Third trumpet: A flaming star named Bitterness fell from the sky. It landed on one-third of the rivers and on the springs of water, turning one-third of the earth's water supply so bitter that many deaths resulted (8:10-11).

Fourth trumpet: When the fourth angel blew his trumpet, one-third of the sun, one-third of the moon, and one-third of the stars turned dark. This phenomenon darkened one-third of the day and one-third of the night (8:12).

Fifth trumpet: A star representing someone fell from the sky and received the key to the abyss. He unlocked the abyss to release dense smoke and a plague of terrifying locusts. Unlike other locusts, these locusts from the abyss were commanded to attack only human beings who had not received the seal of God's protection. This locust army plagued humanity for five months. They had received permission to torment, but not kill, their victims. Nevertheless, the torment was so severe that many people tried to end their lives. Their appearance alone was enough to strike terror in hearts, and their tails delivered a sting like that of scorpions (9:1-11).

Sixth trumpet: An army of 200 million creatures emerged from the Euphrates River and killed a third of humanity. Survivors did not repent of their murders or witchcraft or immorality or thefts (9:13-21).

A Sweet Roll and Two Servers
(Revelation 10:1–11:14)

Between the sounding of the sixth and seventh trumpets, John saw a strong angel descend from heaven. A rainbow was on his head, his face was like the sun, and his feet resembled pillars of fire (Revelation 10:1). He planted his right foot on the sea and his left foot on the land and was holding a small scroll. After roaring like a lion, he announced that God would delay no longer (10:2-7). Then a voice from heaven commanded John to take the scroll from the angel and eat it. John did so, and found the scroll sweet to his taste but bitter in his stomach (10:8-10). The voice informed John that he must prophesy again concerning many people, nations, languages, and kings (10:12).

Revelation 11:1-14 describes the power of two men in Jerusalem who served God faithfully. They had power to burn their enemies to a crisp. Also, they were able to withhold rain and smite the earth with plagues. As you might guess, their popularity rating was lower than Death Valley. After concluding their three-and-a-half-year ministry of prophesying and testifying, they were killed by the Beast from the abyss, and their bodies were left lying in the street. Unbelievers joyfully celebrated their deaths by exchanging gifts. But three days later, God resurrected the bodies of His two servants and transported them to heaven while their enemies watched. Then a devastating earthquake rocked Jerusalem. One-tenth of the city fell, and 7,000 residents perished. However, the survivors refused to turn to God.

IN CASE YOU'RE WONDERING
WHO ARE THOSE AMAZING PROPHETS?

Because so much of their ministry resembles that of Moses and Elijah, many Bible scholars identify the two prophets of Revelation 11 as Moses and Elijah. Others point to Hebrews 9:27 as evidence that every person must die once. Since Moses died before the Israelites entered Canaan, they insist that Moses cannot be one of the two witnesses. They suggest that Enoch, who did not die, and Elijah, who did not die, will be the two witnesses who experience death in Jerusalem.

INFO BYTE
1,260 DAYS
Those who teach that the Tribulation precedes Jesus' return to earth refer to this period of 1,260 days (three and a half years) as the Great Tribulation or the second half of the Tribulation.

Back to the Brass Ensemble
(Revelation 11:15-19)

The seventh angel blew his trumpet, and loud praise announced that Christ was ready to take possession of earth's kingdoms. The elders fell down and worshiped, and the temple of God opened to reveal the ark of the covenant. Lightning, thunder, an earthquake, and a hailstorm marked the occasion.

Dragon on the Loose (Revelation 12–13)

According to Revelation 12:1-7, John witnessed a sign in heaven depicting a woman clothed with the sun, with the moon under her feet, and a crown of 12 stars on her head. She was in labor. A second sign featured a huge red dragon with seven heads, ten horns, and seven crowns. The dragon dragged down one-third of the stars and threw them onto the earth. He waited for the woman to give birth so he might devour her child. The woman gave birth to a boy destined to rule the world with a rod of iron, and He was caught up to God. So the dragon turned his fury on the woman, but she fled to the wilderness where God protected her for 1,260 days.

John witnessed a spiritual war in heaven between Michael (the archangel) and his angels and the dragon (the devil) and his angels. Michael and his angels expelled the dragon and his angels from heaven and threw them down to the earth (12:7-9). This expulsion delighted the hosts of heaven, but it infuriated the devil. He directed his fury at the woman who had given birth to the child. However, she was able to flee to a safe sanctuary in the wilderness. The dragon then unleashed his fury on all who professed faith in Jesus Christ (12:10-17).

Revelation 13 introduces two evil beasts (personalities). John saw the first beast rise from the sea. He had seven heads, ten horns, and ten crowns. On each head was a name that blasphemed God. This beast looked like a leopard, had bear's feet and a lion's mouth. His power came from the dragon. Because the beast's heads recovered from a deadly wound, people worshiped the dragon—his power source—and the

beast. The beast's power was limited to 42 months (three and a half years), but he made the most of his time to blaspheme God and wage war against God's people—the few who refused to worship the beast.

A second beast arose from the earth. He had two horns like a lamb but spoke like a dragon and directed worship to the first beast. He deceived worshipers by performing miracles. He even erected a statue in honor of the first beast and gave the statue life and a voice. He forced everyone to be marked on the right hand and forehead in order to buy or sell. His number was 666 (13:11-18).

IN CASE YOU'RE WONDERING
WHO IS THE ANTICHRIST?

Most teachers of prophecy identify the first beast as the Antichrist. However, two factors should be considered: 1) The Bible does not identify the Antichrist. 2) Every biblical teaching mentioning *antichrist* or *antichrists* portrays this evil role as one of religious deception and false doctrine. For this reason. the second beast, called the false prophet, may better fit the term Antichrist. Imitating Christ, who directed worship to the Father by the power of the Holy Spirit, the false prophet instead directs worship to the first beast by the power of the devil.

The Beginning of the End (Revelation 14–15)

How bad can things get? John had reason to be encouraged. He saw the Lamb and the 144,000 sealed servants of God stand on Mount Zion (Revelation 14:1-5), and he heard angels proclaim judgment and forecast the collapse of Babylon the Great and the Beast's control (14:9-11). Suddenly, John saw someone resembling the Son of Man sitting on a white cloud. He had a gold crown on his head and a sickle in his hand. An angel called to Him to swing the sickle into the earth's harvest. The sickle swept across the earth and harvested it. Then another angel called for the sickle to gather the clusters of grapes ripe for judgment. When the sickle cut through the grapes and they were stomped down in the winepress, blood flowed 180 miles long and reached as high as a horse's bridle (14:14-20).

John witnessed another sign in heaven. A crowd of victors over the Beast sang the song of Moses and the song of the Lamb, and then seven angels carrying seven bowls came out of the temple. The bowls were full of God's wrath (Revelation 15).

Bowling Seven Strikes in a Row
(Revelation 16–18)

A loud voice emanated from the temple, commanding the angels to pour their bowls onto the earth (Revelation 16:1). Here's what John observed:

Bowl Judgments

First bowl: Dreadful, malignant sores erupted on those who followed the Beast (16:2).

Second bowl: The sea became like blood, and everything in it died (16:3).

Third bowl: The rivers and springs of water became blood (16:4).

Fourth bowl: The sun scorched everyone. Everyone cursed God and refused to repent (16:8-9).

Fifth bowl: The Beast's kingdom was plunged into such thick darkness that his subjects ground their teeth. They cursed God but refused to repent (16:10-11).

Sixth bowl: The Euphrates River dried up so that eastern armies could march westward. Evil spirits persuaded world leaders to gather at Armageddon to battle the Lord (16:12-16).

Seventh bowl: A devastating earthquake of unprecedented magnitude split the city of Babylon into three pieces, and cities around the world collapsed. Every island sank, mountains fell flat, and hailstones weighing 75 pounds each pummeled the earth's population (16:17-21).

Chapters 17 and 18 of Revelation describe Babylon, both the collapse of its religious system and its commerce. Earth's unbelievers mourned the loss of Babylon, but heaven, the people of God, and the apostles and prophets were told to rejoice because God had judged Babylon.

The King Is Coming (Revelation 19–20)

Heaven rejoiced because Babylon had bitten the dust by the power of the Lord God Almighty, and the marriage supper of the Lamb was about to take place (Revelation 19:1-9). Then John saw heaven open, and the King of kings and Lord of lords rode a white horse and led the armies of heaven into battle. The King was ready to destroy the earth's armies with a sharp sword that protruded from His mouth (19:11-16). Anticipating the King's victory, an angel summoned the birds of the air to feast on the corpses of the earth's fallen soldiers (19:17-18). John witnessed the marshaling of the armies of the Beast and his allies against the rider on the white horse, but the Beast and the false prophet were apprehended and thrown alive into the lake of fire. The rest of the evil military force was killed by the King's sword, and the birds gorged themselves on their flesh (19:19-21).

Following this decisive battle, an angel took hold of Satan, chained him, and incarcerated him in the abyss for 1,000 years (20:1-3). John saw God's faithful people and His resurrected martyrs rewarded with positions of authority. After 1,000 years, a resurrection for judgment took place (20:4-6).

The Thousand Years

The word "millennium" is based on the period of 1,000 years referred to in Revelation 20:2-3, but Bible scholars line up on several sides when interpreting the events associated with the 1,000 years.

- *Premillennialists* teach that Jesus will take his church first to be with him before He returns to the earth to reign for the 1,000 years. However, premillennialists are not in unanimous agreement about when this snatching away, or Rapture, will occur.
- *Amillennialists* interpret the 1,000 years figuratively, believing that Jesus' reign takes place in the hearts of believers, both in heaven and on earth.
- *Postmillennialists* believe the gospel will triumph over evil and usher in a golden age. The 1,000-year reign of Christ and the return of Christ put the finishing touches on history.

John testified that Satan was released from prison after the 1,000-year period but proved once again that he is incorrigibly wicked. Satan deceived people worldwide and led them against God's people at Jerusalem. However, fire from heaven destroyed the devil's followers, and the devil was cast into the lake of fire to be punished forever (20:7-10).

John also saw the dead stand at God's great white throne.

Because their names were not recorded in the Book of Life, they were thrown into the lake of fire (20:11-15).

Wrapping Everything Up Once and Forever
(Revelation 21–22)

John described in chapters 21 and 22 the end of the world as we know it and the introduction of a new heaven and earth. He focused especially on the New Jerusalem, a beautiful, eternal city, which will be the home of God's people. The city was measured at 1,400 miles wide, long, and high (21:16)—about the distance from New York City to Dallas. It may be a cube or a pyramid, but its design is out of this world! No one will have to pay a utility bill there, because the glory of God illuminates it, and its lamp is the Lamb (21:23). Residents will not have to lock their doors there, because nothing offensive will enter the city (21:27).

John saw a pure river of water flowing from the throne of God and the Lamb (22:1). He also saw fruit trees (22:2). The curse imposed in the Garden of Eden will be a thing of the past, John reported. The throne of God and the Lamb will be in the city, and God's servants will serve Him and behold His face (22:3-4). Basking in the light provided by God, God's servants will reign forever (22:5).

John concluded the book of Revelation by passing along Jesus' promise to come again and reward His followers (22:12-14). He also extended an invitation from the Spirit and the Bride (the church) to come to Christ and receive the water of life (22:17). He warned against tampering with God's Word (22:18-19), echoed Jesus' promise to come again (22:20), and closed with a benediction of grace (22:21).

LET'S GET TESTY

Take a Number, Please!

Give the correct number for each of the following in the book of Revelation.

___ 1. The number of the Beast.

___ 2. The number of letters sent to churches.

___ 3. The number of churches that received those letters.

___ 4. The number of miles in the length of the New Jerusalem.

___ 5. The number of elders.

___ 6. The number of living creatures around God's throne.

___ 7. The number of chapters in Revelation.

___ 8. The number of years in the Great Tribulation.

___ 9. The number of trumpet judgments.

___10. The number of God's servants sealed for protection.

(Answers: 1. 666; 2. 7; 3. 7; 4. 1,400; 5. 24; 6. 4; 7. 22; 8. 3½; 9. 7; 10. 144,000)

Handy Tools for Bible Study

Congratulations, you made it all the way through this study guide! Now you know the basics of what the Bible is all about. So go to a mirror, smile, and give yourself a high five. You deserve it. But where do you go from here if you want to increase your knowledge of the Bible? Well, you may be happy to learn that some handy Bible study tools are available to help you get the job done. Visit a Christian book supplier in your area for the books listed and described here. If you enjoy using a computer, ask the supplier about the availability of Bible study tools on disk or CD-ROM.

- **Bible.** That's no surprise, right? But Bibles come in all shapes and sizes, small print, regular print, and large print, and in many translations—with or without study notes. Browse until you find the one you that seems best for you.
- **Bible Atlas.** Basically, a book of colorful maps of Bible lands, this handy tool directs you to the location of almost every place mentioned in the Bible. You may know where Philadelphia, Pennsylvania is located, but where is the Philadelphia mentioned in Revelation 3:7?

Suppose you are reading 1 Kings 18:41–19:4 and discover that when Jezebel put a contract on his life, Elijah took off running and went from Jezreel to Beersheba and then a day's journey into the desert. Checking the locations of Jezreel and Beersheba in a Bible atlas, you find that Elijah actually left Israel, where Jezebel lived, and ran to the southernmost town in Judah and then traveled even further. A light goes on in the upper story. Elijah was so terrified that he fled Jezebel's country!

In addition to showing locations, a good Bible atlas also gives helpful information about Bible lands such as climate, elevation, agriculture, and history.

- **Concordance.** This Bible study tool lists Bible words alphabetically from Aaron to Zuriel, and gives the Scripture references where each word is found. For example, if you want to know where to look in the Bible to read that Jesus wept, look up "wept" in the concordance and *presto!* you learn that John 11:35 is the place.
- **Commentaries.** These tools offer the comments of Bible scholars on books of the Bible. Unless you are familiar with Greek and Hebrew, your best plan is to select commentaries that don't throw a whole bunch of Greek and Hebrew words at you. Browse until you find commentaries offering insightful explanations in everyday language.
- **Bible Dictionary.** So you want to know something about Baal, the false god Elijah opposed. A Bible dictionary will supply the information. Like a regular dictionary, a Bible dictionary lists topics alphabetically. When you find Baal under "B," you will also find what you want to know about Baal.
- **Topical Bible.** This handy Bible study tool alphabetically lists topics and subtopics featured in the Bible. If you want to know at a glance what the Bible teaches about love, for example, look up the word "love." The topical Bible will present all the Bible has to say about this subject.

This list of study tools could be expanded, but those we have listed in this guide are certainly adequate for a meaningful study of the Bible. Enjoy!

A Few Easy Bible Study Methods

How will you study the Bible on your own? Unless you have unlimited free time, you won't be able to read huge chunks of the Bible at a time. But, if you can devote 20 minutes or more per day to Bible study, you can make terrific progress in your understanding and enjoyment of this wonderful book. Here are a few study methods you might try.

Devotional Method. This is the most personal way to study Scripture. If you use it, you should target a book of the Bible and progress through that book several verses at a time. As you do so, keep a journal of what you learn. The following questions can guide you through this discipline:

- What is this passage's central teaching?
- How does this passage relate to the preceding passage? to the passage that follows?
- What does this passage teach about God?
- What does it teach about human nature?
- What does it teach about me?

269

- What can I learn from this passage that will help me become a stronger believer?
- What privileges do I have, according to this passage?
- What responsibilities do I have, according to this passage?

You may not find answers to all of these questions in every passage you read, but you will find enough to help you personalize God's Word for any given day.

An optional way to organize your journal for devotional Bible study is to list four categories and answer questions in each category. For example, consider the following categories and questions:

Context
- What is the central theme of the passage?
- What precedes this passage?
- What follows this passage?
- Who is speaking?
- To whom is the passage addressed?
- What are the circumstances?

God
- What characteristics of God does this passage reveal?
- What are His resources?
- What are His promises?
- What does He require?
- What does He promise?

Myself
- What am I like, according to this passage?
- What changes does God want to see in my life?

Others
- What does this passage teach about others?
- What are my responsibilities toward others?

You may wish to arrange your journal simply by answering these questions based on your reading:
- Is there a promise to claim?
- a command to obey?

- a difficulty to investigate?
- a prayer to offer?
- a failure to avoid?
- a principle to live by?

Biographical Bible Study. As the name implies, this Bible study method consists of reading what the Bible says about a person. If you choose to study the life of Abraham, for example, you would find every passage and verse in the Bible that mentions Abraham. Then you would read about Abraham, describe his life in the form of a narrative or character profile, and note the ways he interacted with God. You can see how a concordance, Bible dictionary, or topical Bible would be very helpful for this kind of Bible study.

Inductive Bible Study. This method trains the student of the Bible to approach a passage of Scripture without preconceived notions and biases. If you use this method, select a passage of Scripture, give it a title, and write down the following:

- Background information
- Analysis (context, theme, writer, addressees, key words, major teachings, etc.)
- Observations
- Interpretation
- Application(s)

Doctrinal Bible Study. Following this method, you would choose a doctrine—sin or salvation or God or Jesus Christ or the Holy Spirit or heaven or hell or judgment or the church—and research what the Bible teaches about it.

Although other Bible study methods exist, the ones described here will enable you to get well acquainted with God's Word. However, as you study, remember the apostle James's advice: When you look into the mirror of God's Word and see yourself there, don't forget to make whatever adjustments to your life the mirror calls for (James 1:22-25). Putting the Bible into everyday life is what really counts!

A One-Year Bible Reading Program

January 1
Genesis 1:1–2:25
Matthew 1:1–2:12
Psalm 1:1-6
Proverbs 1:1-6

January 2
Genesis 3:1–4:26
Matthew 2:13–3:6
Psalm 2:1-12
Proverbs 1:7-9

January 3
Genesis 5:1–7:24
Matthew 3:7–4:11
Psalm 3:1-8
Proverbs 1:10-19

January 4
Genesis 8:1–10:32
Matthew 4:12-25
Psalm 4:1-8
Proverbs 1:20-23

January 5
Genesis 11:1–13:4
Matthew 5:1-26
Psalm 5:1-12
Proverbs 1:24-28

January 6
Genesis 13:5–15:21
Matthew 5:27-48
Psalm 6:1-10
Proverbs 1:29-33

January 7
Genesis 16:1–18:15
Matthew 6:1-24
Psalm 7:1-17
Proverbs 2:1-5

January 8
Genesis 18:16–19:38
Matthew 6:25–7:14
Psalm 8:1-9
Proverbs 2:6-15

January 9
Genesis 20:1–22:24
Matthew 7:15-29
Psalm 9:1-12
Proverbs 2:16-22

January 10
Genesis 23:1–24:51
Matthew 8:1-17
Psalm 9:13-20
Proverbs 3:1-6

January 11
Genesis 24:52–26:16
Matthew 8:18-34
Psalm 10:1-15
Proverbs 3:7-8

January 12
Genesis 26:17–27:46
Matthew 9:1-17
Psalm 10:16-18
Proverbs 3:9-10

January 13
Genesis 28:1–29:35
Matthew 9:18-38
Psalm 11:1-7
Proverbs 3:11-12

January 14
Genesis 30:1–31:16
Matthew 10:1-23
Psalm 12:1-8
Proverbs 3:13-15

January 15
Genesis 31:17–32:12
Matthew 10:24–11:6
Psalm 13:1-6
Proverbs 3:16-18

January 16
Genesis 32:13–34:31
Matthew 11:7-30
Psalm 14:1-7
Proverbs 3:19-20

January 17
Genesis 35:1–36:43
Matthew 12:1-21
Psalm 15:1-5
Proverbs 3:21-26

January 18
Genesis 37:1–38:30
Matthew 12:22-45
Psalm 16:1-11
Proverbs 3:27-32

January 19
Genesis 39:1–41:16
Matthew 12:46–13:23
Psalm 17:1-15
Proverbs 3:33-35

January 20
Genesis 41:17–42:17
Matthew 13:24-46
Psalm 18:1-15
Proverbs 4:1-6

January 21
Genesis 42:18–43:34
Matthew 13:47–14:12
Psalm 18:16-36
Proverbs 4:7-10

January 22
Genesis 44:1–45:28
Matthew 14:13-36
Psalm 18:37-50
Proverbs 4:11-13

January 23
Genesis 46:1–47:31
Matthew 15:1-28
Psalm 19:1-14
Proverbs 4:14-19

January 24
Genesis 48:1–49:33
Matthew 15:29–16:12
Psalm 20:1-9
Proverbs 4:20-27

January 25
Genesis 50:1–Exodus 2:10
Matthew 16:13–17:9

Psalm 21:1-13
Proverbs 5:1-6

January 26
Exodus 2:11–3:22
Matthew 17:10-27
Psalm 22:1-18
Proverbs 5:7-14

January 27
Exodus 4:1–5:21
Matthew 18:1-22
Psalm 22:19-31
Proverbs 5:15-21

January 28
Exodus 5:22–7:25
Matthew 18:23–19:12
Psalm 23:1-6
Proverbs 5:22-23

January 29
Exodus 8:1–9:35
Matthew 19:13-30
Psalm 24:1-10
Proverbs 6:1-5

January 30
Exodus 10:1–12:13
Matthew 20:1-28
Psalm 25:1-15
Proverbs 6:6-11

January 31
Exodus 12:14–13:16
Matthew 20:29–21:22
Psalm 25:16-22
Proverbs 6:12-15

February 1
Exodus 13:17–15:18
Matthew 21:23-46
Psalm 26:1-12
Proverbs 6:16-19

February 2
Exodus 15:19–17:7
Matthew 22:1-33
Psalm 27:1-6
Proverbs 6:20-26

February 3
Exodus 17:8–19:15
Matthew 22:34–23:12
Psalm 27:7-14
Proverbs 6:27-35

February 4
Exodus 19:16–21:21
Matthew 23:13-39
Psalm 28:1-9
Proverbs 7:1-5

February 5
Exodus 21:22–23:13
Matthew 24:1-28
Psalm 29:1-11
Proverbs 7:6-23

February 6
Exodus 23:14–25:40
Matthew 24:29-51
Psalm 30:1-12
Proverbs 7:24-27

February 7
Exodus 26:1–27:21
Matthew 25:1-30

Psalm 31:1-8
Proverbs 8:1-11

February 8
Exodus 28:1-43
Matthew 25:31–26:13
Psalm 31:9-18
Proverbs 8:12-13

February 9
Exodus 29:1–30:10
Matthew 26:14-46
Psalm 31:19-24
Proverbs 8:14-26

February 10
Exodus 30:11–31:18
Matthew 26:47-68
Psalm 32:1-11
Proverbs 8:27-32

February 11
Exodus 32:1–33:23
Matthew 26:69–27:14
Psalm 33:1-11
Proverbs 8:33-36

February 12
Exodus 34:1–35:9
Matthew 27:15-31
Psalm 33:12-22
Proverbs 9:1-6

February 13
Exodus 35:10–36:38
Matthew 27:32-66
Psalm 34:1-10
Proverbs 9:7-8

February 14
Exodus 37:1–38:31
Matthew 28:1-20
Psalm 34:11-22
Proverbs 9:9-10

February 15
Exodus 39:1–40:38
Mark 1:1-28
Psalm 35:1-16
Proverbs 9:11-12

February 16
Leviticus 1:1–3:17
Mark 1:29–2:12
Psalm 35:17-28
Proverbs 9:13-18

February 17
Leviticus 4:1–5:19
Mark 2:13–3:6
Psalm 36:1-12
Proverbs 10:1-2

February 18
Leviticus 6:1–7:27
Mark 3:7-30
Psalm 37:1-11
Proverbs 10:3-4

February 19
Leviticus 7:28–9:6
Mark 3:31–4:25
Psalm 37:12-29
Proverbs 10:5

February 20
Leviticus 9:7–10:20
Mark 4:26–5:20

Psalm 37:30-40
Proverbs 10:6-7

February 21
Leviticus 11:1–12:8
Mark 5:21-43
Psalm 38:1-22
Proverbs 10:8-9

February 22
Leviticus 13:1-59
Mark 6:1-29
Psalm 39:1-13
Proverbs 10:10

February 23
Leviticus 14:1-57
Mark 6:30-56
Psalm 40:1-10
Proverbs 10:11-12

February 24
Leviticus 15:1–16:28
Mark 7:1-23
Psalm 40:11-17
Proverbs 10:13-14

February 25
Leviticus 16:29–18:30
Mark 7:24–8:10
Psalm 41:1-13
Proverbs 10:15-16

February 26
Leviticus 19:1–20:21
Mark 8:11-38
Psalm 42:1-11
Proverbs 10:17

February 27
Leviticus 20:22–22:16
Mark 9:1-29
Psalm 43:1-5
Proverbs 10:18

February 28
Leviticus 22:17–23:44
Mark 9:30–10:12
Psalm 44:1-8
Proverbs 10:19

March 1
Leviticus 24:1–25:46
Mark 10:13-31
Psalm 44:9-26
Proverbs 10:20-21

March 2
Leviticus 25:47–27:13
Mark 10:32-52
Psalm 45:1-17
Proverbs 10:22

March 3
Leviticus 27:14–Numbers 1:54
Mark 11:1-25
Psalm 46:1-11
Proverbs 10:23

March 4
Numbers 2:1–3:51
Mark 11:27–12:17
Psalm 47:1-9
Proverbs 10:24-25

March 5
Numbers 4:1–5:31

Mark 12:18-37
Mark 12:18-37
Psalm 48:1-14
Proverbs 10:26

March 6
Numbers 6:1–7:89
Mark 12:38–13:13
Psalm 49:1-20
Proverbs 10:27-28

March 7
Numbers 8:1–9:23
Mark 13:14-37
Psalm 50:1-23
Proverbs 10:29-30

March 8
Numbers 10:1–11:23
Mark 14:1-21
Psalm 51:1-19
Proverbs 10:31-32

March 9
Numbers 11:24–13:33
Mark 14:22-52
Psalm 52:1-9
Proverbs 11:1-3

March 10
Numbers 14:1–15:16
Mark 14:53-72
Psalm 53:1-6
Proverbs 11:4

March 11
Numbers 15:17–16:40
Mark 15:1-47
Psalm 54:1-7
Proverbs 11:5-6

March 12
Numbers 16:41–18:32
Mark 16:1-20
Psalm 55:1-23
Proverbs 11:7

March 13
Numbers 19:1–20:29
Luke 1:1-25
Psalm 56:1-13
Proverbs 11:8

March 14
Numbers 21:1–22:20
Luke 1:26-56
Psalm 57:1-11
Proverbs 11:9-11

March 15
Numbers 22:21–23:30
Luke 1:57-80
Psalm 58:1-11
Proverbs 11:12-13

March 16
Numbers 24:1–25:18
Luke 2:1-35
Psalm 59:1-17
Proverbs 11:14

March 17
Numbers 26:1-51
Luke 2:36-52
Psalm 60:1-12
Proverbs 11:15

March 18
Numbers 26:52–28:15
Luke 3:1-22

Psalm 61:1-8
Proverbs 11:16-17

March 19
Numbers 28:16–29:40
Luke 3:23-38
Psalm 62:1-12
Proverbs 11:18-19

March 20
Numbers 30:1–31:54
Luke 4:1-30
Psalm 63:1-11
Proverbs 11:20-21

March 21
Numbers 32:1–33:39
Luke 4:31–5:11
Psalm 64:1-10
Proverbs 11:22

March 22
Numbers 33:40–35:34
Luke 5:12-28
Psalm 65:1-13
Proverbs 11:23

March 23
Numbers 36:1–Deuteronomy
1:46
Luke 5:29–6:11
Psalm 66:1-20
Proverbs 11:24-26

March 24
Deuteronomy 2:1–3:29
Luke 6:12-38
Psalm 67:1-7
Proverbs 11:27

March 25
Deuteronomy 4:1-49
Luke 6:39–7:10
Psalm 68:1-18
Proverbs 11:28

March 26
Deuteronomy 5:1–6:25
Luke 7:11-35
Psalm 68:19-35
Proverbs 11:29-31

March 27
Deuteronomy 7:1–8:20
Luke 7:36–8:3
Psalm 69:1-18
Proverbs 12:1

March 28
Deuteronomy 9:1–10:22
Luke 8:4-21
Psalm 69:19-36
Proverbs 12:2-3

March 29
Deuteronomy 11:1–12:32
Luke 8:22-39
Psalm 70:1-5
Proverbs 12:4

March 30
Deuteronomy 13:1–15:23
Luke 8:40–9:6
Psalm 71:1-24
Proverbs 12:5-7

March 31
Deuteronomy 16:1–17:20
Luke 9:7-27

Psalm 72:1-20
Proverbs 12:8-9

April 1
Deuteronomy 18:1–20:20
Luke 9:28-50
Psalm 73:1-28
Proverbs 12:10

April 2
Deuteronomy 21:1–22:30
Luke 9:51–10:12
Psalm 74:1-23
Proverbs 12:11

April 3
Deuteronomy 23:1–25:19
Luke 10:13-37
Psalm 75:1-10
Proverbs 12:12-14

April 4
Deuteronomy 26:1–27:26
Luke 10:38–11:13
Psalm 76:1-12
Proverbs 12:15-17

April 5
Deuteronomy 28:1-68
Luke 11:14-36
Psalm 77:1-20
Proverbs 12:18

April 6
Deuteronomy 29:1–30:20
Luke 11:37–12:7
Psalm 78:1-31
Proverbs 12:19-20

April 7
Deuteronomy 31:1–32:27
Luke 12:8-34
Psalm 78:32-55
Proverbs 12:21-23

April 8
Deuteronomy 32:28-52
Luke 12:35-59
Psalm 78:56-64
Proverbs 12:24

April 9
Deuteronomy 33:1-29
Luke 13:1-21
Psalm 78:65-72
Proverbs 12:25

April 10
Deuteronomy 34:1–
Joshua 2:24
Luke 13:22–14:6
Psalm 79:1-13
Proverbs 12:26

April 11
Joshua 3:1–4:24
Luke 14:7-35
Psalm 80:1-19
Proverbs 12:27-28

April 12
Joshua 5:1–7:15
Luke 15:1-32
Psalm 81:1-16
Proverbs 13:1

April 13
278 *Joshua 7:16–9:2*

Luke 16:1-18
Psalm 82:1-8
Proverbs 13:2-3

April 14
Joshua 9:3–10:43
Luke 16:19–17:10
Psalm 83:1-18
Proverbs 13:4

April 15
Joshua 11:1–12:24
Luke 17:11-37
Psalm 84:1-12
Proverbs 13:5-6

April 16
Joshua 13:1–14:15
Luke 18:1-17
Psalm 85:1-13
Proverbs 13:7-8

April 17
Joshua 15:1-63
Luke 18:18-43
Psalm 86:1-17
Proverbs 13:9-10

April 18
Joshua 16:1–18:28
Luke 19:1-27
Psalm 87:1-7
Proverbs 13:11

April 19
Joshua 19:1–20:9
Luke 19:28-48
Psalm 88:1-18
Proverbs 13:12-14

April 20
Joshua 21:1–22:20
Luke 20:1-26
Psalm 89:1-13
Proverbs 13:15-16

April 21
Joshua 22:21–23:16
Luke 20:27-47
Psalm 89:14-37
Proverbs 13:17-19

April 22
Joshua 24:1-33
Luke 21:1-28
Psalm 89:38-52
Proverbs 13:20-23

April 23
Judges 1:1–2:9
Luke 21:29–22:13
Psalms 90:1–91:16
Proverbs 13:24-25

April 24
Judges 2:10–3:31
Luke 22:14-34
Psalms 92:1–93:5
Proverbs 14:1-2

April 25
Judges 4:1–5:31
Luke 22:35-53
Psalm 94:1-23
Proverbs 14:3-4

April 26
Judges 6:1-40
Luke 22:54–23:12

Psalms 95:1–96:13
Proverbs 14:5-6

April 27
Judges 7:1–8:17
Luke 23:13-43
Psalms 97:1–98:9
Proverbs 14:7-8

April 28
Judges 8:18–9:21
Luke 23:44–24:12
Psalm 99:1-9
Proverbs 14:9-10

April 29
Judges 9:22–10:18
Luke 24:13-53
Psalm 100:1-5
Proverbs 14:11-12

April 30
Judges 11:1–12:15
John 1:1-28
Psalm 101:1-8
Proverbs 14:13-14

May 1
Judges 13:1–14:20
John 1:29-51
Psalm 102:1-28
Proverbs 14:15-16

May 2
Judges 15:1–16:31
John 2:1-25
Psalm 103:1-22
Proverbs 14:17-19

May 3
Judges 17:1–18:31
John 3:1-21
Psalm 104:1-23
Proverbs 14:20-21

May 4
Judges 19:1–20:48
John 3:22–4:3
Psalm 104:24-35
Proverbs 14:22-24

May 5
Judges 21:1–Ruth 1:22
John 4:4-42
Psalm 105:1-15
Proverbs 14:25

May 6
Ruth 2:1–4:22
John 4:43-54
Psalm 105:16-36
Proverbs 14:26-27

May 7
1 Samuel 1:1–2:21
John 5:1-23
Psalm 105:37-45
Proverbs 14:28-29

May 8
1 Samuel 2:22–4:22
John 5:24-47
Psalm 106:1-12
Proverbs 14:30-31

May 9
1 Samuel 5:1–7:17
John 6:1-21

Psalm 106:13-31
Proverbs 14:32-33

May 10
1 Samuel 8:1–9:27
John 6:22-42
Psalm 106:32-48
Proverbs 14:34-35

May 11
1 Samuel 10:1–11:15
John 6:43-71
Psalm 107:1-43
Proverbs 15:1-3

May 12
1 Samuel 12:1–13:23
John 7:1-30
Psalm 108:1-13
Proverbs 15:4

May 13
1 Samuel 14:1–14:52
John 7:31-53
Psalm 109:1-31
Proverbs 15:5-7

May 14
1 Samuel 15:1–16:23
John 8:1-20
Psalm 110:1-7
Proverbs 15:8-10

May 15
1 Samuel 17:1–18:4
John 8:21-30
Psalm 111:1-10
Proverbs 15:11

May 16
1 Samuel 18:5–19:24
John 8:31-59
Psalm 112:1-10
Proverbs 15:12-14

May 17
1 Samuel 20:1–21:15
John 9:1-41
Psalms 113:1–114:8
Proverbs 15:15-17

May 18
1 Samuel 22:1–23:29
John 10:1-21
Psalm 115:1-18
Proverbs 15:18-19

May 19
1 Samuel 24:1–25:44
John 10:22-42
Psalm 116:1-19
Proverbs 15:20-21

May 20
1 Samuel 26:1–28:25
John 11:1-54
Psalm 117:1-2
Proverbs 15:22-23

May 21
1 Samuel 29:1–31:13
John 11:55–12:19
Psalm 118:1-18
Proverbs 15:24-26

May 22
2 Samuel 1:1–2:11
John 12:20-50

May 23
Psalm 118:19-29
Proverbs 15:27-28

May 23
2 Samuel 2:12–3:39
John 13:1-30
Psalm 119:1-16
Proverbs 15:29-30

May 24
2 Samuel 4:1–6:23
John 13:31–14:14
Psalm 119:17-32
Proverbs 15:31-32

May 25
2 Samuel 7:1–8:18
John 14:15-31
Psalm 119:33-48
Proverbs 15:33

May 26
2 Samuel 9:1–11:27
John 15:1-27
Psalm 119:49-64
Proverbs 16:1-3

May 27
2 Samuel 12:1-31
John 16:1-33
Psalm 119:65-80
Proverbs 16:4-5

May 28
2 Samuel 13:1-39
John 17:1-26
Psalm 119:81-96
Proverbs 16:6-7

May 29
2 Samuel 14:1–15:22
John 18:1-24
Psalm 119:97-112
Proverbs 16:8-9

May 30
2 Samuel 15:23–16:23
John 18:25–19:22
Psalm 119:113-128
Proverbs 16:10-11

May 31
2 Samuel 17:1-29
John 19:23-42
Psalm 119:129-152
Proverbs 16:12-13

June 1
2 Samuel 18:1–19:10
John 20:1-31
Psalm 119:153-176
Proverbs 16:14-15

June 2
2 Samuel 19:11–20:13
John 21:1-25
Psalm 120:1-7
Proverbs 16:16-17

June 3
2 Samuel 20:14–21:22
Acts 1:1-26
Psalm 121:1-8
Proverbs 16:18

June 4
2 Samuel 22:1–23:23
Acts 2:1-47

Psalm 122:1-9
Proverbs 16:19-20

June 5
2 Samuel 23:24–24:25
Acts 3:1-26
Psalm 123:1-4
Proverbs 16:21-23

June 6
1 Kings 1:1-53
Acts 4:1-37
Psalm 124:1-8
Proverbs 16:24

June 7
1 Kings 2:1-3:2
Acts 5:1-42
Psalm 125:1-5
Proverbs 16:25

June 8
1 Kings 3:3-4:34
Acts 6:1-15
Psalm 126:1-6
Proverbs 16:26-27

June 9
1 Kings 5:1-6:38
Acts 7:1-29
Psalm 127:1-5
Proverbs 16:28-30

June 10
1 Kings 7:1-51
Acts 7:30-50
Psalm 128:1-6
Proverbs 16:31-33

June 11
1 Kings 8:1-66
Acts 7:51–8:13
Psalm 129:1-8
Proverbs 17:1

June 12
1 Kings 9:1–10:29
Acts 8:14-40
Psalm 130:1-8
Proverbs 17:2-3

June 13
1 Kings 11:1–12:19
Acts 9:1-25
Psalm 131:1-3
Proverbs 17:4-5

June 14
1 Kings 12:20–13:34
Acts 9:26-43
Psalm 132:1-18
Proverbs 17:6

June 15
1 Kings 14:1–15:24
Acts 10:1-23
Psalm 133:1-3
Proverbs 17:7-8

June 16
1 Kings 15:25–17:24
Acts 10:24-48
Psalm 134:1-3
Proverbs 17:9-11

June 17
1 Kings 18:1-46
Acts 11:1-30

Psalm 135:1-21
Proverbs 17:12-13

June 18
1 Kings 19:1-21
Acts 12:1-23
Psalm 136:1-26
Proverbs 17:14-15

June 19
1 Kings 20:1–21:29
Acts 12:24-13:15
Psalm 137:1-9
Proverbs 17:16

June 20
1 Kings 22:1-53
Acts 13:16-41
Psalm 138:1-8
Proverbs 17:17-18

June 21
2 Kings 1:1–2:25
Acts 13:42–14:7
Psalm 139:1-24
Proverbs 17:19-21

June 22
2 Kings 3:1–4:17
Acts 14:8-28
Psalm 140:1-13
Proverbs 17:22

June 23
2 Kings 4:18–5:27
Acts 15:1-35
Psalm 141:1-10
Proverbs 17:23

June 24
2 Kings 6:1–7:20
Acts 15:36–16:15
Psalm 142:1-7
Proverbs 17:24-25

June 25
2 Kings 8:1–9:13
Acts 16:16-40
Psalm 143:1-12
Proverbs 17:26

June 26
2 Kings 9:14–10:31
Acts 17:1-34
Psalm 144:1-15
Proverbs 17:27-28

June 27
2 Kings 10:32–12:21
Acts 18:1-22
Psalm 145:1-21
Proverbs 18:1

June 28
2 Kings 13:1–14:29
Acts 18:23–19:12
Psalm 146:1-10
Proverbs 18:2-3

June 29
2 Kings 15:1–16:20
Acts 19:13-41
Psalm 147:1-20
Proverbs 18:4-5

June 30
2 Kings 17:1–18:12
282 *Acts 20:1-38*

Psalm 148:1-14
Proverbs 18:6-7

July 1
2 Kings 18:13–19:37
Acts 21:1-17
Psalm 149:1-9
Proverbs 18:8

July 2
2 Kings 20:1–22:2
Acts 21:18-36
Psalm 150:1-6
Proverbs 18:9-10

July 3
2 Kings 22:3–23:30
Acts 21:37–22:16
Psalm 1:1-6
Proverbs 18:11-12

July 4
2 Kings 23:31–25:30
Acts 22:17–23:10
Psalm 2:1-12
Proverbs 18:13

July 5
1 Chronicles 1:1–2:17
Acts 23:11-35
Psalm 3:1-8
Proverbs 18:14-15

July 6
1 Chronicles 2:18–4:4
Acts 24:1-27
Psalm 4:1-8
Proverbs 18:16-18

July 7
1 Chronicles 4:5–5:17
Acts 25:1-27
Psalm 5:1-12
Proverbs 18:19

July 8
1 Chronicles 5:18–6:81
Acts 26:1-32
Psalm 6:1-10
Proverbs 18:20-21

July 9
1 Chronicles 7:1–8:40
Acts 27:1-20
Psalm 7:1-17
Proverbs 18:22

July 10
1 Chronicles 9:1–10:14
Acts 27:21-44
Psalm 8:1-9
Proverbs 18:23-24

July 11
1 Chronicles 11:1–12:18
Acts 28:1-31
Psalm 9:1-12
Proverbs 19:1-3

July 12
1 Chronicles 12:19–14:17
Romans 1:1-17
Psalm 9:13-20
Proverbs 19:4-5

July 13
1 Chronicles 15:1–16:36
Romans 1:18-32

Psalm 10:1-15
Proverbs 19:6-7

July 14
1 Chronicles 16:37–18:17
Romans 2:1-24
Psalm 10:16-18
Proverbs 19:8-9

July 15
1 Chronicles 19:1–21:30
Romans 2:25–3:8
Psalm 11:1-7
Proverbs 19:10-12

July 16
1 Chronicles 22:1–23:32
Romans 3:9-31
Psalm 12:1-8
Proverbs 19:13-14

July 17
1 Chronicles 24:1–26:11
Romans 4:1-12
Psalm 13:1-6
Proverbs 19:15-16

July 18
1 Chronicles 26:12–27:34
Romans 4:13–5:5
Psalm 14:1-7
Proverbs 19:17

July 19
1 Chronicles 28:1–29:30
Romans 5:6-21
Psalm 15:1-5
Proverbs 19:18-19

July 20
2 Chronicles 1:1–3:17
Romans 6:1-23
Psalm 16:1-11
Proverbs 19:20-21

July 21
2 Chronicles 4:1–6:11
Romans 7:1-13
Psalm 17:1-15
Proverbs 19:22-23

July 22
2 Chronicles 6:12–8:10
Romans 7:14–8:8
Psalm 18:1-15
Proverbs 19:24-25

July 23
2 Chronicles 8:11–10:19
Romans 8:9-25
Psalm 18:16-36
Proverbs 19:26

July 24
2 Chronicles 11:1–13:22
Romans 8:26-39
Psalm 18:37-50
Proverbs 19:27-29

July 25
2 Chronicles 14:1–16:14
Romans 9:1-24
Psalm 19:1-14
Proverbs 20:1

July 26
2 Chronicles 17:1–18:34
Romans 9:25–10:13

July 27
2 Chronicles 19:1–20:37
Romans 10:14–11:12
Psalm 21:1-13
Proverbs 20:4-6

July 28
2 Chronicles 21:1–23:21
Romans 11:13-36
Psalm 22:1-18
Proverbs 20:7

July 29
2 Chronicles 24:1–25:28
Romans 12:1-21
Psalm 22:19-31
Proverbs 20:8-10

July 30
2 Chronicles 26:1–28:27
Romans 13:1-14
Psalm 23:1-6
Proverbs 20:11

July 31
2 Chronicles 29:1-36
Romans 14:1-23
Psalm 24:1-10
Proverbs 20:12

August 1
2 Chronicles 30:1–31:21
Romans 15:1-22
Psalm 25:1-15
Proverbs 20:13-15

Psalm 20:1-9
Proverbs 20:2-3

August 2
2 Chronicles 32:1–33:13
Romans 15:23–16:9
Psalm 25:16-22
Proverbs 20:16-18

August 3
2 Chronicles 33:14–34:33
Romans 16:10-27
Psalm 26:1-12
Proverbs 20:19

August 4
2 Chronicles 35:1–36:23
1 Corinthians 1:1-17
Psalm 27:1-6
Proverbs 20:20-21

August 5
Ezra 1:1–2:70
1 Corinthians 1:18–2:5
Psalm 27:7-14
Proverbs 20:22-23

August 6
Ezra 3:1–4:24
1 Corinthians 2:6–3:4
Psalm 28:1-9
Proverbs 20:24-25

August 7
Ezra 5:1–6:22
1 Corinthians 3:5-23
Psalm 29:1-11
Proverbs 20:26-27

August 8
Ezra 7:1–8:20
1 Corinthians 4:1-21

Psalm 30:1-12
Proverbs 20:28-30

August 9
Ezra 8:21–9:15
1 Corinthians 5:1-13
Psalm 31:1-8
Proverbs 21:1-2

August 10
Ezra 10:1-44
1 Corinthians 6:1-20
Psalm 31:9-18
Proverbs 21:3

August 11
Nehemiah 1:1–3:14
1 Corinthians 7:1-24
Psalm 31:19-24
Proverbs 21:4

August 12
Nehemiah 3:15–5:13
1 Corinthians 7:25-40
Psalm 32:1-11
Proverbs 21:5-7

August 13
Nehemiah 5:14–7:60
1 Corinthians 8:1-13
Psalm 33:1-11
Proverbs 21:8-10

August 14
Nehemiah 7:61–9:21
1 Corinthians 9:1-18
Psalm 33:12-22
Proverbs 21:11-12

August 15
Nehemiah 9:22–10:39
1 Corinthians 9:19–10:13
Psalm 34:1-10
Proverbs 21:13

August 16
Nehemiah 11:1–12:26
1 Corinthians 10:14-33
Psalm 34:11-22
Proverbs 21:14-16

August 17
Nehemiah 12:27–13:31
1 Corinthians 11:1-16
Psalm 35:1-16
Proverbs 21:17-18

August 18
Esther 1:1–3:15
1 Corinthians 11:17-34
Psalm 35:17-28
Proverbs 21:19-20

August 19
Esther 4:1–7:10
1 Corinthians 12:1-26
Psalm 36:1-12
Proverbs 21:21-22

August 20
Esther 8:1–10:3
1 Corinthians 12:27–13:13
Psalm 37:1-11
Proverbs 21:23-24

August 21
Job 1:1–3:26
1 Corinthians 14:1-17

Psalm 37:12-29
Proverbs 21:25-26

August 22
Job 4:1–7:21
1 Corinthians 14:18-40
Psalm 37:30-40
Proverbs 21:27

August 23
Job 8:1–11:20
1 Corinthians 15:1-28
Psalm 38:1-22
Proverbs 21:28-29

August 24
Job 12:1–15:35
1 Corinthians 15:29-58
Psalm 39:1-13
Proverbs 21:30-31

August 25
Job 16:1–19:29
1 Corinthians 16:1-24
Psalm 40:1-10
Proverbs 22:1

August 26
Job 20:1–22:30
2 Corinthians 1:1-11
Psalm 40:11-17
Proverbs 22:2-4

August 27
Job 23:1–27:23
2 Corinthians 1:12–2:11
Psalm 41:1-13
Proverbs 22:5-6

August 28
Job 28:1–30:31
2 Corinthians 2:12-17
Psalm 42:1-11
Proverbs 22:7

August 29
Job 31:1–33:33
2 Corinthians 3:1-18
Psalm 43:1-5
Proverbs 22:8-9

August 30
Job 34:1–36:33
2 Corinthians 4:1-12
Psalm 44:1-8
Proverbs 22:10-12

August 31
Job 37:1–39:30
2 Corinthians 4:13–5:10
Psalm 44:9-26
Proverbs 22:13

September 1
Job 40:1–42:17
2 Corinthians 5:11-21
Psalm 45:1-17
Proverbs 22:14

September 2
Ecclesiastes 1:1–3:22
2 Corinthians 6:1-13
Psalm 46:1-11
Proverbs 22:15

September 3
Ecclesiastes 4:1–6:12
2 Corinthians 6:14–7:7

Psalm 47:1-9
Proverbs 22:16

September 4
Ecclesiastes 7:1–9:18
2 Corinthians 7:8-16
Psalm 48:1-14
Proverbs 22:17-19

September 5
Ecclesiastes 10:1–12:14
2 Corinthians 8:1-15
Psalm 49:1-20
Proverbs 22:20-21

September 6
Song of Songs 1:1–4:16
2 Corinthians 8:16-24
Psalm 50:1-23
Proverbs 22:22-23

September 7
Song of Songs 5:1–8:14
2 Corinthians 9:1-15
Psalm 51:1-19
Proverbs 22:24-25

September 8
Isaiah 1:1–2:22
2 Corinthians 10:1-18
Psalm 52:1-9
Proverbs 22:26-27

September 9
Isaiah 3:1–5:30
2 Corinthians 11:1-15
Psalm 53:1-6
Proverbs 22:28-29

September 10
Isaiah 6:1–7:25
2 Corinthians 11:16-33
Psalm 54:1-7
Proverbs 23:1-3

September 11
Isaiah 8:1–9:21
2 Corinthians 12:1-10
Psalm 55:1-23
Proverbs 23:4-5

September 12
Isaiah 10:1–11:16
2 Corinthians 12:11-21
Psalm 56:1-13
Proverbs 23:6-8

September 13
Isaiah 12:1–14:32
2 Corinthians 13:1-13
Psalm 57:1-11
Proverbs 23:9-11

September 14
Isaiah 15:1–18:7
Galatians 1:1-24
Psalm 58:1-11
Proverbs 23:12

September 15
Isaiah 19:1–21:17
Galatians 2:1-16
Psalm 59:1-17
Proverbs 23:13-14

September 16
Isaiah 22:1–24:23
Galatians 2:17–3:9

Psalm 60:1-12
Proverbs 23:15-16

September 17
Isaiah 25:1–28:13
Galatians 3:10-22
Psalm 61:1-8
Proverbs 23:17-18

September 18
Isaiah 28:14–30:11
Galatians 3:23–4:31
Psalm 62:1-12
Proverbs 23:19-21

September 19
Isaiah 30:12–33:9
Galatians 5:1-12
Psalm 63:1-11
Proverbs 23:22

September 20
Isaiah 33:10–36:22
Galatians 5:13-26
Psalm 64:1-10
Proverbs 23:23

September 21
Isaiah 37:1–38:22
Galatians 6:1-18
Psalm 65:1-13
Proverbs 23:24

September 22
Isaiah 39:1–41:16
Ephesians 1:1-23
Psalm 66:1-20
Proverbs 23:25-28

September 23
Isaiah 41:17–43:13
Ephesians 2:1-22
Psalm 67:1-7
Proverbs 23:29-35

September 24
Isaiah 43:14–45:10
Ephesians 3:1-21
Psalm 68:1-18
Proverbs 24:1-2

September 25
Isaiah 45:11–48:11
Ephesians 4:1-16
Psalm 68:19-35
Proverbs 24:3-4

September 26
Isaiah 48:12–50:11
Ephesians 4:17-32
Psalm 69:1-18
Proverbs 24:5-6

September 27
Isaiah 51:1–53:12
Ephesians 5:1-33
Psalm 69:19-36
Proverbs 24:7

September 28
Isaiah 54:1–57:14
Ephesians 6:1-24
Psalm 70:1-5
Proverbs 24:8

September 29
Isaiah 57:15–59:21
Philippians 1:1-26

Psalm 71:1-24
Proverbs 24:9-10

September 30
Isaiah 60:1-62:5
Philippians 1:27-2:18
Psalm 72:1-20
Proverbs 24:11-12

October 1
Isaiah 62:6-65:25
Philippians 2:19-3:3
Psalm 73:1-28
Proverbs 24:13-14

October 2
Isaiah 66:1-24
Philippians 3:4-21
Psalm 74:1-23
Proverbs 24:15-16

October 3
Jeremiah 1:1-2:30
Philippians 4:1-23
Psalm 75:1-10
Proverbs 24:17-20

October 4
Jeremiah 2:31-4:18
Colossians 1:1-17
Psalm 76:1-12
Proverbs 24:21-22

October 5
Jeremiah 4:19-6:15
Colossians 1:18-2:7
Psalm 77:1-20
Proverbs 24:23-25

October 6
Jeremiah 6:16-8:7
Colossians 2:8-23
Psalm 78:1-31
Proverbs 24:26

October 7
Jeremiah 8:8-9:26
Colossians 3:1-17
Psalm 78:32-55
Proverbs 24:27

October 8
Jeremiah 10:1-11:23
Colossians 3:18-4:18
Psalm 78:56-72
Proverbs 24:28-29

October 9
Jeremiah 12:1-14:10
1 Thessalonians 1:1-2:8
Psalm 79:1-13
Proverbs 24:30-34

October 10
Jeremiah 14:11-16:15
1 Thessalonians 2:9-3:13
Psalm 80:1-19
Proverbs 25:1-5

October 11
Jeremiah 16:16-18:23
1 Thessalonians 4:1-5:3
Psalm 81:1-16
Proverbs 25:6-8

October 12
Jeremiah 19:1-21:14
1 Thessalonians 5:4-28

Psalm 82:1-8
Proverbs 25:9-10

October 13
Jeremiah 22:1-23:20
2 Thessalonians 1:1-12
Psalm 83:1-18
Proverbs 25:11-14

October 14
Jeremiah 23:21-25:38
2 Thessalonians 2:1-17
Psalm 84:1-12
Proverbs 25:15

October 15
Jeremiah 26:1-27:22
2 Thessalonians 3:1-18
Psalm 85:1-13
Proverbs 25:16

October 16
Jeremiah 28:1-29:32
1 Timothy 1:1-20
Psalm 86:1-17
Proverbs 25:17

October 17
Jeremiah 30:1-31:26
1 Timothy 2:1-15
Psalm 87:1-7
Proverbs 25:18-19

October 18
Jeremiah 31:27-32:44
1 Timothy 3:1-16
Psalm 88:1-18
Proverbs 25:20-22

October 19
Jeremiah 33:1–34:22
1 Timothy 4:1-16
Psalm 89:1-13
Proverbs 25:23-24

October 20
Jeremiah 35:1–36:32
1 Timothy 5:1-25
Psalm 89:14-37
Proverbs 25:25-27

October 21
Jeremiah 37:1–38:28
1 Timothy 6:1-21
Psalm 89:38-52
Proverbs 25:28

October 22
Jeremiah 39:1–41:18
2 Timothy 1:1-18
Psalms 90:1–91:16
Proverbs 26:1-2

October 23
Jeremiah 42:1–44:23
2 Timothy 2:1-21
Psalms 92:1–93:5
Proverbs 26:3-5

October 24
Jeremiah 44:24–47:7
2 Timothy 2:22–3:17
Psalm 94:1-23
Proverbs 26:6-8

October 25
Jeremiah 48:1–49:22
288 *2 Timothy 4:1-22*

Psalms 95:1–96:13
Proverbs 26:9-12

October 26
Jeremiah 49:23–50:46
Titus 1:1-16
Psalms 97:1–98:9
Proverbs 26:13-16

October 27
Jeremiah 51:1-53
Titus 2:1-15
Psalm 99:1-9
Proverbs 26:17

October 28
Jeremiah 51:54–52:34
Titus 3:1-15
Psalm 100:1-5
Proverbs 26:18-19

October 29
Lamentations 1:1–2:19
Philemon 1:1-25
Psalm 101:1-8
Proverbs 26:20

October 30
Lamentations 2:20–3:66
Hebrews 1:1-14
Psalm 102:1-28
Proverbs 26:21-22

October 31
Lamentations 4:1–5:22
Hebrews 2:1-18
Psalm 103:1-22
Proverbs 26:23

November 1
Ezekiel 1:1–3:15
Hebrews 3:1-19
Psalm 104:1-23
Proverbs 26:24-26

November 2
Ezekiel 3:16–6:14
Hebrews 4:1-16
Psalm 104:24-35
Proverbs 26:27

November 3
Ezekiel 7:1–9:11
Hebrews 5:1-14
Psalm 105:1-15
Proverbs 26:28

November 4
Ezekiel 10:1–11:25
Hebrews 6:1-20
Psalm 105:16-36
Proverbs 27:1-2

November 5
Ezekiel 12:1–14:11
Hebrews 7:1-17
Psalm 105:37-45
Proverbs 27:3

November 6
Ezekiel 14:12–16:41
Hebrews 7:18-28
Psalm 106:1-12
Proverbs 27:4-6

November 7
Ezekiel 16:42–17:24
Hebrews 8:1-13

Psalm 106:13-31
Proverbs 27:7-9

November 8
Ezekiel 18:1–19:14
Hebrews 9:1-10
Psalm 106:32-48
Proverbs 27:10

November 9
Ezekiel 20:1-49
Hebrews 9:11-28
Psalm 107:1-43
Proverbs 27:11

November 10
Ezekiel 21:1–22:31
Hebrews 10:1-17
Psalm 108:1-13
Proverbs 27:12

November 11
Ezekiel 23:1-49
Hebrews 10:18-39
Psalm 109:1-31
Proverbs 27:13

November 12
Ezekiel 24:1–26:21
Hebrews 11:1-16
Psalm 110:1-7
Proverbs 27:14

November 13
Ezekiel 27:1–28:26
Hebrews 11:17-31
Psalm 111:1-10
Proverbs 27:15-16

November 14
Ezekiel 29:1–30:26
Hebrews 11:32–12:13
Psalm 112:1-10
Proverbs 27:17

November 15
Ezekiel 31:1–32:32
Hebrews 12:14-29
Psalms 113:1–114:8
Proverbs 27:18-20

November 16
Ezekiel 33:1–34:31
Hebrews 13:1-25
Psalm 115:1-18
Proverbs 27:21-22

November 17
Ezekiel 35:1–36:38
James 1:1-18
Psalm 116:1-19
Proverbs 27:23-27

November 18
Ezekiel 37:1–38:23
James 1:19–2:17
Psalm 117:1-2
Proverbs 28:1

November 19
Ezekiel 39:1–40:27
James 2:18–3:18
Psalm 118:1-18
Proverbs 28:2

November 20
Ezekiel 40:28–41:26
James 4:1-17

Psalm 118:19-29
Proverbs 28:3-5

November 21
Ezekiel 42:1–43:27
James 5:1-20
Psalm 119:1-16
Proverbs 28:6-7

November 22
Ezekiel 44:1–45:12
1 Peter 1:1-12
Psalm 119:17-32
Proverbs 28:8-10

November 23
Ezekiel 45:13–46:24
1 Peter 1:13–2:10
Psalm 119:33-48
Proverbs 28:11

November 24
Ezekiel 47:1–48:35
1 Peter 2:11–3:7
Psalm 119:49-64
Proverbs 28:12-13

November 25
Daniel 1:1–2:23
1 Peter 3:8–4:6
Psalm 119:65-80
Proverbs 28:14

November 26
Daniel 2:24–3:30
1 Peter 4:7–5:14
Psalm 119:81-96
Proverbs 28:15-16

November 27
Daniel 4:1-37
2 Peter 1:1-21
Psalm 119:97-112
Proverbs 28:17-18

November 28
Daniel 5:1-31
2 Peter 2:1-22
Psalm 119:113-128
Proverbs 28:19-20

November 29
Daniel 6:1-28
2 Peter 3:1-18
Psalm 119:129-152
Proverbs 28:21-22

November 30
Daniel 7:1-28
1 John 1:1-10
Psalm 119:153-176
Proverbs 28:23-24

December 1
Daniel 8:1-27
1 John 2:1-17
Psalm 120:1-7
Proverbs 28:25-26

December 2
Daniel 9:1-11:1
1 John 2:18-3:6
Psalm 121:1-8
Proverbs 28:27-28

December 3
Daniel 11:2-35
1 John 3:7-24

December 4
Daniel 11:36-12:13
1 John 4:1-21
Psalm 123:1-4
Proverbs 29:2-4

December 5
Hosea 1:1-3:5
1 John 5:1-21
Psalm 124:1-8
Proverbs 29:5-8

December 6
Hosea 4:1-5:15
2 John 1:1-13
Psalm 125:1-5
Proverbs 29:9-11

December 7
Hosea 6:1-9:17
3 John 1:1-15
Psalm 126:1-6
Proverbs 29:12-14

December 8
Hosea 10:1-14:9
Jude 1:1-25
Psalm 127:1-5
Proverbs 29:15-17

December 9
Joel 1:1-3:21
Revelation 1:1-20
Psalm 128:1-6
Proverbs 29:18

Psalm 122:1-9
Proverbs 29:1

December 10
Amos 1:1-3:15
Revelation 2:1-17
Psalm 129:1-8
Proverbs 29:19-20

December 11
Amos 4:1-6:14
Revelation 2:18-3:6
Psalm 130:1-8
Proverbs 29:21-22

December 12
Amos 7:1-9:15
Revelation 3:7-22
Psalm 131:1-3
Proverbs 29:23

December 13
Obadiah 1:1-21
Revelation 4:1-11
Psalm 132:1-18
Proverbs 29:24-25

December 14
Jonah 1:1-4:11
Revelation 5:1-14
Psalm 133:1-3
Proverbs 29:26-27

December 15
Micah 1:1-4:13
Revelation 6:1-17
Psalm 134:1-3
Proverbs 30:1-4

December 16
Micah 5:1-7:20
Revelation 7:1-17

Psalm 135:1-21
Proverbs 30:5-6

December 17
Nahum 1:1–3:19
Revelation 8:1-13
Psalm 136:1-26
Proverbs 30:7-9

December 18
Habakkuk 1:1–3:19
Revelation 9:1-21
Psalm 137:1-9
Proverbs 30:10

December 19
Zephaniah 1:1–3:20
Revelation 10:1-11
Psalm 138:1-8
Proverbs 30:11-14

December 20
Haggai 1:1–2:23
Revelation 11:1-19
Psalm 139:1-24
Proverbs 30:15-16

December 21
Zechariah 1:1-21
Revelation 12:1-17
Psalm 140:1-13
Proverbs 30:17

December 22
Zechariah 2:1–3:10
Revelation 12:18-3:18
Psalm 141:1-10
Proverbs 30:18-20

December 23
Zechariah 4:1–5:11
Revelation 14:1-20
Psalm 142:1-7
Proverbs 30:21-23

December 24
Zechariah 6:1–7:14
Revelation 15:1-8
Psalm 143:1-12
Proverbs 30:24-28

December 25
Zechariah 8:1-23
Revelation 16:1-21
Psalm 144:1-15
Proverbs 30:29-31

December 26
Zechariah 9:1-17
Revelation 17:1-18
Psalm 145:1-21
Proverbs 30:32

December 27
Zechariah 10:1–11:17
Revelation 18:1-24
Psalm 146:1-10
Proverbs 30:33

December 28
Zechariah 12:1–13:9
Revelation 19:1-21
Psalm 147:1-20
Proverbs 31:1-7

December 29
Zechariah 14:1-21
Revelation 20:1-15
Psalm 148:1-14
Proverbs 31:8-9

December 30
Malachi 1:1–2:17
Revelation 21:1-27
Psalm 149:1-9
Proverbs 31:10-24

December 31
Malachi 3:1–4:6
Revelation 22:1-21
Psalm 150:1-6
Proverbs 31:25-31